# Nicole Kidman

## Other Biographies by James L. Dickerson

*Ashley Judd: Crying on the Inside*

*Natalie Portman: Queen of Hearts*

*Just for a Thrill: Lil Hardin Armstrong, the First Lady of Jazz*

*Colonel Tom Parker: The Curious Life of*
*Elvis Presley's Eccentric Manager*

*Dixie Chicks: Down-Home and Backstage*

*Faith Hill: Piece of My Heart*

*That's Alright, Elvis: The Untold Story of Elvis's First*
*Guitarist and Manager, Scotty Moore* (with Scotty Moore)

# Nicole Kidman

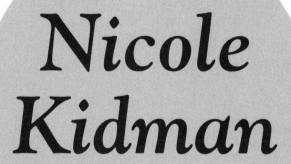

## JAMES L. DICKERSON

CITADEL PRESS
Kensington Publishing Corp.
www.kensingtonbooks.com

CITADEL PRESS BOOKS are published by

Kensington Publishing Corp.
850 Third Avenue
New York, NY 10022

All Kensington titles, imprints, and distributed lines are available at special quantity dis-
counts for bulk purchases for sales promotions, premiums, fund-raising, educational, or
institutional use. Special book excerpts or customized printings can also be created to fit
specific needs. For details, write or phone the office of the Kensington special sales manager: Kensington Publishing Corp., 850 Third Avenue, New York, NY 10022, attn: Special Sales Department, phone 1-800-221-2647.

CI ff.

10 9 8 7 6 5 4 3 2 1

Printed in the United States of America

Library of Congress Control Number: 2002115771

ISBN 0-8065-2490-1

*To Betty Keith*

# Contents

Acknowledgments  •  IX

CHAPTER ONE
The Early Years: Revenge of "Stalky"  •  1

CHAPTER TWO
First Flirtations with Movie Success  •  15

CHAPTER THREE
The Calm Before the Storm  •  24

CHAPTER FOUR
Tom Cruise Arrives with *Days of Thunder*  •  37

CHAPTER FIVE
*Far and Away:* Tarnished Dream  •  59

CHAPTER SIX
At Last, A Juicy Role *To Die For*  •  79

CHAPTER SEVEN
The Making of *Eyes Wide Shut*  •  100

CHAPTER EIGHT
A Gamble on *Moulin Rouge*  •  130

CHAPTER NINE
Days Asunder: Divorce Hollywood Style • 143

CHAPTER TEN
Heels'-Eye View: Life Without Tom • 162

Filmography • 177

Bibliography • 201

Index • 211

# Acknowledgments

I would like to thank the following people for their help with this book: Denny Lawrence, Di-Anne Reynolds, Tania Djipalo, and Rebecca Mostyn at the Australian Film Commission; Gary Goba, Stuart Freeman, Brown Burnett; my agent for this project Alison Picard; my editor Miles Lott; Dr. Mardi Allen, for supplying me with good counsel and tasty cookies; Howard Mandelbaum at Photofest; Monica O'Kelly, Jerrianne Hayslett, Rachel Skinner, and Amanda Armstrong.

CHAPTER ONE

# The Early Years: Revenge of "Stalky"

Nicole Kidman got her American citizenship the old-fashioned way—by drawing her first breath of life on American soil. Born June 20, 1967, in Honolulu, Hawaii, to Australian parents, Antony and Janelle Kidman, she had the wispy red hair and fair complexion of her father and the porcelain facial features of her beautiful mother.

Eventually, Nicole would reach a height near that of her six-foot-two father, a marathon runner, and the feistiness and stubborn self-determination of her feminist mother, but, at birth, the chubby-faced and always smiling infant looked like she would forever remain a pink bundle of joy.

Antony and Janelle were in America on educational visas when Nicole was born, thus providing her with dual Australian-American citizenship. Her birth was something of a surprise. They had been married for six years by the time she was conceived and had become increasingly discouraged about their ability to have children.

Nicole could not possibly have arrived at a more turbulent time. In 1967, both America and Australia were experiencing social unrest because of the war in Vietnam. By summer, there were 463,000 American troops in Vietnam, with another 15,000 scheduled for assignment before the end of the year. Australia had approximately 6,300 troops in Vietnam by 1967, a number that rose to 8,000 by the end of the year.

In both countries, those troops were being supplied by conscription, soldiers drawn from families that were becoming increasingly opposed to the war. In October, American civil rights leader Martin Luther King, Jr., held a press conference in Washington at which he said that if the government did not shut down the war, the government would have to be shut down by the people. Americans by the thousands took to the streets, often in violent protest, to express that very sentiment. Much the same thing was going on in Australia, where a 1967 Morgan Gallup poll found that while 63 percent of Australians favored conscription, only 37 percent favored sending draftees to Vietnam. As in America, opposition to the war was expressed with protests and resistance to the conscription laws.

Among those Australians opposed to the war were Antony and Janelle. Australia's conscription laws were different from those in the United States in that draftees were chosen by a lottery system; those who were opposed to the war basically had three choices—they could go to prison, they could leave the country and seek asylum in countries that did not have a draft, or they could seek educational deferments.

Antony's draft status in 1967 is unknown, primarily because neither he nor Nicole has ever talked publicly about it, but since he was twenty-seven that year, an advanced age for conscription, it is unlikely that it was a factor in his decision to study and work in America. Shortly after Nicole's birth— Antony was attending the University of Hawaii on a scholarship—the family moved to Washington, D. C., where Antony accepted a work-study position with the National Institutes of Health while he doggedly pursued a Ph.D. in biochemistry.

Antony and Janelle were in Washington during some of the biggest anti-war demonstrations in the country's history. Even though their immigration status in the United States was subject to review because of "political" activity, Antony and Janelle remained true to their convictions and joined the protesters in the streets.

Nicole has said that her earliest childhood memory is of playing in the snow in Washington, but following close on the heels of that are her memories of attending antiwar and feminist protest demonstrations with her parents, especially one that occurred in 1969, when she was two years of age. Her parents were involved in "a lot of movements," says Nicole proudly. "Great social consciences, both of them."

Although he was pursuing a degree in biochemistry, Antony was still searching for his professional niche. Breast cancer research was his main focus, but he was interested in much more than the pathology of the disease; he was interested in how negative emotional states, such as depression and anxiety, contribute to cancer recurrence. That interest would subsequently lead him to a second advanced degree, this time in clinical psychology.

Janelle, a nursing instructor, shared his interests, both socially and professionally. After meeting on a blind date in 1961, they discovered that they had an immediate attraction to each other. They were married later that year and parlayed that initial infatuation into a mature love based on mutual interests. Over the years, they experienced both traumas and triumphs, but their marital bond remained strong and they spent few days apart.

In 1971, their last year in Washington, Janelle gave birth to another daughter, Antonia. Her hair and skin were darker than Nicole's, but she had the same infectious smile and indomitable personality. That same year, Antony and Janelle decided they had had enough of America. It was time to return to Sydney, so that the Australization of Nicole and Antonia could begin in earnest.


At a time when many of Australia's new residents were arriving in prison shackles, the Kidmans emigrated to New South Wales in 1839 from Ireland as free settlers. The year after the first Kidmans arrived, New South Wales, one of six states in Australia, banned the importation of convict labor. In later years, it irked Nicole that she could not claim convicts as her ancestors, like most of her friends. Actually, her family is about as close as one can get in Australia to having aristocratic roots.

Over the years, the Kidmans did quite well financially in and around Sydney. One of her ancestors, her great-grandfather Sidney Kidman, was sometimes referred to as Australia's "cattle king." Not only did Sidney make a fortune raising and selling cattle, he became a shipbuilder simply by virtue of owning port-friendly land that was in the right place for the growth of a shipbuilding industry. It was not a pleasant experience for him, however, and he ended up losing money when one of his ships had to be towed out to sea and burned because of faulty workmanship.

Sidney's next big project involved the construction of the Sydney Harbour Bridge, the longest and widest single-span bridge in the world. It was erected in the early 1930s and quickly became a symbol of Australian nationalism. At the bridge's opening, which was attended by Australian premier Jack Land, a right-wing royalist who was upset about independence galloped toward the ribbon-cutting ceremony on a horse and cut the ribbon before Land could do so, thus giving the Crown a rather dubious claim to the bridge. Today there are rumors that the bridge is rusting from the inside out, but no one seems to pay much attention to that. It has stood for more than sixty years and Sydney residents cannot imagine not having it as part of the city's skyline.

Nicole is inordinately proud of the bridge. She often takes American visitors to see it up close. There is a museum and viewing platform on one of the art deco pylons on the south side and private companies offer guided tours through the bridge's inner workings. Nicole has been spotted more than once wearing a regulation jumpsuit on the tours, pointing out, along the way, the work her great-grandfather may or may not have contributed toward the bridge's construction. Make fun of her height, if you want to—she's used to that—but don't dare make a disparaging remark about her bridge!

When Antony and Janelle moved back to Australia in 1971, they bought a house in the upper-middle-class North Short district, where they still live today. Four-year-old Nicole was enrolled in ballet and acting classes and she made her stage debut at the age of six playing a sheep in a Christmas pageant. Janelle constructed her costume out of an old sheepskin car seat, which was fine with Nicole. Wearing the car seat, she bleated her heart out and followed Mary about the stage like an adoring lamb.

Acting wasn't the only activity that Janelle selected for Nicole. An ardent feminist—she read all the feminist authors of the day: Germaine Greer, Betty Friedan, and Gloria Steinem—she took Nicole with her when she went to street demonstrations. Often Nicole was asked to hand out pamphlets, a dubious honor, in her eyes at least, because passersby sometimes responded in a scornful manner to Janelle's feminist viewpoints. Occasionally, Nicole rebelled against those beliefs, like the time she wanted a Barbie doll for Christmas more than anything else in the world and Janelle refused to buy it for her because it was a politically incorrect toy. Nicole resolved that problem by stealing one from a store.

Even though she was sometimes embarrassed by her mother's feminist activism, she saw the experience in a more positive light in later years. "I've never been intimidated by a man," she told a writer for *Telegraph Magazine* in 1996. "My father was gentle but strong, a good role model. So I've always liked men. I wasn't brought up to hate them. But I never thought that because I was a woman I wouldn't be able to achieve something."

Nicole was raised a Catholic and attended mass every Sunday with her father, while Janelle remained at home. Although she converted to Catholicism when she married Antony (the Kidman family was fiercely Catholic), Janelle later became an agnostic. In later years, Antony did her one better and became an atheist. Despite those spiritual readjustments, neither parent allowed his or her dwindling faith in organized religion to prejudice the children—Nicole and Antonia were both enrolled in convent schools and encouraged to attend church.

As parents, Antony and Janelle did not believe in corporal punishment. They subscribed to the theory that children will respond to discipline that shows them the logical results of misbehavior. When Nicole and Antonia misbehaved, their parents held part or all of their allowance or restricted television viewing; they did not scold them or tell them they were stupid or wicked. They avoided imposing layers of guilt on them because they felt it would not be constructive.

"Guilt has long been regarded as an essential to good conduct," Antony once wrote. "Take away guilt, and it is thought that morality will collapse. There is no proof of this whatsoever. Millions of crimes and immoral acts are committed by people who have experienced intense guilt over their past transgressions, but who go on breaking moral codes. If guilt is so efficient in controlling behavior, why do you have so much misbehavior? Guilt can be used to control behavior in children, but the costs and the emotional turmoil associated with that control often outweigh the benefits."

Antony and Janelle were not always able to control Nicole's behavior—she was willful, determined, and at times reckless—but they made certain that she did not grow up experiencing a sense of guilt over mistakes she made. Nicole either learned from her mistakes—or she did not. Either way, she went forward without a sense of shame.

In some respects, Nicole's biggest problem as a child was Nicole herself. By the time she started school, she already was taller than everyone else in her class. By the time she started junior high school, at the age of thirteen, she was five feet nine, hardly a functional height from which to blend into her surroundings.

Because she was so tall and gawky, her classmates nicknamed her "Stalky." She was such a pariah that one of her classmates once had to be dragged kicking and screaming across the room to dance with her. It was bad enough that she was the last girl left chosen to dance, but, when the young man protested so vociferously to having any association with her, it left her humiliated and perplexed about her future as a woman, a situation not helped by the fact that her platinum blond and brunette friends seemed to have perfect heights and body shapes.

Nicole's younger sister didn't help with that situation either. "She has brown skin and beautiful brown hair, and I was always sort of the one who needed to have a personality," Nicole told *People* magazine. "We'd walk down the street and people would go, 'Oh, Nicole, isn't your sister gorgeous?'"

Then there was the matter of her thick, curly red hair. While Nicole was growing up, everyone took turns tugging on her curls. She hated that immensely. It made her feel awkward and ugly, sort of freakish. One day she bunched her hair onto the top of her head into a wild configuration. It attracted so much attention that the principal had to issue her a dire hair-alert warning. She let her hair down the way the school wanted it, but she began dying her curly tresses a variety of colors, sometimes creating a punky rainbow effect.

Despite the drama of her acting-out challenges to the established order, she remained a very shy person, sort of a female James Dean. Sometimes, when she went to parties by herself, she waited outside in the car, watching the people come and go into the brightly lit rooms that pulsated with music and adolescent hormones, wishing she could be more like *them*. Sometimes she mustered the courage to go inside, but more often than not, she ended up turning around and going back home. It was the same situation on the school bus. If she had a friend with her, everything was fine; but if she ever had to board a bus alone, she continued the journey in stony silence, fearful someone would say something about her frizzy hair or her constantly blushing face.

Nicole compensated for what she considered unfortunate physical attributes by being more daring, more willing to try new experiences, than her classmates, male and female. Once she decided to give skydiving a try, but

Janelle thwarted that adventure by refusing to sign the parental consent form. Another time, while out of sight from her parents, she went to a black-market snake farm and allowed handlers to drape a boa constrictor around her shoulders. The snake entwined about her neck, but, thankfully, did not proceed into a deadly constriction. Nicole thought it was a hoot. She was invincible. Nothing could possibly stop her from experiencing life to its fullest.

After he became a clinical psychologist, Antony acquired well-thought-out theories of child development, especially as applied to adolescents. He wrote several popular self-help books, all directed at conflict resolution and healthy living.

"It is partly through comparisons with other group members that adolescents learn about themselves and evaluate their experiences in school, at home and in the broader peer group," he wrote in *Family Life: Adapting to Change*. When that happens, he says, adolescents sometimes learn that life with their friends' parents might be even more difficult than life with their parents. "As a point of reference, [children] may well revise their opinion of their mother and father and perhaps even change the way they behave toward them."

Nicole didn't have to have conversations with her peers to know that her parents were different from theirs. She was very much aware of that from an early age, perhaps dating back to when she was recruited by her mother to hand out feminist literature on the street. Nicole's problems with her parents had less to do with them than with her own evolving concept of the type of person she was going to be as an adult.

She was always closer to her mother, but that was probably because her father was out of the house more often. One of the things that set her apart from her father was the subject of predetermination. As a psychologist, he is compelled to believe that one's behavior can change one's lot in life. Nicole, on the other hand, felt that everything in life, the good and the bad, is already predetermined. Asked by Australian television show host Ray Martin if she felt she could change her fate, she answered, "Oh, yeah. You can affect it, of course. [But] I do think there are certain things and people that you are drawn to that are meant to be in your life. My dad...would say that's hogwash. I challenge him on everything."

"Do you really?" asked Martin.

"I always have. My father is very pragmatic. Mostly my parents are very pragmatic, so I can be airy-fairy—I'm allowed. I like to believe in all those kinds of things. Just in terms of fate and those sorts of things. I'm a romantic, basically."

When you look at Nicole's childhood, at the part about her acting out her fantasies and believing that there is a place in the world that is meant for her and her alone, the inevitability of her chosen profession is difficult to deny. She was not so much made into an actress by her life experiences as she made her life experiences into a launching pad for becoming an actress. It is the classic escape route for an emotional "outsider," which is what Nicole was growing up.

Nicole was always hearing the voices of happiness and excitement; they literally surrounded her at school and in her neighborhood, but seldom did she ever feel a part of it and seldom did she ever make an effort to join in with her peers.

Ballet was her first escape. She took dance lessons and tried to get all the neighborhood fitted in tutus. Then it was mime that grabbed her attention. She became fascinated with a professional mime company that worked the streets of Sydney. Antony was quietly supportive of Nicole's acting ambitions, but Janelle played an active role in helping her daughter realize her dream of becoming an actress.

From ballet lessons to mime to acting, Janelle encouraged and supported Nicole's childhood and adolescent dreams. Nicole was a youth member of St. Martins' Theatre in Melbourne, and she tried out for and won roles in community theater productions in Sydney at the Phillip Street Theater and the Australian Theater for Young People.

"Each weekend I'd go to the theater at Phillip Street," she told the Australian edition of *Rolling Stone*. "I used to lock myself in there for the whole weekend. I thought it was fantastic. I'd be teased, 'cause I'd be going off to the theater instead of going to the beach with the boys and all the girls. I felt like an outsider because of that. But it's character building not to be a pretty child. You can't rely on batting your eyes and saying, 'Please, can I have this?'"

As a result of her devotion to the theater, she experienced her first kiss, not on the sandy beaches around Sydney and Melbourne, but onstage in front of an audience. She relished that kiss and thought about it constantly when she was not onstage. When she arrived at the theater, all she could think about was the upcoming kiss, how the boy's lips would feel against hers, and how she would feel inside when she received the kiss.

Actually, everything she learned about sex in those early years, she learned in the theater. Once, in a production of Frank Wedekind's *Spring Awakening*, a story about sexual repression in the 1800s, Nicole startled her grandmother, who was sitting in the audience—and perhaps even herself—when she yelled out, as required for the character, "Beat me! Harder! Harder! Harder!" Afterward, to her surprise, her grandmother told her that she quite liked it.

As a teenager, she appeared in a wide range of stage plays, including *Sweet Bird of Youth* and *The Seagull*. After one particularly strong performance at the Philip Street Theater, Nicole received a letter of praise from audience member Jane Campion, who was then a film student and would become an acclaimed director.

Nicole was an avid reader in her teens. When she was not at one of the three theaters that she worked out of, she devoted her time to books. It was only natural that she would try her hand at writing. At the age of thirteen, she entered—and won—a short story competition. Her story was about a young girl who got involved with an older man. Teachers gasped, she told *USA Today,* and said things such as "What is this?" and "Who wrote this?" They chastised her for venturing into adult themes, but she was not intimidated because it was a subject that she was interested in at the time.

By the age of fourteen, Nicole had every wannabe actor's dream—an agent. She fantasized about going to America to become a movie star. Few people encouraged that line of thinking, but they did make her feel that success of some kind was within her grasp, if only in Australia where the competition was not so intense. One of her first offers came from aspiring director Jane Campion, who hired her for a role in a film school project; but nothing came of it because Nicole dropped out because of exams. Though disappointed, Campion sent her a postcard that said she hoped to some day direct her in a "classic."

After two years of struggling to balance her duties at school with her ambitions to become an actress, Nicole made the first major decision of her life.

At the age of sixteen, she decided to drop out of high school and pursue act-ing full-time. Her mother was supportive of her decision, happy that Nicole had a dream to follow, but her father was not so supportive, feeling that she would regret not getting an education. Neither Nicole nor her father has ever said much publicly about his position on the matter, but whatever his level of opposition, he clearly did not stand in her way.

"I was a nightmare to my parents," Nicole told *Movieline* magazine. "I lied to them. There was a time when my mother said, 'I can't live in the same house with her.' It wasn't all roses. But that also put me in good stead [for the future]. Because I grew up in a family that yelled a lot, I don't cower [now]. People would lose their tempers in our house, things would be thrown, and an hour later we'd sit around and have a laugh."

As Nicole's dreams of stardom intensified, so did her hormone production. Boys who had scorned her in years past now saw redeeming value in her pale blue eyes and in her long, coltish legs. Nicole responded to the long-awaited attention and fell into her moments of boy craziness. Her first boyfriend was named Doug. He was a surfer and a carpenter and she was especially attracted to his workingman's hands.

"I do have a hand fetish," she told *Rolling Stone*. "Powerful hands that can be gentle. Oooooh. Girls' hands I don't care about. I can appreciate their beauty, but I'm not interested. Men's hands playing guitar? Watching the hands move on a guitar?" That, she said, is what attracts her.

Antony and Janelle had what many people would consider an unusual at-titude toward Nicole's dates. Because Janelle was concerned about men who drink and drive, she insisted that Nicole's dates stay overnight in their home—not in the guest room, mind you, but in Nicole's bedroom. Of course, the young men were admonished to sleep in a separate bed and behave them-selves.

Antony's progressive attitudes toward Nicole's dating habits were con-firmed in his writings. "Dating is a valuable source of experience for the ado-lescent," he once wrote. "A moderate degree of dating, with serious involvement delayed until late adolescence, appears to be a good pattern...For many young adults, moving in with a boyfriend or girlfriend is now seen as yet an-other stage in the development of a relationship, somewhere between going steady and marriage."

Nicole's romance with Doug lasted about six months, then she moved on and established a new relationship with a boy named Rick. Antony and Janelle watched and waited. They were liberal parents, but their willingness to accommodate Nicole during her trek through adolescence seems to have had little to do with ideology—or even Antony's professional beliefs as a psychologist. Clearly they did what they did because they loved her and feared losing her during what they correctly perceived to be a confusing time in her life.

Dropping out of school put a lot of pressure on Nicole to succeed in her chosen career. As a result, she was tireless in her quest to land a role in a movie. She networked with people who were associated with the theaters—and she went door to door. Mostly, she encountered rejections, but occasionally she received words of support.

Finally, at the age of sixteen, she got the break she had been hoping for when she was hired to play the role of Helen in the made-for-television movie *Bush Christmas* (re-titled *Prince and the Great Race* when it was released in video). Filmed north of New South Wales in Beaudesert Shire, Queensland, it was a Disney-style movie about the adventures of a horse named Prince.

The plot in this well-crafted film is straightforward. As Christmas approaches, the Thompson family learns it is in danger of losing its farm if it cannot raise the money to pay the mortgage before January 1. Their only hope is to win an upcoming horse race that offers a cash purse. Nicole is one of three children on the farm. In one of the early scenes, before the adventure begins, the entire family goes to a barn-style dance, where an up-tempo country music band named Bushwacker performs.

Sixteen-year-old Nicole whirls about the dance floor doing a two-step, her bushy, dark hair seemingly out of place in conservative surroundings. The interesting thing about the band is that the lead singer is dressed in a Garth Brooks–style hat and shirt—and he sings in a style that predates Brooks's music by at least six years. It is not known if Brooks ever saw *Bush Christmas*, but, if he did not, it is an amazing coincidence that he would develop such a similar style.

Overnight, two horse thieves steal Prince. When they awaken the next morning, Nicole, her two brothers, and an aborigine named Manalpuy go after the horse. It is a classic children's odyssey, pitting the determined children against the wily horse thieves.

At one point they stumble upon a place sacred to the aborigine. Manalpuy pushes her away because it is forbidden to females. He tells her that she must pretend she never saw it. Nicole walks away in a huff, but later apologizes. "I'm sorry about your sacred place," she says. "I didn't know. Can you forgive me?"

"I will, but my people will not," he replies solemnly.

That night, they dine on lizard and insects, and the next morning they celebrate Christmas (thus the title *Bush Christmas*). They eventually catch up with the thieves and rescue the horse. That done, their task is to get the horse back in time for the race.

*Bush Christmas* was not the kind of film that could catapult Nicole into international stardom, but it went over very well in Australia and has since become a Christmas classic, telecast each holiday with the same reverence afforded *It's a Wonderful Life* in the United States.


Nicole's second movie role in 1983 was in *BMX Bandits*. She played the part of Judy, a young girl who gets involved, literally by accident, with a teenage bicycle "gang." She first appears pushing a grocery cart at the store at which she works. Her first line in the movie is "Hi!" and it is delivered to a chubby male coworker. She meets the bicycle gang when they accidentally crash into the grocery carts she is gathering. She gets fired as a result and tags along with the guys to see where that takes her.

At five feet ten, sixteen-year-old Nicole has a luminous presence in the film. She was a good three and four inches taller than the boys, even taller than all the adults, with the exception of one or two men who were about her same height. For this role, in which the entire focus was on teens, she wore her curly hair pulled up on top of her head in the same configuration that had caused her so much trouble in high school.

In later years, Nicole often spoke of how awkward and ill at ease she felt as a teen. Those feelings are clearly evident in the film, where the gawky and flat-chested actress sometimes appears to think that her biggest challenge in life is simply to move her body from one place to another. She has said that she felt that she was "ugly" at that age, but clearly that was not the case, for she had a beautiful face that was filled with starry-eyed wonderment. The ugliness in her memories is probably due to the way she felt trying to make her body move with as much grace as her thoughts.

Shortly after she joins up with the bicycle gang, they discover a cache of high-tech two-way radios that are meant to be picked up by bank robbers. They sell the radios, one at a time, to other teens with the hope that they will raise enough money for Nicole to purchase a bike of her own.

Soon it becomes apparent to the teens that the crooks—and a very bad gang of crooks they are—are hunting them down to recover the radios. They finally catch up with Nicole in a warehouse, where she tries to talk her way out of the situation, then fights her way to freedom. She is more physical in this movie than she was in *Bush Christmas*. She runs, rides a bike, fights off attackers—everything that a sixteen-year-old would do when chased by vicious killers. She is eventually captured again and kidnapped by the dimwitted crooks, an event that puts her in a position to be rescued by the entire Australian biker nation.

Directed by British-born Brian Trenchard-Smith, who previously had directed *Day of the Assassin* and *The Love Epidemic*, *BMX Bandits*—along with *Bush Christmas*—made Nicole an instant celebrity among Australia's youth. She was very quickly signed up to do a series of television programs in 1984, including *Chase Through the Night* (movie), *Matthew and Son* (movie), *Five Mile Creek* (series), and *A Country Practice* (series).

*Five Mile Creek*, which required her to be in front of a camera five days a week for seven months, probably had the biggest impact on her personal development because it gave her the confidence to take chances and make mistakes without disastrous results.

When she emerged from her first year as an independent teenager, it was with a sense of confidence. At seventeen, she was famous in Australia, the wunderkind of her generation, and she had her own apartment and her own personal bank account. She also had a relationship with a thirty-seven-year-old man. Perhaps to flex her newfound independence, she undertook the first reckless adventure of her life: she left Australia and went to Amsterdam with her boyfriend.

When they arrived in Amsterdam, Nicole decided that she no longer knew how she felt about things (perhaps it was too much closeness on the long flight). "I said, 'I really think we should just be friends,'" she told *Premiere* magazine. As can be imagined, that pronouncement did not go over too well with the boyfriend. Asked if her boyfriend went for the new arrangement, she said no and then burst out laughing. "I naively did not understand male sexuality at that age."

While in Amsterdam, Nicole went to a flea market and purchased an antique brocaded gown made in the 1930s. She thought it would make a beautiful wedding gown—and so it did several years later. "I thought I was going to marry the guy I was with—and I didn't. Thank God . . . 'Cause I'm sure he says, 'Thank God' too. But I knew it was the dress for me."

CHAPTER TWO

# First Flirtations with Movie Success

For decades, there has existed in Australia the story of a legendary race-horse that travels a long distance, under harsh conditions, to Melbourne to win the year's biggest race—not once, but twice in consecutive years. With time, the horse became a mythic source of great national pride, so it was perhaps inevitable that someone would offer up a fictionalized account for a motion picture.

"This is a story that is part of Australian folklore, so I had known about it for a long time," says director Denny Lawrence, who signed on to do the film *Archer* (later changed to *Archer's Adventure* for release in the United States). "The idea of a horse walking such a long distance and then winning a race by such a margin, and doing it again the next year, is of course appealing. Australia was a wild frontier still in those days—like the U.S.A.—with outlaws and many natural obstacles to battle and overcome."

Lawrence, one of Australia's most respected writers and directors—and currently chairman of the Australian Film Institute—says that the main challenge making the film was "slightly fictionalizing the account without betraying the historical fact—and still telling a good dramatic story within the parameters of 'family viewing' as well."

As *Archer's Adventure* begins, Dave, a stable boy played by Brett Climo, talks his employer into allowing him to take Archer on a five-hundred-mile trip to Melbourne to race in the Melbourne Cup. The countryside, while beautiful, is filled with natural dangers and human predators. Brett is robbed of his money on the first day out. On the second day, he comes across a farm, where he asks for food and lodging for himself and his horse, even though he no longer has the money to pay for it.

While at the farm, he meets a young girl named Catherine (played by Nicole), who is there to visit her uncle. They hit it off almost instantly and by nightfall they find themselves in a romantic setting.

"You can kiss me if you like," says Nicole.

"Are you sure?" he answers, not believing what he heard.

Nicole turns away, no longer looking at him. "No," she says playfully. "I've changed my mind."

"Too late," he says, and kisses her.

The next morning they part company, although with an expectation that they will meet again. She tells him that he would be welcome to visit her at her parents' farm, which lies on the road to Melbourne. Before they meet again, Brett has an adventure with a married woman who is burying her child when he rides up to her farm. He builds a coffin for the child and digs the grave. Then he learns that her husband left home to make money for the family, even though the wife needed him more at the farm. Brett decides to look for the husband when he resumes his journey to Melbourne so that he can tell the man about the death of his child and how much his wife needs him.

When Brett rides onto the farm owned by Nicole's parents, everyone is in the middle of a wedding celebration. Nicole encourages him to put Archer in the barn so that he can dance with her. That night, a herd of wild horses spooks Archer into breaking free and joining the herd. With the help of Nicole's parents, Brett locates Archer and resumes his journey to Melbourne.

The entire film was shot on location near Sydney—some of the wilderness locations are today bustling suburbs—but since it was done in the winter, the cast had to wear many different layers of clothing.

The film was beautifully photographed and the Australian scenery is often spectacular. "The landscape was integral to the story and an allegory as well as a reality," explains Lawrence. "To go from temperate coastal regions through the mountains (with snow—very strange to the horses, needless to say) across the tablelands and interior plains to the river flats of Melbourne, was an epic journey."

Nicole did not have a large role in this film, but she was incredibly poised in every scene, becoming the focus even when that was unintended. Lawrence chose her for the role after viewing a sneak preview of *BMX Bandits*. "I thought she was terrifically exciting and charismatic," he says. "I then met with her and found her modest and shy in person, with qualities that were essential to a young woman of those times. She was equally appealing to a modern audience I felt, the character required a bit of 'sass.' She was also tremendously photogenic."

Lawrence was not certain what to expect from her once filming began. "She was very open and easy to direct and work with, but already had confidence and good craft skills which made it easy to get good outcomes," he says. "She was a thorough professional from the word go."

The only scenes that gave her a hard time, he says, were those in which she had to ride a horse and wear long frocks and petticoats. "Like a lot of actors, she was quiet and serious about her work and because she was a little shy I was slightly concerned that she might balk at the 'kissing' scene, but, as at all other times, she was proficiently 'in the moment' and so suddenly 'bold' that it threw Brett a bit, which was perfect for the scene. I had wondered about whether there was enough 'justification' for this little plot element, but by the time we finished the film we all wished we'd had more of Nicole in there—and the audiences loved her, of course."

Actually, it wasn't the actors that gave Lawrence a difficult time during the filming. "Horses are especially flighty and sensitive, even with the best training," he says. "And such thoroughbreds tire easily and get bored and have to be protected. Also, like all of us, they are better at some things than others."

Actually, there were three "Archers" in the film, he says—the main one and a couple of doubles that were used for different tasks such as running, jumping, or crossing rivers. "One funny note is that the lead actor, Brett, was allergic to horses."

Nicole's next movie was *Wills & Burke*, a comedy directed by Bob Weis. It must have been a real clunker because no one in Australia today will discuss it and it cannot be purchased on videocassette in the United States. It has literally vanished from public sight. All actors have movies in their past that they would like to pretend never happened, and for Nicole that movie would appear to be *Wills & Burke*.

As sometimes happens in the movie business, Nicole went from that experience to one that would radically change her life. She was signed for the lead role in the television miniseries *Vietnam*, a drama that re-created the passions that had so inflamed the country, including her own parents, in the 1960s and early 1970s. She was given the role of Megan, a young woman who sees her life profoundly affected by the war. Also co-starring in the series was Brett Climo, who had worked with Nicole in *Archer's Adventure*, and Alyssa-Jane Cook, who went on to become one of Australia's most respected actresses and television personalities.

When the story begins, Megan is fourteen, an awkward schoolgirl who seems unaffected by the war, but when it ends she is twenty-four and very much involved in bringing it to an end. For Nicole, playing the role was a challenge that required her, for the first time in her life, to do outside research on a character.

"It really made a big difference to me to work with a three-dimensional character and flesh out the comic and dramatic aspects of the role," Nicole told *Cosmopolitan* magazine. "I became obsessive about acting. I did all sorts of research about the mores and culture of the Sixties. I wasn't even born yet when the Beatles became popular, so I had to sit down and study life in the Sixties, as if for a term paper."

The highlight of the series occurs when Megan, by then a vociferous opponent of conscription, is a guest on a radio call-in show. As she participates in the listener discussions about the war and the draft, a Vietnam veteran calls in to express his opinions. Megan recognizes the voice: it is her estranged brother, whom she has not seen or talked to in a long time. The point from which she recognizes the voice and then breaks down in tears lasts for six minutes.

It was a masterful scene that required Nicole to express an array of emotions, using only her face; beautifully done, it was accomplished in one take and established Nicole as an actress to be reckoned with. When the miniseries aired, Australians reacted very emotionally to the scene and quickly elevated Nicole to star status. The Australian Film Institute responded by presenting her with an award—her first—Best Performance by an Actress in a Leading Role in a Television Drama.

* * *

After the success of *Vietnam*, Nicole showed up for work in Perth for her next project overflowing with enthusiasm and optimism. *Windrider*, directed by veteran Australian cinematographer Vincent Monton, was a windsurfing movie directed toward the youth market. Nicole signed on to play the role of Jade, a rock singer who falls for a windsurfer (Tom Burlinson) who works at his father's engineering firm.

Burlinson, who was thirty when filming began, was born in Toronto, Canada, to British-born parents, who subsequently moved to New Jersey, then back to England, then on to Australia, where they divorced and Burlinson remained with his father. After doing television in his early twenties, he got his big break in 1981 when he was cast as Jim Craig in *The Man From Snowy River*, starring Kirk Douglas. He had made two additional movies by the time he signed on for *Windrider*, but, for some reason, his career had cooled considerably by then.

*Windrider* begins with Nicole watching Burlinson do a 360-degree turn on a windsurfing board. There is almost no plot development in this movie and Nicole has very few good lines. Mostly, she stands around looking pretty, saying things like "What are you doing, mate?" She still has a deep Australian accent at this point in her career and she plays that up, sometimes looking like a caricature of an Aussie punk rocker on the make. She does no singing in the film, but she does lip-synch to the music.

The most notable thing about this movie is that eighteen-year-old Nicole does her first nude scene, ever. It occurs with Burlison in a shower, where she is covered with soap lather. Subsequently, she does other nude scenes in which she displays her still-growing breasts and barely legal buttocks, clearly her biggest physical asset at that point in her life.

Probably not until the movie was released did Nicole know she had made a mistake. Reviews were typical of the one written by Desmond Ryan for the *Philadelphia Inquirer*: "*Windrider*, an Australian production that proves that Hollywood has no monopoly on airhead entertainment, doesn't have much more content than the average balloon... [it] would have done everyone a favor by forgetting its silly plot and following the wave created by *The Endless Summer*. In this case, facts would make a stronger movie than fiction."

Nicole's judgment in making the film may have been impaired after shooting began because she began dating her costar, Tom Burlinson. It was the first big romance of her life and lasted for nearly three years. She was enthusiastic about the romance and transferred that enthusiasm to a film that was not worthy of it.

*Windrider* ended up becoming a turning point in Burlinson's career. He made only four feature films after that, and although he worked in several Australian television series, he put less emphasis on acting as the years went by (he has not made a movie in over ten years) to focus on his singing career. He has a singing voice that is remarkably similar to Frank Sinatra's—he was chosen to be the voice of the "young" Sinatra in the American miniseries produced by Tina Sinatra—and recently he has made a nice living in Australia with a stage show he created, "The Sinatra Story in Song."

In a 1989 interview with *Rolling Stone*, Nicole was philosophical about both Burlinson and the movie: "I accepted roles when I was younger, which I don't regret, because on everything I've done I've learnt something or I've met someone who's been quite instrumental in molding my career. On *Windrider*, I met someone that...was really important to me and helped me to grow. So you've got to look at things positively. I did do some things that weren't of really high quality, but I learnt a lot."

The relationship with Burlinson ended in 1988 when he asked her to marry him and she said no. Shortly after her breakup with Burlinson, she began dating actor Marcus Graham. Four years older than Nicole, the Perth-born actor had made only one film at that point, *Dangerous Game*, but he would go on to make numerous movies, including 2001's *Mulholland Drive* and 2002's *Horseplay*. For Nicole, the relationship was different from the one she enjoyed with Burlinson. Although she had lived with Burlinson and set up housekeeping, she chose to live separately from Graham during their romance, citing career needs and a wish for more personal space.


In addition to all the career and relationship issues swirling about Nicole in 1985, she experienced her first real family emergency. She was on the set of *Windrider* when she received an urgent telephone call from her mother. Janelle told her that she had some bad news. She was in the hospital, where she had been diagnosed with breast cancer. Nicole was devastated. She dropped the telephone and found the producers and pleaded with them to allow her to return home. They rejected her request on the grounds that they could not afford a break in production.

Nicole stuck it out until production was completed, then hurried home to be with her mother. "Suddenly the person that you love most in the world is losing her hair and sobbing every night," Nicole told *Premiere* magazine. "It was very hard on me and it still remains a big thing in my life."

Janelle underwent a lumpectomy, a new procedure at that time in Australia, then followed up with chemotherapy and radiation, convinced that she was going to die. How ironic it was that Antony's early research had been on the effects of anxiety and stress on breast cancer. Perhaps fearing that her decision to drop out of school had somehow created the anxiety that triggered the disease, Nicole nursed and took care of her mother with uncompromised compassion, even going to the trouble of qualifying as a masseuse so that she could massage her mother's aching muscles every day.

"It was very hard to see your mother going through such pain," Nicole told *Good Weekend* magazine. "It opened my eyes to mortality, and to pain and suffering, and from that point on I was determined to support and be a part of and in some way help. Janelle's cancer changed the family in profound and lasting ways."

One result of Janelle's illness was that Antony resumed his research on breast cancer in order to find out if cognitive behavior therapy could be effective on women with advanced stages of the disease. Like most psychologists, Antony was much better at intellectualizing the problem and looking for solutions outside the family than he was in providing one-on-one support (it is a drawback of the profession). Another outgrowth was Antony's decision to embrace "psychoncology," a new field in which therapists work with cancer patients and their families in an effort to help them better cope with the disease. The best way to help Janelle, Antony concluded, was to find new approaches to treating the disease. As it happened, Janelle's cancer did not recur and today, more than fifteen years later, she is still cancer free.

By this point in their marriage, it had become obvious that Janelle had affected Antony's professional life in a variety of ways. His new focus on breast cancer was an obvious example. Not so obvious was the influence she had on his viewpoints about the changing dynamics of family life in general. He began to see the anxieties and conflicts experienced by women in a more personal context.

"Although women are more positive than men about the prospect of marriage, they are generally less content with the reality of it," Antony wrote in his 1995 book, *Family Life: Adapting to Change*. "The dual goals of career and family are more easily achieved by men. For women these goals conflict and can cause severe problems. The fact that more women than men seek professional help during the years of child rearing, when their children reach adulthood and leave home, and when their spouses retire or die, reflects the great stresses brought to bear on women who carry the emotional responsibility for most family relationships."

Antony understood in 1995 what had perhaps escaped his attention while he and Janelle were busying raising Nicole and Antonia—and trying to pursue their individual careers, one more successfully than the other—namely, that Janelle had paid a high personal price for her devotion to the family unit.

After the release of *Windrider*, it was clear to everyone that Nicole was on a roll—downhill. Her next film, *Watch the Shadows Dance* (also known as *Nightmaster* in the United States), was directed by Russian-born filmmaker Mark Joffe. He had directed two television series—*Fast Lane* and *Carson's Law*—but *Watch the Shadows Dance* was his first feature film.

Nineteen-year-old Nicole was asked to play the role of Amy Gabriel, a high school student who gets involved with a group of fellow students that play war games with paint guns. The male lead was played by Tom Jennings, whose first film role was in *Mad Max Beyond Thunderdome*. After completing work on *Watch the Shadows Dance*, he did one feature film and two television shows, then dropped out of public sight.

Also costarring with Nicole was Joanne Samuel, a twenty-nine-year-old veteran of ten feature films and television series, including *The Young Doctors* and *Mad Max*. Like Jennings, she did two more projects after work on *Watch the Shadows Dance* wrapped, then she, too, dropped out of sight.

The plot of *Watch the Shadows Dance* revolves around the machinations of a mysterious karate teacher and the paint-gun wars, two separate themes that finally merge to create the dramatic tension in the story.

Nicole does not have a single good line in the movie, but the camera loved her face and her mannerisms, despite the contrived tensions that constantly surrounded her. Some of the scenes seem to have been written especially for her. When a young man puts the moves on Nicole, commenting on her legs and arms, one of her "club" members steps in to protect her. Nicole keeps her cool, but when the guy leaves, she chastises her friend for stepping in. "I can look after myself without your help," she says. "I'll do my own fighting, thank you."

As it turns out, the karate teacher is a crazed war veteran, a cocaine addict who kills a drug pusher (coincidentally the same youth who accosted Nicole earlier in the film). Jennings witnesses the murder and tells the karate teacher what he saw. Not wishing to be convicted of murder, the karate teacher shows up at the paint-gun games to silence Jennings. From that point on, the resolution of the conflict proceeds along an entirely predictable course.

The acting in *Watch the Shadows Dance* was not spectacular, but it was within the limits of other, more successful films in this genre. The idea of a story based on paint-gun warriors was a good one and the sound track, most of which was written and sung by Paul Kelly, was above average. The problems with the film lay in the manner in which it was directed and edited. Visually, it never achieved a life of its own.

For Nicole, it represented another regrettable lapse in judgment. Her mother had been diagnosed with breast cancer and she had made two bad films in a row. By the time 1986 ended, Nicole, although only nineteen, was pondering the end of life as she knew it.

CHAPTER THREE

# The Calm Before
# the Storm

Nineteen eighty-seven was a make-or-break year for Nicole. From the
emotional high of *Vietnam*, she had tumbled into the despair of
*Windrider* and *Watch the Shadows Dance*. She had seen it happen so
many times before with Australian actors—a high-profile role, followed by
local public acclaim, then a free-fall tumble into obscurity.

It was around this time that the twenty-year-old actress began dreaming of
stardom in America. She did not want to become a local has-been; she
wanted to perform in the international arena—and the key to that, at least in
her case, was to make a name for herself in America. And why not? Legally,
she was as much an American as she was an Australian. Hollywood was her
birthright, was it not?

Nicole's next movie was a comedy entitled *The Bit Part*. Costarring Chris
Haywood and Katrina Foster—and directed by Brendan Maher—it did nothing to advance Nicole's career. The film disappeared from public view almost
overnight and today it is next to impossible to find on videocassette.

Nicole took that hit on the chin and kept going. Her next project was a
part on the television series *Room to Move*. She played the role of Carol Trig,
a high school track star who meets a new girl who makes her question her
dedication to the sport. Also co-starring in the show was Alyssa-James Cook,
with whom Nicole had worked in *Vietnam*.

Artistically, Nicole's fortunes improved somewhat when she signed on to do the feature film *Flirting*, a coming-of-age story about adolescent romance between two boarding school students. In the wrong hands, the film could have been another teen exploitation film such as *Windrider* and *Watch the Shadows Dance*, but director John Duigan rescued it from that fate, primarily by writing the script himself. Actually, *Flirting* was the second film in a planned trilogy about Danny Embling, an awkward adolescent prone to stuttering and attacks of knee-jerk nerdiness.

In 1987, Duigan was ranked among Australia's "new wave" filmmakers. He got his start in the mid-1970s with a government grant that allowed him to direct low-budget films such as *The Firm Man* and *Trespassers*. With a deft hand for merging detail with the bigger picture, he quickly gained a reputation for "serious" films that dealt with issues. *Sirens*, staring Hugh Grant, Sam Neill, Elle Macpherson, and Portia de Rossi, is one of his better post-*Flirting* efforts. Released in 1994, the film explored religious and sexual issues from the viewpoint of a young British reverend.

The Australian film community is minuscule compared to its counterparts in America and England, so it is not uncommon for directors to use the same actors over and over again, especially if they have a public following. Nicole had no reservations about signing on for *Flirting* because Duigan also had been her director in *Room to Move* and *Vietnam*.

Nicole was given the role of Nicola Radcliffe, an older student at the girls' school where the female lead, played by fifteen-year-old Thandie Newton, attends classes. *Flirting* was Newton's first motion picture. The daughter of a Zimbabwean mother, a princess of the Shona tribe, and an English father, she lived in Zambia until political and social unrest forced her family to move to England. Before going to Australia to star in her first film, she received a degree in anthropology from Cambridge University. She went on to appear in another film with Nicole, 1996's *The Leading Man*, and, ironically, she did a love scene in 2000 with Tom Cruise in *Mission: Impossible II*.

The male lead in *Flirting* was played by Noah Taylor, who had originated the character in *The Year My Voice Broke*. The British-born actor went on to appear in nearly two dozen films, including *Lara Croft: Tomb Raider* (2001) and *Vanilla Sky* (2001).

*Flirting* begins at the boys' school with a number of boys, including Danny, reporting to the headmaster's office for a sound whipping. After the caning, Danny lies in bed and mulls over the complexities and absurdities of life, finally turning his thoughts to the girls' school located across the lake. To Danny, with his suppressed sexuality, the two schools stare at each other across the lake like "brooding volcanoes."

When the scene switches to the girls' school, Thandiwe, who is the only black student in the school, feigns sleep as a group of white girls gather around her and wonder aloud if the black girl with an African past would be interested in a banana.

Danny, an awkward boy who sometimes stutters, is attracted to Thandiwe, the more aggressive of the two. As if to prove that, she breaks away from a dance to sneak into his dormitory. They sit on his bed to talk for a while, then she excuses herself to go to the bathroom. While she is gone, the other boys return from the dance, leaving Thandiwe trapped in the bathroom. Danny goes in to rescue her, and they both get trapped in a stall when several boys enter the room to shower.

Danny and Thandiwe soon become pen pals. When one of the other boys steals one of her letters and reads it to everyone, she is mortified. She blames Danny and when they put on a coed play, she chooses Nicola's suitor as her partner. Nicola ends up with Danny, a development that does not please her.

One of the movie's best scenes occurs when Nicola and Thandiwe come together as dance partners. As the dance teacher yells out instructions for the girls to look "sultry" and "smolder," the two girls spar with eye contact. Nicola is magnificent in her body language and facial interactions. Finally, after peppering her foe with haughty attitude, she gets to the point. "I think we should swap partners in the musical," suggests Nicola, who goes on to explain that Danny did not read the letter aloud—it was taken from him. Later that evening, Nicola catches Danny and Thandiwe kissing.

One night Danny and Thandiwe have a sexual encounter in which she relieves his tensions with her hand. When she returns to the dormitory, Nicola asks her if anything happened. Thandiwe, overcome with guilt, coughs and says, "I beg your pardon."

"No, it's all right. You don't have to tell me. I think if I liked some boy enough, I'd want to."

"Have you ever?"

"Of course, not."

"Almost?"

"Well...do you remember the young guy who was fixing the bell tower? I used to take him a cup of tea each morning before assembly. I rather liked him, although he never said anything much. I used to . . . close my eyes and sit on a chair and let him touch me all over as long as he promised not to take anything off. I thought it was so exquisitely daring I'd almost faint. I'd have to sit down because I'd be trembling so much my legs would have given way. Afterward, I'd be reading a lesson convinced all the teachers must know because I was so shivery delicious all over."

"I'm amazed," says Thandiwe.

"So am I when I think of it, which is most of the time, especially at mass." Nicola offers up a toast. "Here's to risks," she says bravely.

Nicole's eyes dance the entire time she tells the story about the boy in the bell tower. Her concept of on-screen sexuality had changed over the past couple of years; for the first time we are given a glimpse of a more mature actress, one who understands the nature of the connection between her brain and her vagina. If the truth is told, no one *talks* about sex better than Nicole Kidman; utilizing those skills, she would make an amazing dominatrix at a dead poets' society.

The movie ends predictably enough, but not before Thandiwe is seen topless in bed with Danny, a surprise since the actress was only fifteen at the time.

*Flirting* was not released in the United States until 1991. For the most part, reviewers were enthusiastic about the film. Wrote Roger Ebert for the *Chicago Sun-Times:* "So often we settle for noise and movement from the movie screen, for stupid people indulging unworthy fantasies. Only rare movies like *Flirting* remind us that the movies are capable of providing us with the touch of other lives, that when all the conditions are right we can grow a little and learn a little, just like the people on the screen. This movie is joyous, wise and life-affirming, and certainly one of the year's best films."

*Flirting* is a film to "make you believe in love again," wrote Michael Morrison for the Edinburgh University Film Society. "It's all been done before," he wrote. "But this film is refreshingly original. *Flirting* is intelligent, witty, tender and beautifully understated."

Hal Hinson, writing for the *Washington Post*, called the film "brilliant." He praised one "touch and kiss" scene and wrote, "Every event has that urgent desperation of adolescent hyperbole when every sensation is a new one, and so the whole movie has this drunk-dizzy, head-over-heels quality."

* * *

Australian filmmaker Phillip Noyce began making short films and documentaries as a teenager, but he was twenty-six before he made his first feature, *Backroads* (1977). He followed that up the following year with *Newsfront*, a film about the movie newsreel industry; that effort won him Australian awards for best film, best director, and best screenplay. For the next decade, he did a couple of feature films, but for the most part, he worked in television, most successfully on *The Hitchhiker*.

When he was chosen to be the director for *Dead Calm*, a thriller based on Charles Williams's novel, he knew he had his hands on something special. Technically, it would be a challenge to film, he knew, but that was the least of his problems. Since it was basically a three-person story—two men and a woman—everything would ride on casting. A mistake there would nullify even the best camera work and direction.

For the female lead, the role of Rae Ingram, Noyce and the producers considered a number of "name" actresses such as Debra Winger and Sigourney Weaver, but the more they discussed it among themselves, the more Nicole Kidman's name came up. Her performance in *Vietnam* had affected Noyce greatly.

After watching the emotional radio scene in which Nicole carries six minutes of the action simply by virtue of her facial expressions, he was so moved by her performance that he wept. She had never attempted a role as complicated and as psychological demanding as the one required in *Dead Calm*, but he had no doubts about her ability to handle it, despite her youth.

Veteran actor Sam Neill, then forty years of age, was chosen to play opposite Nicole as Rae Ingram's husband, John Ingram. The Irish-born actor had made nearly twenty feature films, including *Omen III: The Final Conflict* and *The Good Wife*—and he had appeared in about as many television series—so he was considered a safe choice.

When it came to the second male lead, the villainous role of Hughie Warriner, the *Dead Calm* brain trust decided to go with Billy Zane, another newcomer. The American-born Zane had appeared in only two feature films, *Critters* (1986) and *Back to the Future* (1985), but he had done several television shows, including "The Case of the Hillside Stranglers" and "Police Story: Monster Manor," that had demonstrated a propensity for creating offbeat characters. At twenty-one, dark and emotionally unpredictable, he would be an effective counterpoint foil for Nicole.

As *Dead Calm* begins, Nicole's character, Rae Ingram, is in an automobile accident that kills her young child. Disconsolate over the loss, she and her husband, John, take a long cruise so that they can be alone with each other. Three weeks at sea, they spot their first ship. Dead in the water, it appears to be deserted. As they stare at the schooner, they spot a man in a dinghy rowing toward their ship. When he comes aboard, he tells them that his name is Hughie Warriner. There was a disaster aboard the schooner, he explains, and all five crew members died of food poisoning. To make matters worse, he insists that the schooner is sinking. All he wants is to get as far away as possible.

When Hughie goes to sleep, John rows over to check out the ship. What he discovers alarms him and he heads back to his ship, but before he can reach it Hughie knocks Rae unconscious and takes over the boat. John makes a desperate move to get aboard, and, to his horror, he fails.

As the ship sails away with Rae unconscious and Hughie at the wheel, John returns to the schooner and tries to get the ship operational again.

Rae is horrified when she awakens and sees that the schooner is no longer in sight. "Would you just tell me one thing?" she asks. "I just need to know if that boat is sinking."

"No," Hughie answers, looking at his watch. "Past tense would do, but, yeah, it is. Why don't you believe me?"

"Yeah, I believe you. 'Course I do. That's why we've got to go back. To get John."

"There's no going back."

Rae locates the schooner on the radar screen, but the radio contact with John is only one way (he can hear her, but she can't hear him). He uses clicks to talk to her. One of the auditory delights of the movie occurs when she talks to him on the radio, her whispers of "Are you there?" cutting straight to the bone.

In an attempt to get control of the situation, Rae allows Hughie to make love to her. Whether the sex is a seduction on her part or a form of rape is left up to the viewer to determine. Nicole is nude during this scene, her by-then famous posterior exposed for maximum benefit.

Once Hughie lets down his guard, Rae drugs him and then tries to load a shotgun, only they end up fighting over it. He tries to choke her, but passes out from the drugs. While he is unconscious, Rae ties him up and nails down the hatch to the cabin. She tries to start the engine, but it won't start. She hoists the sails and turns the boat around.

Eventually, Hughie gets free and goes after her once again. This time she wounds him with a speargun and sets him adrift in a rubber raft. Of course, this being a thriller, there is much more action to come.

Nicole's physical acting in this movie is suburb. It is really the first time she had been asked to display anger, panic, and resolve with her body—and she rises to the task, even in those scenes, so uncharacteristic of Nicole, in which she has to go toe-to-toe with Hughie in physical combat.

"She was absolutely focused on that picture, which is remarkable for a twenty-year-old," says assistant director Stuart Freeman. "She handled everything like a trooper [and] under pretty hard conditions. I did a picture with Vanessa Redgrave in Alaska many years ago and Nicole reminds me so much of Vanessa in the tenacity to get the performance. She's so focused on getting a performance that she is unaware of being cold or being roughed up because she is so focused on the performance. That was in 1987—now the world knows how focused she is."

That is high praise coming from an assistant director as experienced as Freeman. Born in Great Britain, where he began his film career, he moved to Australia in 1981; by 2002 he had worked on over sixty feature films in twenty-nine countries and had completed more than two hundred hours of television.

Although Freeman had lived in Australia six years before production began on *Dead Calm*—and was familiar with Nicole's work—he had never met her. That occurred in the producer's office in Sydney while they were in preproduction. They did not meet again until everyone arrived on location in Queensland, a resort area in northeastern Australia just inside the Great Barrier Reef.

The actors and film crew stayed on Hamilton Island for the duration of the twelve-week shoot, living in chalets and block apartments usually rented to tourists. The island is one of the most popular in the area and features a high-rise hotel and a jet airstrip with direct access to Australia's major cities.

They knew from the start that it would be a difficult shoot—most of the action takes place aboard a schooner and working with boats is sometimes as worrisome as working with animals—but there was no way during preproduction for them to prepare for their worst enemy, bad weather.

"We shot it when the trade winds were full on," says Freeman. "When we did the storm sequence, we actually sidled out and caught the edge of a storm, which was happening daily. That was the remarkable thing about it—the storm sequences were virtually for real."

Working at sea is one of the hardest things to do on film, he explains. "It doesn't matter what happens; if you miss the mark, you can't just put the brakes on—you have to turn around 360 degrees to come back again and you are subject to the wind, the waves, the elements. The most difficult thing [for the actors] was being able to concentrate on the performance when everything else was against them, the way the weather was treating us."

When the weather was bad, they simply filmed on a set they built on the island. They constructed it from scratch around a seventy by forty–foot water tank. Buoyed by empty oil drums, the sets floated on the water, thus providing a sense of realism. When the actors walked, the make-believe boat rocked and rolled, generating a realistic movement comparable to what they would have experienced aboard the ship.

The first acting challenge Nicole faced was as a car accident victim. Lying in the emergency room of a hospital, tubes connected to her body and her face battered and bruised, she convincingly portrayed a mother who had just lost her only child.

"When a good actor focuses, they become that character," observes Freeman. "Nicole mentally put herself into that position. Obviously, Phil Noyce would have set the scene, the tempo, but it doesn't matter what the director does because in the long run it has to be the ability of the actor to pull it off. It comes down to ability. She showed that amazing ability at such a tender age. In terms of the style of acting in such an oppressive, if you like, psychological aspect of the movie, it was astounding that she had the ability. I've often wondered if she knew she had the ability."

Another tough scene to make realistic was the sex scene between Nicole and Zane, which was filmed on a set designed to look like the interior of the ship. Nicole's character initiated the seduction, perhaps with the intention of making him trust her, but shortly after it began (she removed her shirt and he ripped away her shorts), she left him to go up on deck, only to return to complete the act. The scene was tough on Nicole, not because of the nudity—she had appeared nude in movies before—but because of the emotions involved, the fact that she would be having sex with a man she despised.

"All the crew that had to be there were there," says Freeman. "Everyone respected [her feelings] and that was another thing that she handled superbly. Those that have to be there to do their job, do their job, and part of her job was to do that scene. So it was a matter of doing it and doing it professionally. Again, for her tender years, she was so mature."

Although Nicole was somewhat shy in her personal relations with the other actors and crew, when it came to the work product, she was surprisingly assertive. "I remember there were many times when there were discussions about a particular scene that she and Phil would have a very, very deep and meaningful conversation while we were doing lighting or getting the positions right," says Freeman. "Sometimes they would go off and just discuss the performance."

The subject matter of the film was not the only difficult consideration. Simply dealing with the sea and its many moods was time consuming. Typically, the crew and actors put in fifteen-hour days. Already located a good twenty miles from the mainland, they had to travel an hour by boat from Hamilton Island to reach the lea of another island, where most of the filming took place.

"We had a boat for makeup, support boats, divers, people in the water, camera boats—and our catering was brought out by boat," says Freeman. "We had a massive boat for our base and we had other boats to take us out—it was absolutely colossal."

On weekends, they all let down their hair and partied on Hamilton Island. No one ever thought about leaving the island to go to the mainland. "There were fun times, singing and partying, but nothing extraordinary," recalls Freeman. The only person who did not seem to relax was Nicole's costar Billy Zane. "He was very intense in those days," says Freeman. "The part he was playing, he put his heart and soul into it, and it was hard for him to get out of it."

Nicole had a different take on Zane's apparent isolation. "Phil Noyce manipulated us in certain ways, so that Sam [Neill] and I got on very, very well, and Billy, well, we didn't get on," she told *Rolling Stone*. "But Billy and I were playing characters that were in conflict constantly. And I think there was an unspoken agreement between us that we weren't going to get on. I don't think you can be buddy-buddy with someone you're meant to be struggling with, and feeling so much animosity towards."

To keep in character, Nicole made it a point to be in bed by ten P.M. each night. For Zane, who remained in character twenty-four hours a day, Nicole's standoffishness was a challenge and he constantly exhorted Nicole to come out and play past her bedtime. It annoyed her because, as she later admitted, she secretly wanted to be the wild one.

Sixteen years after the fact, Freeman's strongest memories about the film revolve around Nicole's relationship with his daughters—Rachel and Joanna, who were four and five years of age at the time of filming. He recalls that Nicole would complete terrifying scenes in which she was fighting for her life, then she would sit down to watch the dailies and invite Rachel and Joanna to sit on her lap. It was an amazing sight to Freeman, who was not used to seeing actresses change emotional gears so quickly. It touched him to see his daughters cling to her and have their affections reciprocated.

"I have nothing but respect for that girl," says Freeman. "She's a very favorite lady of mine because of the things she had to do [in the film] and the conditions she had to do them in. When we saw the dailies and she sat the girls on her knees, you wouldn't know that she'd been putting on that ordeal the way she was smiling and playing with my girls. She's an amazing woman...Nicole Kidman is one of my happiest memories. I have nothing but respect for her."

Costar Neill was left with much the same impression. "She can do anything, but she does have that extra thing, which is that she is a star," he told CNN. "And that's the mysterious factor you can't explain."

When *Dead Calm* was released in the United States in early April 1989, Nicole was almost overwhelmed by the attention she received. Warner Bros. flew her to Los Angeles and treated her like royalty. "I have limousines all the time at my disposal," she told the Australian edition of *Rolling Stone*. "They have two suites for you. 'Which one would you prefer?' 'Well, I don't care!' I said. 'Whatever you think.'" At every turn, she was asked if she needed anything. If she looked the slightest bit tired, they offered to call in a masseuse. They watched her constantly, ready to respond in an instant to any change in her mood, however slight. "It's very hard to cope with it without feeling so guilty. You end up walking around going, 'My God, I don't deserve all this.' And feeling like you're bluffing it."

When *Dead Calm* was released, director Phillip Noyce went to Hollywood to observe audience response at Mann's Chinese Theater. What he saw and heard surprised him. "One woman was yelling, 'I can't stand this! I can't stand this!'" he told Steven Rea of the *Philadelphia Inquirer*. "And the audience was shouting back, 'Well, leave then!' And she was saying, 'I can't leave!' And I honestly thought she was going to have a heart attack... audiences right across America are building up an enormous agitation during this movie—they scream and they shout at the screen, and people stand up and yell out."

Reviews were mixed and displayed some of the same emotions described by Noyce. Wrote Christine Arnold Dolen for the *Miami Herald*: "Somehow you just sense, when a movie begins with an adorable toddler rocketing through the windshield of a car, that you're not about to experience a few hours of wholesome family entertainment... The best that can be said about *Dead Calm* is that director Phillip Noyce maintains nearly constant tension and finds a surprising number of ways to evoke menace in confined spaces. As for me, if I want tension, I'll just drive I-95."

Desson Howe wrote in the *Washington Post*: "*Dead Calm*, an Australian murder mystery about three people, two boats and too many unanswered questions, grabs the hell out of you but slowly releases its grip. For much of the movie, you're enthralled. By the end, you're laughing. This is not good."

Roger Ebert had a different take on the film. "[It] generates genuine tension, because the story is so simple and the performances are so straightforward," he wrote for the *Chicago Sun-Times*. "This is not a gimmick film (unless you count the husband's method of escaping from the sinking ship), and Kidman and Zane do generate real, palpable hatred in their scenes together."

After filming on *Dead Calm* was wrapped, all were optimistic about the work they had done, but the movie business being what it is, they were afraid to be overly optimistic. "Every picture that's made is made by professional people who hope they have made a good product," says assistant director Stuart Freeman. "I don't think that anyone thought that it would be the success that it was, but there were a lot of people hoping that it would be a success."

Although Freeman and others still had postproduction work to do on the film, the actors parted company to pursue new projects. Zane moved on to *Back to the Future II*, where he played Match, and *Memphis Belle*, in which he played bombardier Lt. Val Kozlowski. Neill's next film was *French Revolution*, which he followed up with *The Hunt for Red October*, in which he played Capt. Vasily Borodin.

Nicole moved on to another feature film, *Emerald City*, and the television miniseries *Bangkok Hilton*. In the latter, she played an innocent Australian girl who goes to Thailand in search of the father she never knew. Along the way, she gets involved with a drug trafficker who uses her as a courier. She is eventually caught by authorities and sent to the *Bangkok Hilton* to await trail.

Written by Terry Hayes, who wrote the script for *Dead Calm*, the story also involves a burned-out lawyer, played by Denholm Elliott, who helps navigate the plot through a complex tale of intrigue. When *Bangkok Hilton* first aired in Australia in 1989, Nicole received universal acclaim for her acting. The following year it aired in the United States on cable television's TBS. *Seattle Times* writer John Voorhees called it "one of the best thrillers of the season."

Nicole's next feature film, *Emerald City*, is a drama about success, Australian style. Colin and Kate Rogers are a successful couple—he's a screenwriter and she's in publishing—that move from a small town to a big city and get caught up in the greed and selfishness that was so prevalent in the 1980s. Things start to go wrong for them once they meet Mike McCord, a hack scriptwriter who dreams of the big payoff.

McCord's girlfriend, Helen (played by Nicole), soon becomes the object of Colin's lust, even as Kate (played by Robyn Nevin) sets her sights on her boss. If there is a moral to the story, it is that in the big city you have to choose between having morals or great wealth, since obviously the two concepts are incompatible.

The film did not garner any interest when it was released in the United States, but it did find favor with Australian moviegoers. It was nominated for five awards from the Australian Film Institute, including best actress (Nicole Kidman), best screenplay, best achievement in cinematography, best supporting actor (Chris Haywood, who played Mike McCord), and best actor (John Hargreaves, who played Colin Rogers). Only Haywood took home an award.

At this point in her life, Nicole was not certain where her career was headed. There were only so many movies you could make in Australia and the pool of available actors and filmmakers was small enough that you kept working with the same people.

The kind of stardom that Nicole did not want to achieve was exemplified by Robyn Nevin, her costar in *Emerald City*. Nevin had entered the National Institute of Dramatic Art at the age of sixteen, the same age at which Nicole had unofficially emancipated herself, and over the years she had become one of Australia's most recognizable television and cinematic faces.

When they made *Emerald City*, Nevin was forty-six and really had little to show for her success, except name recognition, among Australian television viewers and moviegoers. She was at the top professionally, but the distance from the middle to the top did not seem like a very big leap. Eventually, she became frustrated and gave up acting entirely to become the artistic director of the Sydney Theatre Company.

That type of life was not what Nicole envisioned for herself. At the age of twenty-one, she already was about as famous as you could get in Australia and that simply was not enough for her! She found herself in a similar place in her personal life. Her romance with Marcus Graham was satisfying and comfortable, but she was not ready to go to the next level—marriage and a house full of kids.

For Marcus, it had been love at first sight. Their adolescent years had been filled with the same nebulous angst—a dyslexic, Marcus had left school at fifteen to work as a hamburger cook—and they had navigated through those turbulent teen years by using the same unlikely compass, drama school and its promise of a fanciful life.

When Marcus looked at Nicole, he saw his soulmate, the person with whom he expected to live the rest of his life. Even though she already lived with him in his luxurious Sydney apartment, he wanted more from her. He wanted her to work on movie projects with him and to extend that professional partnership into a more traditional family relationship.

Nicole's feelings toward Marcus were much more complicated. She was attracted to him because of his dark, smoldering good looks and his James Dean–like affability, but she did not share the same emotional commitment to the relationship, for to do so would be to acknowledge that she somehow had reached the end of the line and was ready to settle into some sort of mindless mediocrity. At twenty-one, the still-coltish Nicole had her inquiring eyes set squarely on the horizon.

# CHAPTER FOUR

# Tom Cruise Arrives with Days of Thunder

In 1989, nearly six months after *Dead Calm* was released in the United States, actor Tom Cruise was invited to a private screening of the film. Rehearsals were scheduled to begin soon for his next movie, a car racing drama entitled *Days of Thunder*, and neither he nor the director was happy about the available choices for the female lead. Warner Bros. had generated a buzz about Nicole Kidman's performance in *Dead Calm* and Tom went to the screening to see what all the fuss was about.

What he saw was a twenty-year-old redhead playing a difficult role written for an older woman and bringing it off with flawless authenticity. He could not believe his eyes. He was so totally mesmerized by her performance that he decided, on the spot, that she would be perfect for *Days of Thunder*. There were plenty of beautiful actresses who were capable of playing a race car driver's girlfriend, but since the girlfriend was also a physician, it was mandatory for the credibility of the character that her face reflect a semblance of professional competence and intelligence.

Nicole was in Japan promoting *Dead Calm* when she received word that Tom Cruise wanted to meet with her about a role in *Days of Thunder*. "I thought, 'Oh yeah, right,'" she told *Premiere* magazine. "I'd been to America before. You go in, you audition, you don't get the job."

Landing a role in a Tom Cruise film could not possibly be as easy as that. Ever the pragmatist, she decided that she would do the audition, but only to spend a few days hanging out with *Dead Calm* director Phillip Noyce and his family—and then go on to England for a long overdue visit with her sister, Antonia.

When Nicole walked into the conference room for a meeting with Tom and five other men, she was suffering from jet lag, the result of the long flight from Tokyo. She felt (but did not appear) disheveled, tired, and oddly out of rhythm. Tom rose to his feet as she entered the room and she walked directly over to him to shake his hand.

At five feet eleven, Nicole was shocked to see how much taller she was than the five-foot-seven leading man. She knew what the movie was about, so she figured she'd lost the part as soon as she walked into the room. Why would they give the role to an actress who was four inches taller than an actor who was going to play the part of a macho race car driver? Casting her in that role made no sense, or so she thought.

Nicole was handed a couple of pages of script to read and told that she was being considered for no role in particular. She gave the reading, then left the conference room, convinced that it all had been a waste of time. At the very least, she thought, she had received a free trip to Los Angeles.

What she did not know—could not possibly know—was that Tom's reaction to her had been instantaneous. "My first reaction to meeting Nic [the name she prefers from family and friends] was pure lust," Tom said over and over again about that audition. "It was totally physical."

The following morning Nicole received a telephone call from one of the producers. The female lead was hers if she wanted it. Nicole was stunned. What about the differences in our height, she asked? The producer said that it did not bother Tom and was of no concern to him or the other producers.

Nicole said yes on the spot. There was nothing to think about. It was only the biggest break of her career.

At age twenty-seven, Tom Cruise was on top of his game. Over the past eight years he had starred or costarred in thirteen feature films, including his first big hit, *Risky Business* (1983), *Top Gun* (1986), *Rain Man* (1988), and the much-heralded *Born on the Fourth of July* (1989), movies that ranked among the top-grossing films of the 1980s.

Careerwise, Tom's success worked both sides of the street. Despite his average height, female moviegoers were attracted to his boyish good looks and his affable, non-threatening sexuality. Male moviegoers liked him because, despite his slick, "pretty boy" image, he seemed to be a man's man at his core, someone to whom they could relate in the ongoing battle against the feminization of America.

Born Thomas Cruise Mapother IV on July 3, 1962, in Syracuse, New York, he never had a stable family life. His father, Thomas Cruise Mapother III, was an engineer at General Electric and considered it his responsibility to relocate whenever the company needed him to participate in a new research project. His mother, Mary Lee, saw her role as wife and mother as a supportive one and she followed her husband about the country without complaint. During the first eleven years of Tom's life, the family, which eventually included three daughters, moved a total of seven times.

In his early years, Tom was a dreamer. He frequently isolated himself from other family members and sought adventures that he could enjoy alone. Mary Lee was a little bit like that herself. Each time they moved to a new city, she sought out the local playhouse and volunteered to participate in any way that was needed. At one point, she even established her own dramatic group. Once she saw that Tom enjoyed a rich fantasy world, she encouraged him to mimic his favorite television characters.

By the time Tom got used to exploring his neighborhood in Syracuse, the family moved to Ottawa, Canada, where Tom got interested in sports, especially skating. Mary Lee was happy to see him engage in extracurricular activities because it became apparent soon after he started school that he was not going to be a good student, at least not academically. What the family did not know then—but later discovered—was that Tom had a learning disorder called dyslexia. Simple reading was a nightmare for him.

The Mapother family lived in Ottawa longer than it had lived anyplace else, thus allowing the children to grow into a comfortable routine with neighborhood friends and classmates, but what fate gave with one hand, it took away with another. When Tom was twelve, Thomas and Mary Lee sat the children down and explained to them that the marriage simply was not working out. They announced plans to get a divorce. After that stunning admission, Thomas took Tom outside to play baseball, probably to distract him, but it only served to alienate him from a world that he no longer saw as safe and secure.

Tom, along with his sisters, was devastated. Things had been going so well. He could not understand how his family could fall apart so quickly. His perception of family, indeed his perception of gender roles, was altered in an instant. What he remembers most about that year are the voluminous tears that flowed.

After the divorce, Mary Lee took the children and moved to Louisville, Kentucky, where she and Thomas had first began their life's journey. It was not a glamorous homecoming, for she had little money and had to move her children into a low-rent house, the best she could afford on a salesclerk's salary.

"After a divorce, you feel so vulnerable," Tom told Christopher Connelly in a 1986 interview for *Rolling Stone*. "And traveling the way I did, you're closed off a lot from other people. I didn't express a lot to people where I moved...I didn't feel like they'd understand me. I was always warming up, getting acquainted with everyone. I went through a period, after the divorce, of really wanting to be accepted, wanting love and attention from people. But I never really seemed to fit in anywhere."

Growing up, Tom had male friends, but he later admitted that he found it easier to trust females. That attitude is due, in part at least, to the fact that after the divorce he grew up in a household in which he was the only male. When he needed comforting and understanding—and for a preteen boy that is fairly often—it always was offered by the females in his life. As a result, his adolescent concept of "maleness" derived from his still evolving concept of self.

By the time he was fourteen, Tom had some serious issues to resolve, both personal and educational. He was not doing well because of his reading problems and his mother did not earn enough money to enroll him in a private school where he could get specialized attention. In addition, he was having a difficult time envisioning where he would fit in as an adult.

The solution to all of his problems, or so it seemed at the time, was to become a Catholic priest. With that in mind, in the fall of 1976 he enrolled in St. Francis Seminary, a Franciscan order located near Cincinnati. There he would get an education and prepare for a vocation as a priest.

Life changed radically for Tom at St. Francis. Now, instead of being surrounded entirely by females, he was in an environment with no females. He slept in a dormitory with about two dozen boys and he went to classes that were taught by male priests. Students were not required to pledge a lifetime of celibacy, and most of the students eventually rejected celibacy, but the percentage of "keepers" was high enough to keep the church supplied with a steady supply of priests.

Tom stayed in the school for only one year. The brothers suspected they were losing him as a potential priest when they discovered that he was sneaking out of the dormitory to go to the homes of local girls. They knew that they had lost him for certain when he asked one of the brothers if he thought girls would be uninterested in him because of his diminutive stature.

When he was sixteen, he moved to Glen Ridge, New Jersey, with his mother, his sisters—and his new stepfather, a plastics worker named Jack South. Tom never took to his stepfather and there always seemed to be tension between the two. Perhaps because of that, Tom began looking for activities outside the family to occupy his time.

At Glen Ridge High School, he took up wrestling and soccer in an attempt to make new friends. He also decided to try out for the school production of *Guys and Dolls*. He landed the role of Nathan Detroit in the stage play and to the great pleasure of his mother and sisters, he demonstrated a real talent for acting.

After the play, a talent agent approached Tom and told him he had natural ability and should pursue a career as an actor. That was all the encouragement that he needed. After graduation from Glen Ridge High School, he told his mother and stepfather that he had decided to go to New York to pursue a career as an actor. They encouraged him to go to college first, but Tom would have none of that. There was nothing in life that he wanted more than to become an actor.

Soon after Nicole signed on for *Days of Thunder* she phoned her boyfriend, Marcus Graham, who was still in Australia, and told him the wonderful news. His first reaction was envy—he was in the midst of a temporary career slump—but he quickly recovered and voiced his support.

When Nicole returned to Australia, it was primarily to pack her bags and visit with her parents. It would not be the first time she had left home, but it somehow felt different this time, as if she were embarking on a something other than a simple trip to the States. Nicole, at age twenty-two, left Australia in November 1989, not sure what the future held but convinced that what-ever happened was a manifestation of her destiny.

That feeling was confirmed shortly after she arrived in Los Angeles, when Sam Cohen, a top New York agent—he represented, among others, Woody Al-len and Meryl Streep—flew to the West Coast to sign her to a contract. She phoned Marcus almost immediately, almost in shock over the attention she was receiving.

Marcus was miserable that fall. Nicole was more than just a girlfriend to him. She was his best friend and a symbol of his future happiness. At first, they spoke often by telephone (his telephone bill soaring to well over $1,000), then it became more and more difficult to get through to her—because of her tough schedule, she explained. As soon as she returned, he promised himself that he would take her away to some exotic tropical island and reinvigorate their relationship.

As the months wore by, Marcus's optimism about a future with Nicole faded with each slowly returned telephone call. When they did talk, it fo-cused on her present and not *their* future. In March 1990, while watching the Academy Awards, Marcus saw Nicole and Tom together at the cere-mony. He phoned to talk to her about it, but he could not get through to her. Finally, as the number of unreturned telephone calls grew, the reality of the situation dawned on Marcus—he and Nicole were done as a cou-ple.

Nicole was never good at breaking up. She preferred to close her eyes and simply wish the unpleasantness away. Sometimes that actually worked!


*Days of Thunder* had a convoluted genesis. Jerry Bruckheimer and Don Simpson, the producers of the box-office smash *Top Gun*, had been pressuring Tom Cruise for quite some time to do a sequel. His response, finally, was to suggest that instead of simply redoing the previous hit, they give the *Top Gun* treat-ment to his latest high-speed passion—car racing, with the goal of making the best race car movie ever made.

The subject had been on Tom's mind for three years, ever since he had driven Rick Hendrick's Winston Cup cars around the track at Daytona. He explained to Bruckheimer and Simpson that he wanted to make a behind-the-scenes movie that focused on the personalities of the drivers, the owners, and the pit crew. He wrote out a brief outline and took it to Paramount so that executives there could approve the project.

Tom hired Warran Skaaren, who had written the screenplay for *Top Gun*, to flesh out his ideas for a script. Skaaren did his best to bring Tom's ideas to life, but the two men had a difficult time seeing eye to eye on the story line. Finally, after several drafts, Skaaren withdrew from the project. Frustrated by the slow progress, Tom approached one of the best-known screenwriters in the business—Robert Towne, who had penned the scripts for classics such as *Bonnie and Clyde* and *The Godfather*. After attending a race with Tom, Towne voiced enthusiasm for working on the project.

Once they had a completed script, Tom and the producers selected a director—Tony Scott, who had directed *Top Gun*—and then put together a cast that included veterans Robert Duvall and Randy Quaid, chosen for their uncanny ability to appeal to working-class moviegoers. Nicole Kidman was the last piece of that puzzle.


*Days of Thunder* begins with a Daytona 500 race and an announcement that a favored driver has dropped out. Car lot owner Tim Daland, played by Randy Quaid, sees an opportunity to enter the race car business and pleads with retired pit boss Harry Hogge, played by Robert Duvall, to build him a car. Hogge tells him that he first needs to find himself a driver—no driver, no car.

Daland arranges for his driver Cole Trickle, played by Tom Cruise, to test-drive another driver's car. Trickle burns up the track, impressing Hogge and the car's regular driver, Rowdy Burns (played by Michael Rooker) with his driving skills. Against his better judgment, Hogge agrees to come out of retirement to work with Trickle.

After several unsuccessful races, Hogge and Trickle have a fight and Trickle storms out of the office. Hogge finds him in a bar and utters the words all drivers (and lovers) dread hearing: "We've got to talk." Hogge asks him why he thinks things are not working out. Trickle expresses frustration that he can't do the "car talk" thing. He admits he knows next to nothing about cars. The paternal Hogge, seeing him in a sympathetic light for the first time, tells him not to worry—they'll figure it out.

After their talk, Trickle enjoys a winning streak and then crashes while dueling on the track with Rowdy. Both drivers are taken to the hospital, where Trickle meets Dr. Claire Lewicki, played by Nicole Kidman.

When she enters his hospital room for her first face-to-face meeting with him, he thinks she is a ringer. A few days earlier Hogge and the boys played a trick on him with a paid escort dressed up like a cop. He assumes the beautiful neurosurgeon is just another good old boy gag. To the horror of his team members, he takes Claire's hand and places it between his legs.

"Isn't this what you're really looking for?" he asks.

"Well, that's interesting enough, Mr. Trickle, but it's just not my speciality," she says, and then leaves the room. Trickle is horrified at his mistake. When he is discharged from the hospital, he sends Claire a roomful of flowers and asks her for a date. She says she doesn't have time, then changes her mind and agrees to fly to Charlotte with him. Later, while they are in bed, she asks, "Tell me what you love so much about racing?"

"The speed—to be able to control it. To know that I can control something that's out of control. I'd really have to show you."

"Show me," she says, and they kiss.

In another scene, after he has scared the hell out of her by racing with an irate cab driver, she yells at him: "Control is an illusion, you infantile egomaniac. Nobody knows what is going to happen next...nobody knows and nobody controls anything. You've gotten a glimpse of that and you're scared."

As the story progresses, Trickle learns that Rowdy has more serious injuries than they first realized. He needs surgery and will be unable to race his car in the Daytona 500. Since Trickle has lost his sponsor, Rowdy asks him to race his car. Trickle reluctantly agrees, but everyone, himself included, wonders if he has lost his nerve as a result of the previous accident.

On the day of the big race, Claire shows up at the racetrack but tells Trickle that she does not plan to stick around to watch the race. Says Trickle, "Claire, I'm more afraid of being nothing than I am of being hurt."

Of course, when Trickle drives out onto the track, Claire changes her mind and joins Hogge in the pit to watch the race and cheer him on to victory.

For Nicole, making the film was an adventure unto itself, for she had never seen a NASCAR race. Not until Tom took her for a 180-mile-per-hour spin around the track did she understand what all the excitement was about.

"It was fantastic," she said in ESPN's *The Making of Days of Thunder*. "I really like things that get my adrenaline pumping. I'd never watched a race before . . . now I can understand why people get hooked on it."

To make *Days of Thunder*, the film company built sixty cars, but by the time production wrapped, they had only two cars left, having wrecked the other fifty-eight. One of those wrecked cars was used for the scene in which Tom experiences a devastating crash. To capture it on film, Tom's car was equipped with a camera and a sawed-off telephone pole that was rigged to dig into the pavement at the appropriate time to send the vehicle tumbling end over end at 120 miles per hour. Taped inside the car was a note for the actual driver: "Turn wheel to left, push button—good luck."

Parts of the movie were filmed during a live television broadcast, so it was always a challenge to keep the movie cameramen out of the way of the television cameramen. Before each scene, director Tony Scott used storyboards and an assortment of toy cars to show the camera crews and stunt drivers exactly what he wanted captured on film. They placed cameras beneath the cars and inside the cars, the goal being to find vantage points that had not yet been exploited by other filmmakers. In all, Scott used an astonishing twenty-eight movie cameras to make the film.

Even with all the technical razzle-dazzle at his disposal, Scott placed a higher premium on making a film that explored the personalities of the men behind the scenes of NASCAR. "The characters that I've written are based on these people and not just cars going around in circles," screenwriter Robert Towne said in the ESPN documentary. "I believe that we have gotten a sense of these people on film."

When *Days of Thunder* was released in June 1990, it did only moderately well at the box office—it took in nearly $89 million domestically when it needed $100 million to show a substantial profit—and reviews were mixed.

"*Days of Thunder* serves up little to think about, much less enjoy," wrote David Sterritt for the *Christian Science Monitor*. "There's a certain novelty in seeing Mr. Duvall give one of his rare mediocre performances, and there's a certain hilarity in watching Australian actress Nicole Kidman impersonate a 'brain doctor,' as the screenplay calls her, whose own brain reels with romance every time Cruise's character comes near."

Desson Howe, writing for the *Washington Post*, found the film to be packed with MTV-like images. "Essentially an encore from the *Top Gun* team, director Tony Scott's *Thunder* is exactly what it promises to be: Not much—but at dizzying speed, stripped down and free of wind-resistant subtlety," he wrote. "There's a certain integrity to that. A certain deafening integrity. Producers Jerry Bruckheimer and Don Simpson, two of Hollywood's more successful antichrists of taste, should be congratulated—and they will be. Watch those box-office receipts pile up."

Some of Cruise's racetrack heroes came to his defense. Former Daytona 500 winner Geoff Bodine, who gave Tom his first ride around the famous track, compared the movie to *Top Gun* in an interview with the *Miami Herald*: "I can just see those Air Force/Navy pilots watching *Top Gun* and saying, 'Ridiculous—that's not the way it is.' I've heard that from some people in the racing community: 'This isn't how it really is.' Of course, it isn't. It's how Hollywood sees it. But it's still pretty realistic. They just made it juicer and more spectacular."

Some people thought it was a little too realistic. Remember race car owner Rick Hendrick, whose friendship with Tom inspired him to make the movie? His crew chief, Harry Hyde, sued Paramount, alleging that he was injured by Tom's using his career as a basis for Duvall's character, Harry Hogge. According to news reports, he took home $40,000 from a settlement with the movie company.

Upon meeting Tom Cruise for the first time, the first words out of Nicole Kidman's mouth were "You're funny!" She quickly forgot what he said that made her laugh, but not the fact that he had made her laugh when she least expected it.

If it wasn't love at first sight, it was a reasonable facsimile. "He took my breath away," she told *Rolling Stone* in a 1999 interview. "I don't know what it was—chemical reaction? Hard to define—hard to resist."

Tom felt it, too, although he was married at the time to actress Mimi Rogers. Nicole was unlike any woman he had ever known. His first response to the mysterious feelings that she stirred inside him was to panic and move out of the Brentwood mansion that he shared with Mimi. Then, feeling that he had overreacted—he had not so much as kissed his new costar, his infatuation with her was little more than a fantasy at that point—he moved back into the house with Mimi, without ever explaining why he had left. The only problem with that was that he could not get Nicole out of his mind. Each time he tried to focus on Mimi, images of Nicole crept back into his thoughts.

Nicole underwent a similar experience in her relationship with Marcus, but since he was thousands of miles away in Australia—and she did not have to face him—she handled the situation much differently. She simply stopped taking Marcus's telephone calls, probably more out of guilt than anything else.

How could she ever justify breaking up with Marcus? Not only was he her lover, he was her best friend. She and Tom had shared no intimate moments— and, besides that, he was married. If she couldn't understand what was going on between herself and Tom, how would she ever be able to explain it to Marcus?

By the time they left for Daytona Beach, Florida, to start shooting *Days of Thunder*, Tom and Nicole's relationship seemed unstoppable. Since Tom was in nearly every scene—and Nicole was not—they were halfway through shooting before they got to spend any time together.

"Our scenes together went very well—we clicked," Nicole told *Cosmopolitan*. "We made each other laugh." Then, perhaps realizing that she was speaking in double entendre, she grinned broadly. "I don't think we would have made it as a couple matched by a computer service. I'm a lousy driver myself. At home, I drove Mum's old VW and put more than a few dents into it while trying to park. I didn't know one car from another and couldn't care less... [Tom] drove me around the Daytona track at one hundred eighty miles an hour. I ended up with a sore neck because at that speed your head gets pulled back. But it did get my adrenaline pumping."

Everyone in the film company knew what was going on between Tom and Nicole. They could see it in the secretive glances Nicole tossed Tom's way and in the way he grinned at her whenever their eyes met. They were so gaga over each other that it would have been embarrassing, if it had not been so entertaining to watch from the sidelines.

Not entertained by the spark-filled romance was Tom's wife, Mimi, who flew to Daytona Beach in December to talk to him about their two-year-old marriage. Six years his senior, she had taken him under her wing in 1987, after Tom had been involved in a high-profile romance with *Risky Business* costar Rebecca De Mornay. High-profile romances were nothing new for Mimi who had been linked by the tabloids with Tom Selleck, Christopher Reeve, and Kennedy clansman Robert Shriver.

Other than a penchant for garnering tabloid headlines, the couple seemed to have little in common except membership in the science fiction–inspired religion of Scientology. When things started going badly in their marriage, Mimi turned to the Scientologists for help. She and Tom attended church-supported counseling sessions in an effort to resolve their difficulties, but nothing seemed to work. Meanwhile, Tom grew more and more distant.

Things did not come to a head until Mimi's trip to Florida. It was then that Tom told her that he had fallen in love with Nicole and wanted a divorce. Stunned by the suddenness of it all, Mimi took the next flight out of Daytona Beach. She had gone to be with Tom to repair their marriage, to do the right thing—instead she was humiliated by his unwillingness to even discuss their relationship.

On January 16, 1990, Tom and Mimi announced their impending divorce in a joint statement that said, in part: "While there have been very positive aspects to our marriage, there were some issues which could not be resolved even after working on them for a period of time. Anyone who has been through this type of situation will understand that it is a complicated and difficult decision."

The divorce was all very clinical, very Hollywoodish and businesslike in its lack of passion. Tom treated it as a changing of the guard. He took responsibility for the failure of the marriage, he was generous to Mimi in the settlement, and he made certain that everyone saw him moving on with his life. "It just seemed right," Tom told writer James Greenberg. "I think anyone who has met Nicole would understand."

Mimi exhibited much the same attitude, insofar as moving on with her life was concerned, although she clearly felt she was the injured party. Stargazers wondered about the divorce because rumors had circulated about the couple ever since they had gotten married. Was Mimi bisexual or perhaps a full-blown lesbian? She had encouraged that line of thinking by holding hands in public with other actresses, most notably *Cheers* costar Kirstie Alley. A *Star* headline once proclaimed: KIRSTIE ALLEY: I LURED MEN BY PROMISING 3-IN-A-BED WITH MIMI ROGERS.

Not until March 1993, when she did a nude layout for *Playboy* magazine, did Mimi address the rumors. She told the magazine that although she and

Kirstie were "wild and crazy single girls," there was no truth to the rumors that she is bisexual or a lesbian.

In the interview, she also addressed rumors about her divorce from Tom. She denied that she had grown tired of him and was responsible for the divorce. Then she dropped a bombshell, one that would prompt speculation that Tom was gay and haunt him for years to come. She and Tom split up, she explained to the magazine, because "Tom was seriously thinking of becoming a monk. At least for that period of time, it looked as though marriage wouldn't fit into his overall spiritual need. And he thought he had to be celibate to maintain the purity of his instrument. Therefore, it became obvious that we had to split."

Was Mimi serious about Tom's lack of interest in sex—or was she simply displaying her wicked sense of humor? If true, it would not necessarily mean that Tom is gay. It could simply mean that Tom had lost interest in her as a sexual partner, perhaps as a result of her celebrated penchant for party hopping.

Of course, none of that was of interest to Nicole, for she had her own agenda. In the blink of an eye, she had been transformed from an obscure Australian actress into the costar of a Hollywood blockbuster—and, as the weeks went by, cast by the tabloids as the love interest of America's sexiest film star. Could life possibly get any sweeter?

At times, she found all the media attention almost overwhelming. "I didn't come from America, so I didn't understand the whole idea of movie stars and the way America deals with it. The scrutiny on your life is...weird," she told the *Los Angeles Times*. "It really was a shock to go to Hollywood. [Before] I was working with really great people like Phillip Noyce and George Miller who were writing roles for me. It never really hit me until a few years into it when people would say to me, 'So your first film was *Days of Thunder*', and I'd say, 'No, I did all this theater and stuff.' It was frustrating having to start again."

Once the first surge of publicity over Tom's divorce subsided, he and Nicole relaxed somewhat when out in public. They were spotted holding hands and smooching in shopping malls. It was during this time that they discovered they had more in common than simple physical attraction. Both are consummate daredevils, risk takers who are willing to put their lives on the line. To Nicole's delight, Tom took her skydiving. At one point, as they fell toward earth in free fall, Tom zoomed in on her and planted a kiss on her mouth, then broke away and yanked his parachute cord. For Nicole, who thrived on adrenaline rushes, romance couldn't possibly get any better than that.

Once Tom and Nicole became an item, Janelle Kidman wasted no time flying to America to get a personal assessment of the situation. Nicole and Tom met her in New York, where she spent two weeks getting to know her daughter's new boyfriend. She was surprised at how much alike they were. She described them as "two peas in a pod" and she told her daughter that it seemed to her that they had found in each what they always had been looking for—a best friend.

Before Janelle returned to Australia, Nicole gave her one more bit of information: She and Tom planned to live together in his $4 million Pacific Palisades home once work on *Days of Thunder* was completed and Tom's divorce was finalized in April. Janelle was not entirely surprised, for when it came to affairs of the heart, her daughter had never been overly cautious. She went after love with the same ferocity and determination with which she went after movie roles.

During her first year as a live-in companion to Tom, Nicole did her best to adapt to stardom Hollywood style. She gave the obligatory interviews, she toned down her Australian accent, and she attended one party after another, although that was her least favorite thing to do. It was during this period that Tom learned that Nicole's cool, confident exterior was little more than camouflage for a cauldron of emotions that she struggled to keep in check while out in public.

She suffers from what psychologists generically call panic attacks. When photographers and reporters press in around her, the strobe lights from the cameras blinding her eyes, her heart races and she struggles to not run away. Typically, people who are in the throes of a panic attack feel a suffocating sense of doom, as if they are going to die if they cannot escape whatever pressure instigated the attack.

Nicole's father, Antony, described panic attacks this way: "Physically, symptoms appear—rapid heart beat, muscle tension, perspiration, trembling. Cognitively the person thinks he may die, go mad or lose control of himself."

Early on in the relationship, Nicole learned to depend on Tom to get her through situations like that. The public saw photographs of Nicole holding Tom's hand, their bodies pressed close together, his lips close to her ear whispering sweet nothings—and they thought it was the most romantic thing imaginable.

Beyond any doubt, Tom and Nicole were very much in love at that point, but those romantic images of them were not always what they seemed. More likely, especially in a public arena, Nicole pressed in close against Tom because she was experiencing a panic attack. Tom helped her get through those times by holding her hand tightly and whispering into her ear that everything was going to be all right.

After weeks of public scrutiny of their relationship, Nicole was relieved when the time came to take Tom to Australia to meet the rest of the family. She gleefully told him that they would encounter no paparazzi in Australia.

When they arrived in Sydney, she felt a great sense of relief, though it turned out to be short-lived. Since Nicole had given her apartment to her sister, Antonia—and since bunking with Tom in her parents' home did not seem a viable option—they checked into a hotel and made an itinerary of all the places they wanted to visit.

Unfortunately, reporters surrounded them the moment they stepped out of the hotel. Nicole was horrified by the intensity of their interest. They were followed every place they went. That had never happened to her before. She had considered Sydney a safe haven and now that bubble had been burst. They did manage to have several fun-filled visits with Antony and Janelle, and Nicole was able to show Tom the places that were important to her, especially the Harbour Bridge.

Then, for some reason, known only to Nicole, she took Tom by Marcus's apartment to meet him. Presumably, she felt that their friendship would survive his broken heart. It did eventually, after a little healing time, but it was much too soon for the friendship card to be played. Marcus, still bruised by the breakup, was at home when they arrived, but he asked a friend to answer the door and say that he was not there. Nicole still had volumes to learn about men.

After a few outings escalated into moblike chaos, Tom and Nicole retreated to their hotel room, where Nicole sat down at the window and wept, gazing out at the skyline that had earlier held so much promise. For the love of a man, she had given up her country, her friends, and her family. Now, facing the painful realization that you really can't go home again, she understood, for the first time, what it meant to be a prisoner of her own fame.

\* \* \*

After a courtship of less than a year, Tom and Nicole were married on December 24, 1990, in a sunset ceremony in Telluride, Colorado. Surrounded by snow in a lily-and-rose arbor outside a cozy cottage they had rented, Nicole wore the off-white, vintage bridal gown she had purchased in Amsterdam years ago and kept in her hope chest.

Antony and Janelle Kidman, along with Nicole's sister, Antonia, who served as her bridesmaid, were in attendance, as were other friends from Australia. Also present were Tom's mother, Mary Lee Mapother, Tom's best man, actor Emilo Estevez, and Dustin Hoffman and his wife.

At age twenty-three, Nicole was embarking on the greatest adventure of her life, although she never really saw it as a radical change in her lifestyle. "We have so much in common that it's almost as if we are the same person," she explained to *Cosmopolitan* not long after the ceremony. "People who know us see that so clearly. Marriage won't change my life. I mean, it is a commitment, but it doesn't really change anything."

Or so Nicole thought. One thing that did change was her concept of religion. Although she and Tom had both been raised Catholics, he had veered in another direction as an adult. Tom was a member of the Church of Scientology, a multibillion-dollar religious organization built on the writings of the late L. Ron Hubbard, whose books, according to his publisher, have sold over 120 million copies in thirty-two languages.

Celebrities have been the organization's recruiting targets almost from the beginning. "Celebrities are well-guarded, well-barricaded, overworked, aloof quarry," Hubbard once wrote. "They are important people because they reach a lot of people. They set trends in society." In addition to Tom Cruise, the church's Hollywood recruits include Michael Jackson, John Travolta, Jenna Elfman, Kirstie Alley, Dustin Hoffman, and Goldie Hawn.

The focus on celebrities is so great, according to *Variety*, that the organization operates an ornate "Celebrity Center" in a building constructed by newspaper tycoon William Randolph Hearst, a magazine entitled *Celebrity*, and a movie production company named Golden Era Studios. With all its high-profile celebrity connections, you would think that the organization would be revered by the mainstream Hollywood media; but that's not the case, primarily because of the organization's sometimes hostile reaction to media coverage of its activities. Books with titles such as *The Scandal of Scientology* by

Paulette Cooper and *L. Ron Hubbard: Messiah or Madman* by Bent Corydon have prompted lawsuits and what Corydon has described as "hounding" by church officials.

L. Ron Hubbard, who died in 1986, seems like an unlikely messiah. For most of his life he financed his research to discover what he called the "basic principle of existence" by writing science fiction novels and short stories. He traveled extensively, and, for three months in 1948, he worked with inmates in a Georgia mental hospital. In 1950, he expressed his theories in a book entitled *Dianetics: The Modern Science of Mental Health*, a bestseller that catapulted him into an international spotlight.

For twenty-five years, Hubbard toured the world, giving lectures and demonstrations of his powers (followers claim to have witnessed him read minds, change his body size, and move objects with telekinetic power). To true believers, he was the reincarnation of the Buddha, a prophet with one foot in the Far East and the other set squarely in the new power center of the new universe—Hollywood, California.

The Church of Scientology is Hubbard's vision of religion in a modern, humanist context. It is based on several principles, including the belief that man is an immortal spiritual being whose experience extends well beyond a single lifetime. Scientology believes that humans are basically good and can find salvation by attaining brotherhood with the "universe." "Scientology holds in common with all great religions the dream of peace on Earth and salvation for man," explains the church's literature. "What is new about Scientology is that it offers a precise path for bringing about spiritual improvement in the here and now and a way to accomplish it with absolute certainty."

Scientologists believe in God, but not necessarily the God found in the Old and New Testaments. "Scientology is not a dogmatic religion in which one is asked to believe anything on faith," says church literature. "An individual discovers for himself that Scientology works by applying its principles and observing or experiencing the results."

Scientology is a religion that Tom Cruise took to, almost immediately, in his mid-twenties. The main attraction to him seems to be its philosophy that it can help repair any difficulty and overcome any adversity. "Life pounds you—you know what I mean?" Tom once told *Vanity Fair* writer Evgenia Peretz. "You come across losses. All of a sudden something happens and now you feel like you cannot go forward or it invalidates you . . . Scientology has helped me be able to figure out tools to understand exactly what a problem is, and how to overcome those problems."

Tom wasted no time early in their relationship exposing Nicole to the teachings of the Church of Scientology, and she promised to keep an open mind about it. In the beginning, there were rumors that she had to embrace Scientology in order to marry Tom, rumors she steadfastly denied. "No way," she told *Rolling Stone*. "I would never have married him if that was it. That would've been forcing me to do something I didn't want to do. He and I allow ourselves to be who we are. Am I someone following one philosophy? No, but there's parts of Scientology that are great."

Nicole did not go into detail about the aspects of the religion that she felt were "great," but one of them certainly must have been the way in which church members network with each other. Her first glimpse of that would have been while she and Tom were filming *Days of Thunder*, because fellow church member John Travolta showed up to pal around with Tom. The second could have been when church member Dustin Hoffman recommended her for a role in his next motion picture, *Billy Bathgate*.

Based on the novel by E. L. Doctorow, *Billy Bathgate* seemed to have all the ingredients for a blockbuster hit. American has a long-standing fascination with organized crime families and it does not take much in the way of a story line to entice them into a movie theater to cinematically commune with the likes of Al "Scarface" Capone, Carlos "Little Man" Marcello, or Benjamin "Bugsy" Siegel.

In the case of *Billy Bathgate*, the focus is on mobster Dutch Schultz, a New York nightclub owner who came under the watchful eye of U.S. Attorney Thomas E. Dewey, one of the toughest prosecutors in the nation. When he learned he was the target of a federal investigation, Schultz put out a contract on Dewey, a clear violation of the Mafia's code of conduct (prosecutors were off limits, for obvious reasons).

The hit man went straight to Mafia godfather Charlie Luciano and told him about Schultz's plans. Fearful that Schultz was out of control, Luciano met with other New York crime families, all of whom agreed that putting out a contract on Schultz was the only solution. In October 1935, Schultz was dining at a New Jersey restaurant with three associates when gunmen cut them down as they sat at the dinner table.

*Billy Bathgate* is the coming-of-age story of a young man of that name who signs on to be a flunkie for Schultz during the time period covered by the federal investigation. The mobster's criminal activities are secondary in the story to the youth's discovery of the jaded and morally gnarled world that surrounds him.

To bring the story to life, producers Arlene Donovan and Robert F. Colesberry hired director Robert Benton, who had demonstrated that he had box-office savvy with hits such as *Kramer vs. Kramer* and *Still of the Night*, both of which he also wrote. Actually, it was as a screenwriter that he was best known, with hits such as *Superman* and *What's Up, Doc?*. With that stellar background, it is a mystery why he wanted Tom Stoppard to write the screenplay for *Billy Bathgate*.

Dustin Hoffman was asked to play the role of Dutch Schultz. He had come off a string of duds—*Ishtar* (1987) and *Dick Tracy* (1990)—and box-office hits such as *Tootsie*, *Kramer vs. Kramer*, and *All the President's Men* (1976). To some movie observers, Hoffman was an enigma, primarily because he sometimes seemed reckless in the judgment he showed during script selection. In truth, he is simply disrespectful of the Hollywood tradition that holds that motion picture stars should play it safe once they have reached a certain level of success. Hoffman likes to roll the dice.

Chosen to play the title role of Billy Bathgate was Loren Dean, a twenty-one-year-old veteran of only two movies, *Plain Clothes* and *Say Anything*. He had just the right amount of fresh-faced, John Boy innocence to make the character believable.

Bruce Willis was added for an important cameo role as Bo Weinberg, Drew Preston's first gangster boyfriend. Although his screen time was slight, the character sets the tone for the remainder of the story and serves as a point of reference.

For the role of Drew Preston, Schultz's girlfriend, the filmmakers needed an actress who could be believable as a society-oriented married woman who is attracted to the adrenaline rushes associated with organized crime. She had to be beautiful, careless with her love, manipulative, and speak with a Park Avenue accent. Nicole Kidman thought she could handle that role just fine. So did the producers and directors who auditioned her for the part, except for the accent. After the reading, Hoffman called his pal Tom to tell him about Nicole's audition. "Ah, man," he intoned. "Where did *she* come from?"

Benton gave Nicole the name of a voice coach and told her she had two weeks to lose her Australian accent. Privately, he was skeptical she would be able to do it. When she returned two weeks later, speaking flawless "American," he could not stop bragging on her. "She was phenomenal," he told *Cosmopolitan*. "Her American accent was perfect. After a long day of shooting, though, she'd revert right back and speak in her natural Australian accent, and the crew was amazed. They asked me, 'Why does Nicole talk like an Aussie? Is it some kind of joke?' "

*Billy Bathgate* begins with Dutch taking Bo out on a tugboat to kill him. As Bo's girlfriend, Nicole makes her first appearance in the movie as New York socialite Drew Preston. She sits and watches as Bo sits tied to a chair, his feet resting in hardening cement. Also present is Billy Bathgate. There is a flashback to show how Billy got involved with the mob. It began simply enough, with Dutch spotting him in the street juggling balls. He tips him and Billy uses the money to buy a pistol.

Nicole's first nude scene in an American movie occurs when Drew is taken home after the murder. She knows better than to tell anyone what she witnessed on the tugboat, especially her homosexual husband who has his own after-hours agenda. Now an accessory to the crime, she does the only safe thing and becomes Dutch's girlfriend.

When Dutch is charged with racketeering in upstate New York, he takes Drew and Billy with him to attend the trial. Shortly after arriving in town, Dutch goes to a local bank to deposit a bag of cash. He introduces Billy to the banker as his "prodigy." After the banker leaves the room, Drew corrects Dutch. "If I make a tiny criticism, do you promise not to get all sulky and pout?" she asks. "It's protégé."

"What did I say?" asked Dutch.

"Prodigy. It means child genius."

So much for gangster rap 1930s style.

At first uncertain why Dutch wanted him along, Billy soon learns that his main job is to baby-sit Drew. In one of the more effective scenes, Billy takes Drew out into the country to get her and himself out of Dutch's sight. She finds a waterfall and sits on the ledge, high above a pool of water. She asks Billy how it was when Bo died.

In a flashback, the scene switches to the moment Bo is pushed off the boat. As he sinks, there is a flashback to the present, where a nude Drew has jumped into the pool. She sinks beneath the water, just as Bo sinks. When she pops out of the water, Billy helps her into her dress.

"Did he really ask you to protect me?" she asks.

"Yes," he says.

"I mean . . . that he would think that I couldn't take care of myself. And you promised him you would?"

"Yes."

"Do you always keep your promises?"

"Yes."

"Do you have a girlfriend?"

Drew turns up the heat on Billy by seducing him. He tells her she does not appreciate the position she is in—"You're Schultz's girl."

"No, I'm not his girl. He's my gangster."

Later, in bed at the hotel, Drew says, "Poor Billy Bathgate. You made a promise to protect me. I'm not making it easy for you, am I?"

"No ma'am, you're not."

Toward the end of the movie, when Billy says about Drew, "She's not like ordinary people. She's not scared of anything," he might well have been talking about Nicole herself. Although the part of the girlfriend was one that she was weary of playing, she never lost sight of the strengths of her character. There was little room for character development as written, but she pushed it to the limits allowed within the story.

The release of the movie was delayed until November 1, 1991, due to decisions made during editing that some scenes needed to be reshot. Reviews were not especially kind. Wrote Rita Kempley for the *Washington Post*: "In the annals of crime-related entertainment, the adaptation of E. L. Doctorow's *Billy Bathgate* ranks up there with Geraldo's TV special on 'The Mystery of Al Capone's Vault.' When thrown open to our prying eyes, the picture, like the vault, is full of nothing but stale air."

Also displeased with the film was Jay Carr, who wrote for the *Boston Globe*: "Every season there's one big-budget movie that attracts disaster rumors like a magnet. This year, it's *Billy Bathgate*, with its re-shot endings and postponed opening dates. [It] isn't a disaster exactly. It's more like handsome taxidermy. Director Robert Benton fills the screen with gorgeously burnished pictures, Tom Stoppard's screenplay transfers the novel's action and many of its lines efficiently, and the production values are first-rate. But the film mostly just sits there."

Most critics were impressed with Nicole's acting, but some questioned whether her character should have been played by an older actress (Nicole was just a year older than Loren Dean, who was supposed to be of high school age). One critic, *Rolling Stone*'s Peter Travers, pointed out what he thought was a Disney first—a glimpse of Nicole's pubic hair.

Even before *Billy Bathgate* was released, Nicole experienced a sudden halt in her career. The phone stopped ringing with offers. News media interest in her seemed to focus on her marriage to Tom and not her career. When she did receive attention, it was borderline negative, as if she had done something wrong by coming to America and marrying Tom. Rumors surfaced again about Tom's sexual orientation. Hollywood gossips said the marriage was little more than a devil's bargain, whereby he got respectability and she got a career by riding on his coattails.

"I went through a period when I didn't get any work for a year," Nicole told *Good Weekend*, an Australian magazine. "It was a very tough time for me and I wanted to go back to Australia, but Tom's career was in America."

Nicole had to decide whether her first priority was her career or her marriage. She came down solidly on the side of her marriage, discrediting her detractors with the single-minded zeal with which she embraced her new life with Tom.

# CHAPTER FIVE

# Far and Away:
# *Tarnished Dream*

With the wind whipping against her nylon jumpsuit and her heart pounding wildly, Nicole climbed out onto the wing of the airplane and—clutching the braces and guide wires that held the biplane together—slowly made her way to the tip of the wing, where just staying on her feet was a major accomplishment.

As Tom kept the airplane on a steady course, Nicole did a nearly perfect arabesque and stepped off the wing. Because the airplane was traveling so fast, she appeared to be suspended in air, still holding the arabesque for what seemed like an eternity as the plane pulled away from her, until the moment she began tumbling to earth and then pulled the rip cord, her parachute snatching her back into reality.

Nicole's romance with Tom began on a Daytona racetrack, where their emotions were jacked up by the addictive adrenaline rush of mind-numbing speed—and it continued that way well into their marriage. From race cars, they moved to skydiving, and then to airplanes, perhaps Tom's biggest passion, and then on to daredevil combinations such as wing walking.

Always, it was about the speed, and about putting everything on the line.

Tom loves to fly, especially a two-seat biplane, the wing of which Nicole used as a platform for her arabesque. His favorite maneuver is a Cuban Eight, in which he puts the plane into a dive, flying straight to the ground—only pulling up at the last minute.

Nicole adored that dangerous quality in Tom—it was so like her mother and so unlike her father—and she made an effort to be at his side whenever he went on a thrill-seeking mission. Asked by *Rolling Stone* if she felt frightened when doing daredevil stunts, she said: "That's the point. Sure, I worry about dying, but that's part of the adrenaline rush. Your whole body is resisting, saying, 'No, no, no, this isn't right.' But you do it anyway. It sounds mad."

When Nicole and Tom first met, the attraction was purely physical, a chemical reaction pure and simple. It was only later that they realized how similar they really were. Nicole had always been a daredevil, willing to try anything, whether it involved wrapping killer snakes around her neck, or traveling halfway around the world to sample different cultures. Dare her to do it, whatever the risk—and you could consider it done.

Of course, married life for Nicole that first year or two was not a constant roller coaster ride. They settled into a life of domestic normality that was almost sitcomish in its predictably. They vowed never to be apart for more than two weeks at a time and they made it a point to eat dinner with each other every day, no matter what was happening in their professional lives. Sundays became a day for family get-togethers, depending on where they were and who was available at the time. It was the day when Nicole did the cooking. Working in the kitchen was something that she enjoyed, something that kept her grounded and in touch with the real world.

Tom's marriage to Nicole was very different from his marriage to Mimi, and those differences were due, in no small measure, to Nicole's concept of marriage, a viewpoint influenced by her psychologist father. Relationship parity is a *must* to Nicole—and it is no mystery where that belief came from.

We know what advice Nicole received from her parents because Antony aired his concepts of marriage in his self-help books. On the matter of parity, he once wrote: "Power and dependency are linked and in any relationship are determined by who controls the reinforcers or resources such as the material goods, the affection and the support. When these resources are roughly equal, the power balance in the relationship will be the same. When they are not, the partner who controls more of the desired resources will have more power in the relationship."

Parity was not the only guiding principle in Nicole's relationship with Tom. Another important belief of hers is that couples should never take each other for granted. Shortly after they got married, Tom was astonished to learn that if he wanted Nicole to accompany him somewhere, he had to ask her out on a date. He could not assume that she always would be available. When she explained the "dating" procedure to him, he shook his head in amused disbelief. "You mean, you might turn me down?" he asked, to which she responded in her deep Aussie accent, "Yep!"

After Nicole completed work on *Billy Bathgate*, she and Tom looked around for another project they could do together. Producers jumped at the chance because the chemistry between the actors in *Days of Thunder* was palpable, there for everyone to see, and the prospect of magnifying that chemistry in an epic production excited everyone.

*Far and Away* seemed to be the perfect vehicle. Directed and cowritten by former child actor Ron Howard, who had just come off a losing streak with *Backdraft* and *Parenthood*, it told the story of two Irish immigrants who come to American in the late nineteenth century to make new lives for themselves.

Tom was asked to play the role of Joseph Donnelly, a young Irishman who left Ireland after being faced with eviction from his father's farm, and Nicole was cast as Shannon Christie, an aristocratic, headstrong girl who goes to America to escape the blandness of her family life, not to mention a suitor who is obsessed with her.

For Nicole, that meant switching from her newly acquired American accent to an Irish one, a creative process she was getting used to. Tom had a more difficult time. He had made a career of playing himself in movies and changing his speech patterns was not as easy as he had expected. Nicole and Tom eased the transition by hanging out with local Irishmen and picking up their speech patterns. When that proved to be inadequate, Tom employed the services of a speech coach who taught him how to master the basics.

For Nicole and Tom, romantic locations like Dublin and County Galway only intensified their continuing infatuation with each other. When they were not reciting their lines before the camera, they hugged and kissed in full view of the crew, except when they disappeared into their trailer for unexplained absences of two hours or more.

Ron Howard had never seen anything quite like it. Sometimes he would call out, "Action," then turn to see the couple clinched in a passionate kiss.

Crew members sometimes jokingly offered to pour buckets of water on them. More than once, the scene would be set with Nicole before the camera and Tom's voice, capped with affectionate awe, would filter over Howard's shoulder with the observation that, "Isn't she beautiful!"

Nicole was just as bad, often making comments to no one in particular about his good looks or, when he was filming his fight scenes, extolling the attractiveness of his bare chest. It was obvious to everyone working on the film that she was very much in love, almost to the point of schoolgirl giddiness. Despite the couple's honeymoon glow, the film did manage to get made.

*Far and Away* begins in Ireland in the 1890s. Joseph is an impoverished farmer who is fighting a losing battle to make a living on rented land. When his father dies, thugs are sent by the landowner to tell the family that their rent is overdue. The thugs burn down the farmhouse and Joseph goes after the landlord to seek revenge.

When he arrives at the landlord's house, he falls asleep in the barn, fully intending to murder the man at the earliest opportunity. Fate intervenes when Shannon encounters him in the barn and stabs him in the thigh with a pitchfork. As a result, Joseph is taken prisoner and held against his will in the house.

One night, Shannon climbs up a ladder to his second-floor room and tells him that she is running away. "Perhaps you are wondering why I'm running away," she says. "I'll tell you. I'm running away because I'm modern. I'm modern and I'm going to a modern place . . . I'm very smart and very modern and that's all you need to know about me."

Joseph is resistant at first, but she perseveres and convinces him to escape her father's house and then to go with her to America. They catch a ship to America, him posing as her servant, a status he is not too keen about.

Once they arrive in Boston, Joseph becomes a boxer to earn money and Shannon takes a job as a chicken plucker. Life in America is harder than they ever imagined and they are forced to take rooms in a brothel. After a string of boxing successes, Joseph loses a big fight and is beaten senseless. He awakens in the street and sees Shannon's Irish suitor, who has traveled to America to find her.

Penniless, Shannon and Joseph are cast out into the street in the dead of winter. They break into a house to get food and the home owner fires a shot that wounds Shannon. Joseph takes her to the suitor's house so that she can be cared for properly, then he disappears, thinking he has done the best thing for her under the circumstances.

Eventually, Joseph gets a job working on a railroad. One day he sees a wagon train on its way to Oklahoma for the land rush and he joins it. At the camp, he spots Shannon, who is there with her family and suitor.

"I wondered if I'd ever see you here," she said. "I suspected that I might." She is cool toward him at first, hiding her anger over his disappearance. She says, "Time takes care of everything, doesn't it, Joseph?"

"Everything's worked out as it should have," he says. "Don't you agree?"

Shannon nods affirmatively, then tells him good luck with his dreams. Of course, they meet again at the end, when they together claim the land they have wanted so much since their arrival in America.

When *Far and Away* was released in May 1992, during Memorial Day weekend, it took in an encouraging $13 million from more than fifteen hundred screens, but that was far less than Universal Pictures expected (by contrast, *Alien 3* took in $23 million the previous weekend and *Lethal Weapon 3* took in $27 million).

Critics were decidely less than enthusiastic about the lumbering epic. Hal Hinson of the *Washington Post* wrote: "*Far and Away* is such a doddering, bloated bit of corn, and its characters and situation so obviously hackneyed, that we can't give in to the story and allow ourselves to be swept away... Cruise has never seemed more lightweight; his job is to embody the virtues of a larger-than-life Hollywood movie star, and yet he has never appeared more inadequate to the task."

Writing in the *Chicago Sun-Times*, Roger Ebert praised the photography and then noted: "Are audiences thought not capable of seeing great pictures and listening to great dialogue at the same time? Are they so impatient they have to be thrown boxing scenes instead of character scenes? Is there any purpose to this movie other than visual spectacle?"

After it became apparent that the movie was not going to do well (it ended up grossing only $58 million in the United States), Ron Howard did a series of interviews to *explain* the movie. "Old-fashioned was what I had in mind," he told the *Philadelphia Inquirer*. "These are the kinds of movies that made me want to become a director, this style of storytelling. *How the West Was Won, The Quiet Man*—it's a certain style of motion picture experience."

Nicole and Tom were not much help promoting the film. For some reason, they had decided before the movie's release not to do any joint interviews. Tom had been antagonistic toward the press for several years—often requiring reporters to sign restrictive contracts before he would talk to them—but Nicole always had a more realistic view toward publicity. She did interviews for *Far and Away*, only not with Tom in the room. "I knew it would be ... difficult ... for my career, when we decided to get married," she explained to *W* magazine. "But I figured, God, you fall in love with somebody and get married once, properly. I'm not going to do it again."

Ironically, the biggest disappointment of *Far and Away* was not a lagging box office; it was the less-than-enthusiastic way in which fans reacted to Tom and Nicole together on screen. Some people said it was because Tom's female fans resented Nicole sharing the spotlight with him. Others pointed to the tepid on-screen chemistry between the two actors and suggested that perhaps they should keep their careers separate.

After *Far and Away*, Nicole expressed regret that she and Tom had teamed up on screen again so soon after *Days of Thunder*. Asked about that by *Movieline*, she said: "I regretted the way I was viewed as just Tom Cruise's wife. In terms of the film and the character, I was very appreciative ... I was trying to have my own identity. I'm sure that happens to a lot of people—I was just experiencing it in a public way."

Losing her professional identity was not something she had counted on. She had gone from being a big fish in a small Australian pond to being Tom's fish in an aquarium illuminated with spotlights. She was in love. Other people who fell in love could do so without losing their identity, so why should that be a special problem for her?

Tom did everything he could to make her feel special. He lavished expensive gifts on her, ostentatious displays of affection such as a red Mercedes, and he gave her a Labrador retriever to cuddle and play with while he was away at work putting together multimillion-dollar movie deals.

Nicole once told him that she did not like to shop, so he went shopping for her, purchasing expensive gowns for her to wear, clothing that he thought would look good on her. There was nothing overtly manipulative in Tom's behavior, no sinister motives, but it was as if he had borrowed a page from Antony Kidman's book *Family Life: Adapting to Change*, which makes the case that classic, gender-based power struggles between men and women sometimes revolve around who controls the purse and the toys.

Nicole was aware of what was happening—she was, after all, her father's daughter—but, truthfully, she did not care. For the first time, she was in a relationship with a man who was both her friend and her lover, and together they were headed down the same creative road, dreaming the same fantasies. She willingly gave up her independence because she felt, for the first time in her life, that she had found someone to love that was going to love her back.

"I'm not sort of running around and going, 'Oh my God, oh my God, who can I be with, where's someone I can spend the rest of my life with?'" she told *Women's Weekly*, an Australian publication. "I've found that person now and it's just a warm, comforting, incredibly trusting and supportive environment. That's given me a base to shoot out from, to grow from. And he's just a great person to be with."

Once Tom had Nicole driving the car he wanted, wearing the clothing he picked out for her, and playing with the puppy of his choice, he went off to make another movie. Next up was a courtroom thriller named *A Few Good Men*, directed by Rob Reiner, who had a major hit in 1989 with *When Harry Met Sally*. The script was based on a true incident that was adapted into a Broadway play by Aaron Sorkin, who wrote the screenplay as well.

Tom was asked to play Lt. Daniel Kaffee, an inexperienced navy lawyer who defends two marines, played by Wolfgang Bodison and James Marshall, who have been charged with murdering a colleague during a hazing incident. The marines claimed that they were following orders and that the death was accidental.

Lieutenant Commander Jo-Anne Galloway, played by Demi Moore, is put in charge of overseeing the marines' defense. She is nudged by her superior officer to assign Kaffee to the case, primarily because he is lazy, the type of bureaucratic legal mind that would rather plea-bargain than fight. With Kaffee in charge, the top brass feel that the case has a better chance of quietly disappearing. However, the deeper that Kaffee and Galloway get into the case, the more convinced they are of their clients' innocence. Kaffee also discovers that he has a real passion for investigative legal work.

A requirement for all good thrillers is an immovable object, someone that has the power to make or break the case. That person, in this instance, is Col.

Nathan Jessup, a hard-line marine played by Jack Nicholson. Did he give his tacit approval for the hazing incident or did he simply look the other way after the fact? The real fireworks of the film are generated by Kaffee's confrontations with Jessup. In the climatic courtroom scene, Jessup lunges at Kaffee and has to be restrained by two marine guards.

Even though Tom was the star—and Nicholson became an important character only toward the end of the movie—it was the older man who had the best lines. At one point, he says: "Son, we live in a world that has walls, and those walls have to be guarded by men with guns... You don't want the truth because, deep down in places you don't talk about at parties, you want me on that wall, you need me on that wall."

In many ways, *A Few Good Men* was Tom's biggest challenge to date. Not just because he had to play opposite a movie legend, but because he had to memorize so many legal phrases and complicated dialogue, not an easy task for someone with reading problems. Costar Kevin Bacon, who played Capt. Jack Ross, the prosecutor assigned to convict the two marines, also had problems with his lines. Sometimes, during make-up, the two men rehearsed each other.

An additional challenge for Tom was the fact that the movie provided him with no opportunity to flash his heralded charm in the face of the opposite sex. His scenes with Demi Moore were businesslike, devoid of romance and sex appeal (indeed it later was suggested the role was originally meant for a male, but was changed to a female without making gender changes in the script). The closest the two characters come to romance is a debate over when an invitation by Galloway for dinner constituted an official date. Galloway said definitely not. Kaffee said it sounded like a date to him. And so it went.

Although there was no romance in the movie, there was plenty on the set whenever Nicole showed up to visit Tom. Typically, they found a dark corner and kissed, while embarrassed crew members tried not to watch. She may not have enjoyed playing the role of the girlfriend in the movies, but she demonstrated a real talent for it in real life.

For the most part, film critics were enthusiastic about *A Few Good Men*. Peter Travers, writing in *Rolling Stone*, described Tom as a "fireball" and Nicholson as a "marvel... coiled to spring." Then he added, "There is no bigger kick in movies right now than watching Nicholson pull out all the stops as he takes on Cruise. Maybe it isn't art. Sometimes witty, suspenseful, knockout entertainment is enough."

Rita Kempley, writing in the *Washington Post*, described the movie as a "brass-buttoned, square-jawed huzzah for military justice that's thankfully free of the messy moralizing of the Vietnam age ... it's a grand undertaking that wrangles with the heavy questions that cropped up at Nuremberg and My Lai, questions that deserve and get lots of imposing shots of monuments and not a little swashbuckling from the big stars."

One notable dissenter was Roger Ebert, writing in the *Chicago Sun-Times*: "Nicholson is always fun to watch, as he barks and snarls and improvises new obscenities. Cruise is an effective contrast, as the immature young officer who discovers himself ... But the movie doesn't quite make it, because it never convinces us that the drama is happening while we watch it; it's like the defense team sneaked an advance look at the script."

For all the grand visions seen in the film by some critics, the ticket-buying public flocked to theaters (it grossed $237 million worldwide) not to see a discourse on the abuse of military power, but rather to see Tom and Nicholson, representing Hollywood's young gun and old guard, clash in face-to-face combat, however symbolic it might be. The most memorable confrontation between the two men, the one that made all the television sound bites, occurred when Kaffee pressed Jessup on the witness stand.

"You want answers?" asks Jessup.

"I think I'm entitled."

"You want answers?"

"I want the truth!" says Kaffee.

"You can't handle the truth!" snarls Jessup.

The financial success of *A Few Good Men* proved the box-office drawing power of stars such as Tom Cruise, Nicholson, Demi Moore, Kevin Bacon, and Kiefer Sutherland, but it raised new questions in Tom's mind about the direction his career should take. He was the star of *A Few Good Men*, but it was Nicholson who got the best lines. When moviegoers left the theater, they did not mimic him saying, "I want the truth"—no, they mimicked Nicholson's, "You can't handle the truth!"

What Tom wanted more than anything else was a role he could really sink his teeth into. For whatever reasons, that continued to elude him. In 1992, no one in Hollywood was any bigger than Tom Cruise—he was a box-office leader, earning in excess of $10 million per film—but he felt that despite his enormous success, he should be doing better things with his talents.

\* \* \*

In January 1992, *Parade* magazine reported that Nicole and Tom were expecting a baby in February. "Not true!" countered a spokeswoman for Nicole.
She demanded a retraction by the magazine. Anyone with half a brain could
see that Nicole was not eight months pregnant.

Actually, there was some truth to the story. The couple, in fact, was expecting a baby—an adopted child—and somehow word had leaked out and
the story had gotten twisted in the telling and the retelling. Horrified by the
story, Nicole and Tom put their secret adoption plans on hold.

For months, the tabloids had been filled with speculation about whether
they could have children of their own. Some stories suggested that the couple
had been tested and had learned that Tom was sterile. Others suggested that
it was Nicole who was unable to conceive. The couple was outraged by the
*Parade* story, which they felt was an invasion of their privacy, because it spot-
lighted their so-called marital inadequacies and made it difficult for them to
pursue adoption.

Heartbroken by the experience, Nicole put her emotions aside and began
work on her next movie project, one that would not feature her husband.
*Malice* is a thriller that was carved from the same psychological putty as *Dead
Calm*. Directed by Harold Becker (*Sea of Love* and *The Onion Field*), it fea-
tured a strong cast made up of Alec Baldwin, George C. Scott, Bill Pullman,
Anne Bancroft, and Bebe Neuwirth.

Nicole had accepted another "girlfriend" role, but this one had a wicked
twist and hardly counted. She was asked to play Tracy Kennsinger opposite
both Pullman, who plays her husband, Andy, and Baldwin, who plays a hot-
shot surgeon named Jed Hill. The supporting cast included Bancroft as
Tracy's mother and newcomer Gwyneth Paltrow as a student murder victim.
It was only Paltrow's third feature film and she would be hardly noticeable in
the film today had she not gone on to better things.

*Malice* begins with a pastoral look at a women's college as classes are let
out and the students pour out onto the campus. With an uplifting chorus in
the background, a student rides her bicycle home, where she is raped and badly
beaten as she feeds her cat. She is rushed to the hospital, where Dr. Jed Hill
saves her life with aggressive sleight-of-hand in the operating room.

When Andy, a dean at the college, shows up at the hospital to inquire
about the student, he meets Dr. Hill and realizes that they attended the same

high school. He offers to rent Dr. Hill a room on the third floor of the house he shares with Tracy until he can find a home of his own.

Tracy voices disapproval over her husband's decision to rent the room because she says it gives them little privacy (he says they need the money), but she seems unconcerned about a young boy in the house next door who sits at the window and watches them have sex.

When Tracy experiences mysterious stomach pains and is taken to the hospital for emergency surgery, it is Dr. Hill who performs the operation. He removes both her ovaries, one of which did not have to be removed. Since that means that Tracy will no longer be able to have children, she gets a lawyer and sues Dr. Hill. She ends up winning a huge settlement from the hospital.

Angry with her husband, whom she also blames for the unnecessary surgery, she goes home to visit her mother. Although Tracy is the focus of the story, it is slow to develop and her best lines occur late in the movie, when her role in the plot is understood.

One of Nicole's best scenes is with Pullman. After she finds a hypodermic needle in the bed, obviously placed there to injure her, she sets up a meeting with Andy and confronts him with her suspicions. "Sweetie, I'm going to talk for a minute, so it'd be better if you didn't interrupt me, okay?" she says, her voice sweetly menacing. "I found a hypodermic needle in my bed. I don't know who put it there. It doesn't matter. What matters is that I didn't think it was funny... So what I'm saying is this—whoever played that joke is playing in a league they're not ready for. Now I came here hoping we can reach an understanding."

Later, fearing that Andy has learned the secret that he and Tracy have, Dr. Hill tells her to pay Andy off. She brushes that suggestion aside and suggests that they commit a murder.

"Do you know what you're saying?" he asks.

"What's the big leap, Jed? You cut me open, stuck your hands in and twisted my ovaries so they'd look all dead..."

Dr. Hill slaps her hard across the face. She responds by pulling a pistol on him.

Clearly, by the end of the movie Tracy is not the woman who began the movie. It is her dark secret that propels the plot and gives the story a surprise ending.

Nicole did a great job of acting in the film, showing anger that never got away from her. It is difficult for an actor to show anger while keeping his or her eyes reflective—and Nicole was able to do that with apparent ease. A lesser actor would have tried to show the anger in her eyes as well as in her face, thus destroying the psychological validity of the character's true mental state.

When the movie was released, critics were generally unkind. Writing for *Rolling Stone*, Peter Travers felt it was too over the top. "Perhaps director Harold Becker thought flashy acting could distract us from the gaping plot holes. Becker gets so intent on confusing us, he forgets to give us characters to care about, the way he did in *Sea of Love*...*Malice* is way out of that classy league. It's got suspense but no staying power."

For Jeff Shannon, writing in the *Seattle Times*, there were problems with the way the plot ended, but Nicole's acting impressed him: "Kidman is a femme fatale for the '90s, giving a deliciously nasty performance. She can't prevent you from forming early suspicions (and neither can Baldwin, whose cocky charisma is used as a smoke screen), but there's just enough doubt to keep things interesting."

The most biting and irreverent comment about the movie came from Roger Ebert, who wrote in the *Chicago Sun-Times*: "Peering into the shadows of *Malice*, I was reminded of a remark at this year's Telluride Film Festival by John Alton, the ninety-two-year-old cinematographer who specialized in using shadows and darkness. 'If I'd used more lights,' he said, 'they would have been comedies.'"

Making the film had been pleasant enough, though there were reports that Tom displayed a little jealousy when he showed up on the set during a love scene between Nicole and Baldwin. "Some of those kissing scenes are a little too strong—and a little too long," Tom said, according to the *Star*. "A kiss shouldn't take a minute and a half—ten seconds is more like it." Baldwin reportedly snapped back with, "Sorry, but Kim [Basinger] is away for five days."

After shelving their adoption plans for almost a year, long enough they thought, to allow public interest to wane, they revived those plans in early December 1992 and filed for adoption in Palm Beach, Florida.

Again, word leaked out. This time their lawyer demanded an investigation into what he called a "blatant breach of confidentiality" and he asked for the dismissal of all court personnel who were involved in leaking the information.

Frustrated by their inability to pursue a private legal procedure that thousands of Americans each year successfully enter into and complete with a minimum amount of stress, Nicole and Tom withdrew their adoption petition. Their lawyer said that they feared that if they continued with the adoption, the birth mother's identity would be discovered and that would have unfortunate repercussions for both them and the child.

Why was their lawyer so willing to make public comments about the fiasco? Was it a smoke screen so that Nicole and Tom could secretly pursue adoption from another angle? Within weeks, they located another child and filed a new petition. This time, the procedure went much more smoothly.

In January 1993, they went to a Miami hospital and picked up a healthy baby girl whom they named Isabella Jane Kidman Cruise. The daughter of a married woman who already had two children, Isabella weighed in at nine pounds. The name Isabella has no family connection; they chose it simply because they liked it.

To Nicole and Tom's surprise, the *National Enquirer* published photos of the couple cuddling the infant wrapped in a blanket. There were reports that Tom made a deal with the photographer, exchanging the hospital photo for the photographer's promise to lay off them in the future, but that seemed ridiculous, since the photo made it more likely that the mother, who did not know the identity of the adopting parents, would be able to recognize her child and cause trouble for the couple at a later date.

Within weeks of arriving home with Isabella, Nicole started work on her next movie project. Written and directed by Bruce Joel Rubin, who had scored a major box-office hit in 1990 with *Ghost*, *My Life* is the story of a terminally ill man who prepares for his death by videotaping interviews with himself and others about his life.

It was only Rubin's second time to direct a film, the first occurring twenty-three years earlier with *Dionysus*. Perhaps because he once spent a year and a half exploring India and Tibet, living for a while in a Nepalese monastery, he had a metaphysical view of life, one that he injected into *My Life*, some would say to the film's detriment.

Although there are more than a dozen supporting characters in the film, it is basically a two-person show—Bob Jones, the dying public relations executive, played by Michael Keaton, and his wife, Gail Jones, played by Nicole Kidman. It is true that it was another "girlfriend' role for Nicole, but she did not bristle at this one for two reasons: first, because Gail is not a sex object (the movie is oddly asexual), and second because she was allowed to straighten her hair, in her mind a symbol of her new maturity.

*My Life* begins with one of Bob Jones's childhood experiences, one in which he prays for a circus to appear in his backyard and then becomes disillusioned with God because it does not happen. The scene is a setup for the true beginning of the film, thirty years later, when Bob, presumably once again let down by God because of his terminal illness, is shown making a video for his unborn child.

Nicole's first appearance occurs when Bob and Gail are in bed talking about his illness. Gail says, "You know at some point we're going to have to tell people."

"Don't forget to tell me when that is, okay?" he says.

"Amazing, isn't it? There's just no appropriate etiquette for this."

He jokes about it and then has a severe pain attack.

Early in the film, it is apparent that Nicole has been told by the director to be subdued and to whisper her lines to emphasize the gravity of the situation. It is a technique that fails, especially since Keaton seems determined to mumble his way through the entire film. Much of what he says is so low and jumbled that it is beyond the capacity of the human ear to detect.

When his doctor tells him that there is nothing else he can do, that he has only about three or four months left, he leaves the doctor's office devastated. Then, as he's walking away, he realizes that attitude is not acceptable. He storms back into the doctor's office and angrily tells him, "Don't take away my hope—it's all I've got left."

Gail suggests he try a Chinese practitioner because she knows other people who have been helped by alternative medicine techniques. Bob is reluctant, but he does it to please her, figuring it is the least he can do under the circumstances.

One day the Chinese practitioner tells him: "The last second of your life is the most important moment of all. It's everything you are, ever said, ever thought, all rolled into one. That is the seed of your next life…until that last moment, you still have time."

Inspired by his conversations with the practitioner, Bob takes his video-camera on the road and gets in touch with the people of his past, ostensibly to leave a record for his child, but just as importantly to try to understand why his life turned out the way it did.

One day Gail finds one of his tapes and watches it, not knowing that it is one in which he tells his unborn child not to be upset if his mother marries again. It hits Gail hard, as could be expected. "I feel like I've already lost you," she tells him. "Like we've lost each other."

"What do you want me to say?"

"Don't say anything. Just hear me. Bob, I need you . . . I can't do this alone. I need you to be there."

Much of the film deals with Bob's inability to relate to Gail about what he is feeling about his eminent demise and what she is going through with the pregnancy. When she tells him that she wants him to go with her to get an ultrasound—they don't yet know the sex of the baby—he frowns.

"I need to share this with you, Bob," says Gail. "Don't make me go through it alone, please. It's our baby. Don't pretend it away."

He responds that he's not— He's setting up a trust fund and preparing for "its" future, to which Gail responds, "Bob, please—love us!"

Because of his cancer Bob wants to embrace life, at least whatever life he has left, but the anger and frustration that he feels set up a defense that keeps others away. Because he is estranged from his family, and he hasn't visited them in four years, Gail encourages him to reestablish contact with them. She tells him his brother is getting married in April.

"You're kidding," he says. "To whom?"

He voices surprise that they were even invited to the wedding. "Forget it—I'll probably be dead by then anyway."

"Great—then you'll have the perfect excuse for not showing up."

Nicole has a few great lines in the film, but her character is so underdeveloped that her performance often seems flat and uninspired. She has appeared in very few films in which she did not develop a strong on-screen chemistry with the leading man. For whatever reason—her marriage to Tom could have been a factor—she and Keaton never connected. That combined with direction to recite their lines in a near whisper proved fatal for the film's artistic vision.

When *My Life* was released, reviews were mixed. *Chicago Sun-Times* critic

Roger Ebert thought parts of the movie were good, but he did not like the way the humor and seriousness of the story were contrived into juxtaposition. "[It] should be a more rigorous and single-minded film," he wrote. "Maybe it started that way, before getting spoonfuls of honey to make the medicine go down. If a character invites us to join him on the most important journey of his life—to parenthood and death—then he shouldn't distract us with little side trips to schtick and funny business."

Desson Howe, writing in the *Washington Post*, was more forgiving: "[Rubin's] latest movie accelerates so rapidly into the serious, you're left dry-mouthed and blown away. You're pulled in deeper and deeper until—by the anguishing conclusion—you're hanging on for dear life, trying to maintain dignity, trying to keep from falling apart."

A *Rolling Stone* reviewer could not wait to twist the knife in the corpse: "There's potential in a movie about a professional deceiver who gets slammed with some scummy facts about who he is by trying to sell an idealized version of himself to his child. Keaton could have played the hell out of that role. But Rubin swallows Bob's PR campaign and then asks us to swallow it, too. No sale."

By all accounts, Nicole was upset by the reviews, not just the negative ones, but even the positive ones that made her realize how limited her character had been in the film. Always insecure about her physical appearance, she concluded that she was not leading lady material. All a leading lady had to do was simply project the right image, at least that was the prevailing wisdom of the day in Tinseltown. Nicole did not see that quality in herself. Her true talent, she decided, was as a character actress, someone who projected different images for different roles.

Nicole had tried to be a "star" opposite Tom in *Days of Thunder* and *Far and Away*—and she had tried it with Alec Baldwin in *Malice* and Michael Keaton in *My Life*—and the results had all been the same . . . a big zero. How could she have fallen so far since the intoxicating victory of *Dead Calm*? Convinced that her film career in America was going nowhere, she thought about returning to Australia. If she had not been happily married to Tom, she surely would have done so.

Unable to flee to Australia and unwilling to stumble into more dead-end roles, where she was expected to shine as a "movie star," she decided to rethink her career. "I took time off and evaluated why I was an actor, and why

I was here, and what I wanted to do," she told the *Boston Globe*. "I didn't re-alize when I made *Far and Away* how much I would then be defined and judged in relation to [Tom]."

Her solution was to focus more on independent films, where women his-torically have been able to explore stimulating new territory as character ac-tresses.

If 1993 was a bad year for Nicole, other than the adoption of Isabella, it was a terrific year for Tom, who signed on to do an unusual—for him, at least—role in *Interview with the Vampire*, based on Anne Rice's best-selling novel. He also wrapped up production on *The Firm*, based on John Grisham's best-selling novel. For a while that year, Tom was the cinematic darling—or an-tichrist, depending on how you looked at it—of America's popular literary establishment.

*The Firm* was based on Grisham's novel about a Memphis law firm and its flirtations with organized crime. It was something the Arkansas-born author knew a little something about, having practiced law in a small Mississippi community just south of Memphis. Although travel magazines promote the city as a center for music, barbecue, and everything Elvis, Memphis has been an organized crime center since the 1920s. Grisham's yarn is fiction, but it is also true in the sense that it is based on activities that have taken place in Memphis for decades and law firms that really do exist.

Director Sidney Pollack and executive producer Michael Hausman knew nothing about that, of course, so they decided to be true to the book and shoot most of the movie in Memphis, with smaller segments earmarked for Boston and the Cayman Islands. When it came to the script, however, they decided to jazz the story up somewhat. They changed the ending, a decision that gave the movie a different perspective, and they made numerous minor changes in the story Grisham had written.

One major change they considered was adding a female lawyer to the Memphis law firm joined by Tom's character, Mitch McDeere, someone who could develop a romance with McDeere and come between him and his wife. Meryl Streep's name came up first, but then it was decided that they needed someone closer to Tom's age.

Rumors circulated that Nicole was promoted for the part. If true, it must have sent the Aussie redhead ballistic. All she needed at that point in her career—to end it—was to make another movie with Tom and play the girlfriend that comes between him and his wife! You could probably have heard Nicole's screams halfway to Australia. For whatever reason, the idea of "another woman" was eventually dropped.

When Tom and his costars—Gene Hackman, Jeanne Tripplehorn, Hal Holbrook, Wilford Brimley, Ed Harris, Holly Hunter, and Gary Busey—arrived in Memphis in the winter of 1992 to begin production, the film company was given the royal treatment by the city—and even by the mobsters they were scripted to unwittingly portray.

"I'm always on location, but I've never been in a city like Memphis where they made it so easy for you and where even your needs were anticipated," Pollack told Donald La Badie, a writer for *The Commercial Appeal.* "I never in my life felt so welcome. People knocked themselves out for you. I'll tell you one thing. It turns out that this Southern hospitality crap isn't crap—or at least it isn't in Memphis."

Unfortunately, the hospitality was not a two-way transaction. Tim Baker, a cardiovascular consultant for a pharmaceutical company in Memphis, stopped by the set to say hello to his old classmate from St. Xavier Catholic boys school in Kentucky and to ask him to do a public service announcement for a dyslexia school in Little Rock.

As he stood in line in an attempt to establish contact with Tom, he was mistaken for an extra and told to move along with the others. As he was rounding a corner, he spotted Tom in a director's chair talking to Pollack. He tried to talk to him, but he could not get close enough. Instead, he wrote out a note and asked a member of the crew to give it to Tom.

Baker did his work as an extra and went home to wait to hear from Tom. A week later, he received his response in the mail—an autographed photograph of Tom playing softball. The rejection did not seem to bother Baker. "[Dyslexia] is a tough thing to live with," he told *The Commercial Appeal.* "Back then, they didn't know what dyslexia was. Our school was advanced, offering several college courses. For him to do as well as he did (as a dyslexic) is remarkable." Asked if Tom was popular at St. Xavier's, he said no: "He was liked but not popular."

Filming proceeded without any major delays or problems and wrapped up in late February 1993, after seventy-seven days of filming. Tom's absence to fly to Florida to help Nicole pick up baby Isabella provided the only behind-the-scenes drama.

When *The Firm* was released in the summer of 1993, reviews were predictable. Jay Carr, writing in the *Boston Globe*, described Tom as "not an actor of great range," but one who can become intense when the situation calls for it. "Owing its popularity more to its arrival during a cultural values shift than to literary merit, [*The Firm*] offers reassurance that there's moral redemption from the greedy go-go '80s," he continued. "*The Firm* doesn't reach and sustain the tension level of a really first-rate thriller. But neither does it bore you. Although far from fully satisfying, it's slick enough to find ways to make you keep watching it."

Joe Brown, writing in the *Washington Post*, saw merit in the film, almost apologetically. "*The Firm* looks like just another variation on Cruise's patented young-hot-shot roles of the past decade," he wrote. "But Cruise has grown substantially as an actor, and *The Firm* means to expose the underbelly of the amorally acquisitive 1980s."

The effect Tom had on Nicole after they were married was fairly obvious and played up by the entertainment press, which continued to depict her as Mrs. Tom Cruise, the Australian wannabe who became a Hollywood star by virtue of her association with Tom. It was not true, of course, but lies are just as hurtful as the truth sometimes.

What the entertainment press did not pick up on was the effect Nicole was having on Tom's career. How could he live with a woman who was so passionate about her craft and not be influenced by her views? Nicole was disillusioned about the Hollywood concept of stardom. Basically, that concept is that people go to movies to see stars be themselves, and not to see great acting. To help her refocus her career, she enrolled in New York's Actors Studio, where she was taught the Method technique of acting. The experience uplifted her spirits and made her even more determined to be an actress as opposed to being a "movie star."

Because Nicole was convinced that character acting was the way to go, she influenced Tom's decision to play the vampire Lestat in *Interview with the Vampire*. For the first time, Tom would play someone other than himself. He would play a villain, a vampire who killed the innocent to feed his own bloodlust. Tom was tired of playing himself. He wanted what Nicole wanted—the opportunity to portray a character who was totally different from what he was in real life.

The news that Tom would play Lestat was greeted with vocal opposition by the book's fans. Author Anne Rice jumped into the fray by telling a reporter that Tom Cruise "is no more my vampire than Edward G. Robinson is Rhett Butler." (After the movie's release she changed her mind and praised Tom's performance.)

When the movie was released, *Rolling Stone* published a review that was typical of most reviews of the film in that it begrudgingly gave Tom credit for his acting abilities. "The movie is hypnotic, scary, sexy, perversely funny and haunting in a way that taps into primal fears," said the magazine. "It can also be gross, snail paced and grindingly glum. You could say the same things—pro and con—about Rice's book."

No one was more pleased than Nicole, character actor advocate that she was. For the first time, she felt that their marriage had a creative direction. As time went by, more and more people wondered what she planned to do next. She gave a hint early in 1994 when she told *Movieline* that she would "Loooove to play a sex kitten." And just so that the tabloid press would not misinterpret that comment, she volunteered to the magazine that she was not a lesbian and she considered Tom to be the best lover she had ever had.

# CHAPTER SIX

# At Last, A Juicy Role
# To Die For

E ven after Nicole and Tom adopted Isabella, Nicole continued to tell journalists that they were still trying to have a child of their own and she denied that either of them had ever undergone fertility tests. She resented the endless questions about an issue that most couples would consider intimate and beyond the perimeters of entertainment news coverage. If her womb was not private, she wondered, whatever would be?

Of course, as far as the media were concerned, their fertility was less an issue than Tom's sexual preference. Those issues were revived in the February issue of *McCall's* magazine in a story that quoted a "prominent movie critic" as saying that the actor's marriage was arranged by his management to halt the gay rumors, while promising Nicole an acting career in return.

Nicole and Tom were shocked by the story, especially since his ex-wife, Mimi Rogers, who had begun the speculation with her comments in *Playboy*, recanted her previous statements in the January/February issue of *Detour* magaazine, saying, "No, he's not gay. I run into people all the time who tell me that . . . I slept with the man for four years, I should know." After being contacted by Tom's lawyers, *McCall's* agreed to run an apology in its April issue.

In February 1995, in the midst of the new gender speculation, Nicole and Tom adopted their second child, an African American boy who was born on February 6 and placed into their home by mid-month. They named him Connor Antony Kidman Cruise.

Not long after that, Nicole went on the offensive over the gay issue with an interview that appeared in *Vanity Fair* magazine, a publication that the previous year had aired Tom's denials of homosexuality. "I'll bet all my money I've ever made, plus his, that he doesn't have a mistress, that he doesn't have a gay lover, that he doesn't have a gay life," she said. "We're both heterosexual. We have a lot of homosexual friends and neither of us would shy away from having a homosexual (movie) role...but I take offense if people say I would marry into a marriage of convenience. I think that's very sexist because they're saying, 'She married for fame and money.'"

But what the magazine offered with one hand, it took away with the other by describing Nicole as a "heat-seeking missile" who pursued her career with "relentlessness." Nicole was livid. She became convinced that magazines were going to print only what they wanted to print, regardless of what she said.

Sometime later, in an interview with the friendly *Good Weekend*, the Sunday supplement of the *Sydney Morning Herald*, she said: "I do think, and I say this to Tom, that you are judged as a woman in this industry so much more than men. I mean, I live with one of the biggest stars in the world and I know how I'm judged in relation to how he's judged. His determination is called intensity; my determination is called ambitious to the point of ruthless."

Nicole's next film role ran counter to what she had been telling reporters for the past year that she was going to focus on character roles and avoid the glitzy movies that used her for window dressing. To the surprise of everyone, she accepted the role of the licentious Dr. Chase Meridian, a criminal psychologist who spars with Batman in *Batman Forever*. After everything she had said, why would she want to play a comic book character in the glitziest movie of the year?

Nicole is very competitive, so the prospect of beating out all-American actress Sandra Bullock for the part may have played a role in her decision. However, a more likely reason can be found in the fact that the movie's director, Joel Schumacher, was best known for character-driven movies such as *St. Elmo's Fire* and *Flatliners*—and Nicole may have wanted to be cooperative, with the view of landing a role more to her liking somewhere down the road.

*Batman Forever* had the look and feel of a box-office smash. In addition to

Nicole, the film featured three leading men types—Val Kilmer as Batman, Tommy Lee Jones as Harvey Two-Face, and Jim Carrey as the Riddler—and a supporting cast that included Chris O'Donnell as Robin and the up-and-coming Drew Barrymore as Sugar.

Kilmer seemed like an unlikely choice to replace Michael Keaton in the title role. His most successful film to date was *Top Gun*, in which he costarred with Tom. His performances as Doc Holliday in *Tombstone*, Elvis in *True Romance*, and Jim Morrison in Oliver Stone's *The Doors* were well received by critics, but they were not the type of roles that projected a traditional leading-man image.

*Batman Forever* begins with Two-Face holding a hostage as his hideout is surrounded by cops. After responding to the bat sign, Batman arrives on the scene and meets Dr. Chase Meridian for the first time. She is elegant and direct, and since Nicole has dyed her hair, she is blond and forbidding or accessible (depending on her mood).

In an effort to save the hostage, Batman falls into a trap and is caught in a metal cylinder that is lifted skyward by a helicopter. After several bad moments, he escapes, only to discover that his own temporary capture has allowed Two-Face to escape during all the confusion.

Back in his straight life as industrialist Bruce Wayne, he turns down Edward Nygma's request for a go-ahead on daring new brain research. Frustrated by the rejection, Nygma transforms himself into the Riddler and devises a plan to get even.

Meanwhile, Dr. Meridian, having decided that she has a personal interest in Batman, summons him with the bat sign. When he realizes that there is no emergency, Batman chastises her for misusing the signal. "You called me here for this? The signal is not a beeper."

"Well, I wish I could say that my interest in you is purely professional," responds Dr. Meridian.

"You trying to get under my cape, doctor?"

"A girl can't live by psychoses alone."

His interest piqued, Batman asks, "The car, right? Chicks love the car."

"What is there about the wrong kind of man?" Dr. Meridian asks herself aloud. "In grade school, it was guys with earrings. College...motorcycles, leather jackets. Now...[she reaches out and feels his breastplate]...black rubber!"

With her blond hair blown by an electric fan off camera, she comes on to Batman. He says he hasn't had much luck with women, to which she responds that perhaps he just hasn't met the right one.

The above exchange was pretty much the extent of what was expected of Nicole in the way of character development. Clearly, she was in the movie to provide eye candy to comic book fans and little else.

*Batman Forever* lived up to expectations by grossing $184 million in the United States and another $149 million in overseas markets, but reviews were mixed, as might be expected. Peter Travers, writing in *Rolling Stone*, thought its overall tone was an improvement over the two previous Batman movies: "There's no fun machine this summer than packs more surprises. Sure, there's a lot missing: *Batman Forever* is more cheery than haunting. The violence, being cartoony and affectless, has no weight or consequence— something the moral finger pointers mysteriously think is a good thing."

Kenneth Turan, writing in the *Los Angeles Times*, felt the film was one of the season's "noisiest efforts," but he found redemption in its quieter moments: "*Batman Forever* is not a film for the ages, but it will do for right now. If nameless dark forces compel a visit to a summer blockbuster, this loud and boisterous comic book confidential is serviceable enough to satisfy."

Writing in the *San Francisco Chronicle*, Mick LaSalle said that he thought Kilmer's Bruce Wayne was younger and more handsome than previous Batmen: "You get the feeling most of his problems would be solved if only he got with the right girlfriend. In this case that's Chase Meridian (Nicole Kidman), who is neither ugly enough nor beautiful enough to do Lauren Bacall, but she gives it a good try."

Nicole generally got good marks for her performance. Indeed, some observers felt it was her stylish and recklessly seductive effort that rescued the film from falling into a mosh pit of adolescent boy-toys and heavy-metal-level sound effects: Swoosh! Bam! Purr! Compared to the other actors, Nicole seemed almost lifelike!

At around this same time, Nicole's acquaintance from acting school, director Jane Campion, told friends in Sydney that she wanted to do a film adaptation of Henry James's *The Portrait of a Lady* and was considering Nicole for the lead role as the stubborn but tragically vulnerable Isabel Archer.

When word of this reached Nicole, she called Campion and told her that *The Portrait of a Lady* was one of her all-time favorite novels. To Nicole's disappointment, Campion voiced second thoughts about the project, saying that she had heard that another film company had an adaptation of the novel in the works.

Nicole was persistent. She told Campion that it did not matter—she insisted that "They can do theirs and we'll do ours." The director was so taken by Nicole's passion for the project that she decided to proceed. She told Nicole that she had the part.

Nicole was elated, the happiest she had been in a long time. She had always, from day one, considered herself a real actress, not the sort of eye candy she had become in films such as *Batman Forever*, *My Life*, *Far and Away*, and even *Days of Thunder*. Her spirits soaring, she began studying for the part, reading everything she could get her hands on, turning over creative possibilities in her mind.

Then, while her emotions were at a peak, Campion called her and dropped a bombshell. She had decided that Nicole was not right for the part! Nicole was stunned, as was Tom, who found the way that Campion handled the matter very upsetting.

Like a rejected lover, Nicole called Campion repeatedly in an effort to restore confidence in her. Nicole assured her that she had both the passion and the ability to become Isabel Archer. It was a superb acting job, because by then Nicole had begun to question her own abilities.

Campion told *Premiere* magazine that she felt "ashamed" about her role in the incident: "I think it just came out of—you know, in the time that Nicole was in Hollywood, she'd made quite a few films I didn't think suited her, and I don't think she felt suited her either."

Finally, Campion agreed to fly to Los Angeles and allow Nicole to audition for the part that she had given her and then taken away. It was an awkward situation for both of them. They spent two days together, with Nicole performing scenes from the film and, at times, improvising, with Campion videotaping everything that Nicole did. It was a humiliating thing for an actress of Nicole's experience to do, but she went after the role as if it were her first.

On the evening of Campion's last day in Los Angeles, the two women went out on the town to relax, ending up at a rock 'n' roll disco where they danced the night away. Before she left town, Campion told her that she wanted a week, without telephone calls, to look over the videotape and make her decision. The fact that she did not tell her if she had the role before leaving was unsettling to Nicole, but she had gone too far with the director to be sidetracked by petty insecurities.

Finally, after she had time to digest the material, Campion called Nicole and told her that she had the part—*again!* Nicole burst into tears. Campion had put her through hell, had in fact broken her spirit and reassembled it to her own liking, but Nicole was so grateful that she forgave her instantly and promised to give the role everything she had.

Meanwhile, work on the project, which did not yet have a completed script or secured financing, was affected by a personal tragedy. Campion's first child, a boy, died soon after birth. Devastated, Campion rebounded by getting pregnant again (this time, she would have a healthy baby girl she named Alice).

When Nicole first read the script for *To Die For*, she was convinced she was perfect for the part. Based on Joyce Maynard's novel about a woman who persuades her teenage lover to murder her husband, it is a true story that Maynard, probably best known for her eyebrow-raising relationship as a young woman with reclusive author J. D. Salinger, adapted to her fictional story with great effect.

The script was written by legendary screenwriter and actor Buck Henry (perhaps best known for writing *The Graduate* and *Catch-22*) and ventured into the dramatically treacherous territory of black comedy, a place few actors are comfortable traveling because of the great creative risks involved.

As if all that was not daunting enough for any actor, the film was going to be directed by Gus Van Sant, best known for off-the-wall films such as *Even Cowgirls Get the Blues* and *Five Ways to Kill Yourself*. One of the few openly gay directors in Hollywood, he played in a rock 'n' roll band called Kill All Blondes and recorded solo albums, one of which is entitled *18 Songs About Golf*. In short, he is a controversial director who likes to push the envelope out past the edge of Hollywood's comfort level. The fact that his favorite filmmaker is Stanley Kubrick speaks volumes about his cinematic vision.

*To Die For* producers offered the lead role of Suzanne Stone Maretto, the slightly crazed weather girl who thought life would be sweeter without her husband, to Meg Ryan, but she turned it down. When Nicole learned that, she called Van Sant and made her case over the telephone why she would be perfect for the part. She told him that she had never been given an opportunity to play a complex character and she saw Suzanne as the role of a lifetime. Their conversation lasted more than an hour, during which Nicole explained her vision for the character.

Van Sant listened patiently as she explained that Suzanne was not some totally screwed-up bitch, but rather a woman with incredible savvy who makes some bad decisions, then he told her over the telephone that she had the part. He liked the fact that she was not an overexposed female lead and he liked the passion that she put into her argument that she was perfect for the part.

Nicole was grateful but stunned with the ease with which he said yes. Van Sant later explained his decision to CNN. "She told me she was destined to play the part of Suzanne Stone...and not wanting to stand in the way of destiny, I thought maybe I should give her the part."

Exhilarated by her good fortune, Nicole researched the role with obsessive determination. She spent three months studying what she called "American women." At one point she and Tom checked into a Santa Barbara, California, hotel and, living entirely off room service, watched television for three days straight.

There were only two rules: the television had to be on twenty-four hours a day and no one could leave the room, no matter what. The idea was to soak up everything, and really experience television as a mind-altering influence.

"I found out that TV deadens you, and it's hypnotic," she explained to *Time* magazine. "I would get involved in the talk shows, yelling back at the screen."

By the time Nicole went to Ontario, Canada, to begin work on the project, she had become the character in the film. She took a notebook and filled it with exercises to do for each scene. Since the character, Suzanne, used a handheld video camera in the movie, Nicole carried one with her as well, learning to edit what she videotaped.

To the dismay of local residents in Brampton, King City, and Toronto, she got so far into the character, as Billy Zane had done in *Dead Calm*, that she was unable or unwilling to get out of character. As a result, local residents reported to the media that Nicole Kidman was a flaky, self-centered bitch who was totally without a sense of humanity. Unaffected by criticism of the character, Nicole told *Juice* magazine: "I actually liked Suzanne. I mean, as sick as that is, she is still a victim of TV and society."

Cast opposite Nicole was Matt Dillon, who played the part of Suzanne's husband, Larry Maretto. As a teen heartthrob, he had won audiences over with his squared-jaw good looks and low-keyed acting style, attributes that were perfect for the role of a pretty-boy husband who lived in ignorance of his wife's dark impulses. The role of Suzanne's teenage boyfriend, Jimmy Emmett, was given to Joaquin Phoenix, and the role of her television boss, Ed Grant, was given to Wayne Knight, known to *Seinfeld* fans as Newman, the ever-present postal worker from hell.

*To Die For* begins with news coverage of Larry Maretto's murder. Family members are interviewed and the story is told through their eyes (including Suzanne's). Each family member gives his or her opinion of the marriage and the events that changed it.

At one point, before Larry and Suzanne got married, he tells his sister that Suzanne is like a "volcano," to which the sister replies, "She can't even bowl."

"She's so pure and delicate and innocent," says Larry, "you just love to look at her and you want to take care of her for the rest of your life."

When Suzanne and Larry get married, she wears a veil that is identical to the one Maria Shriver wore in her real-life wedding. "You're not anybody in America unless you're on TV," says Suzanne. "On TV is where we learn about who we are."

Eventually Suzanne involved three high school students in a documentary for the cable station where she does the weather. Soon she is having sex with Jimmy. After a few encounters, she tells him she can't do it anymore. "I can't go home every night and have him trying to touch me, when all the time I'm just thinking about you, about us."

One evening, while out with Jimmy, she dances in the headlights to Lynard Skynard's "Sweet Home Alabama," her short dress and white panties literally driving the teenager insane. It is one of the visual highlights of the film.

After Larry is murdered, the family gathers at the house, where Suzanne walks from room to room holding her dog, Walter. At the funeral she turns on a boom box, startling mourners with "All By Myself."

After the funeral, Lydia, a teenage girl who was involved in planning the murder, shows up at Suzanne's house and says she wants to talk.

"What do you want to talk about?"

"What we're going to do," says the frightened teen.

"We?"

"You and me and Jimmy—I'm scared."

Suzanne tells her to stay away from her house. "Don't you ever watch *Mystery Theater* or anything?"

Nicole's best lines in the film occur after the teens' arrest, when she is telling her story to her own video camera: "To think that these disadvantaged youngsters, who I had taken under my wing and would only stand to ultimately benefit from my media savvy—to think they might be responsible for this heinous crime. It simply boggles one with disbelief. Of course, I realized and I hope this doesn't sound callous, that the up side to all this, assuming justice prevails, is I would have in my documentary an extremely marketable commodity, something that even PBS would take an interest in."

When the film wrapped, Nicole felt better about *To Die For* than any others she had made. She felt she had come to understand Suzanne better than any character she had ever played. "Here's a woman who's ambitious, but who ends up going down the wrong track," she told the *Atlanta Constitution*. "There are a lot of things in the movie that show you Suzanne is a victim. Of television, certainly. She grew up in a generation that just watched television, and had her morals dictated by TV's moral code. Then, within that, she's a woman who has to pursue whatever she has to to get where she wants to get. In that sense, I see her as very much a victim. Obviously, audiences will make judgments on it differently, but I had to approach it from that way."

The only reservation she had about the part was a fear that people would think that Suzanne was the real Nicole Kidman. It was a risk she felt she had to take.

In March 1995, Nicole took Isabella—she was now being called simply Bella—and Connor to be with Tom in Prague, where he was filming *Mission: Impossible*, then on to London, where they set up housekeeping in an enormous four-story house they reportedly rented for $15,000 a week.

Based on the successful television series, *Mission: Impossible* is about an American agent who is under false suspicion and disloyalty and must expose the real spy without the help of the American government. It costarred Jon

Voight, Henry Czerny, Jean Reno, and Vanessa Redgrave, and it was directed by Brian De Palma, best known for his work with *Carrie* (1976) and *The Untouchables* (1987).

In May 1995, Nicole left their London home to fly to Cannes to attend the film festival and to promote *To Die For*. Wearing a revealing dress that was slit almost to her hip, she made a big splash at the festival. For the first time since her marriage, no one asked her about Tom, who obviously had not made the trip with her; everyone was much more interested in her new film than in her marriage and that suited her just fine.

When *To Die For* was released in September 1995, reviewers were lavish in their praise of the movie and Nicole's acting abilities. Wrote David Ansen in *Newsweek*: "Those who know Kidman only from her one-dimensional roles in *Far and Away* and *Batman Forever* are in for a treat: she's a smashing comedienne. The movie wouldn't work if Kidman overplayed her hand, condescending to the role. But she invests Suzanne with a deliciously self-deluded conviction, a cheerleader's witchy mixture of genuine naiveté, calculated sexuality and lethal cunning. She's a hoot."

Under the headline KIDMAN MONSTROUSLY GOOD IN 'TO DIE FOR', Mick LaSalle wrote for the *San Francisco Chronicle*: "Suzanne is a monster, and a lesser actress might have played her on one note. But Kidman brings to the role layers of meaning, intention, and impulse. Telling her story in close-up—as she does throughout the film—Kidman lets you see the calculation, the wheels turning, the transparent efforts to charm that succeed in charming all the same. Kidman has always been pretty, but in *To Die For*, her beauty and magnetism are electric."

Roger Ebert, writing in the *Chicago Sun-Times*, thought the film was filled with perfect character studies. "*To Die For* is the kind of movie that's merciless with its characters, and Kidman is superb at making Suzanne into someone who is not only stupid, vain and egomaniacal, but also vulnerably human. She represents, on a large scale, feelings we have all had in smaller and sneakier ways. She simply lacks skill in concealing them."

*To Die For* took in $21 million in the United States, with negligible world sales except in Great Britain and France, where the film was a modest success. By contrast, *Mission: Impossible* proved to be an enormous success when it was released in 1996, taking in $180 million in the United States and $422 million worldwide.

＊　＊　＊

For the remainder of 1995, Nicole basked in the glow of praise for her work in *To Die For*, taking in a best actress award from the Boston Society of Film Critics. She also started work on a new film, one that had caused her great anguish in the beginning, but that now offered her hope for a new direction as a serious actress.

*The Portrait of a Lady* began production in London in late summer and then moved on to Rome, Florence, and Tuscany in September. Joining Nicole was a stellar cast of character actors: John Malkovich as Gilbert Osmond, Barbara Hershey as Madame Serena Merle, Mary-Louise Parker as Henrietta Stack-pole, Shelley Duvall as Countess Gemini, John Gielgud as Mr. Touchett, and Shelley Winters as Mrs. Touchett. It was the kind of cast and story that Nicole had dreamed about for years.

In order to focus on the film, she left the children with Tom in London for the first week or so. So that she could feel the pain of being Isabel Archer—a turn-of-the-century heiress who rejects the attention of several appropriate suitors only to fall in love with an abusive scoundrel played by Malkovich— she wore a corset that squeezed her waist in to a mere nineteen inches. Asked to explain, she said it was because she wanted to feel the pain that Isabel felt. At one point, Campion had to stop filming when she noticed Nicole turning pale from the overtightened corset.

Through filming, Nicole played close attention to every detail, including her own makeup. She insisted on looking as plain and unassuming as possible. Occasionally, the pressure she put on herself to excel overflowed onto the set in a disruptive manner.

One day, Martin Donovan was playing opposite Nicole in the stable scene when he noticed that she was walking around with a rather glassy look in her eyes. It was a difficult scene for both actors and drained their emotions. After hours of shooting and re-shooting, they were almost ready to wrap the scene when Donovan looked over and saw Nicole being carried off the set. She had collapsed from exhaustion.

Campion found Nicole's fastidiousness exasperating at times, but she was also dazzled by the results. "I always thought that, somewhere inside me, I was always best for the part," Campion told *Premiere*. "Until about halfway through, when Nicole started doing stuff I couldn't even imagine. She was surprising me and surprising herself. And that's what I wanted for Isabel—to be surprised."

*The Portrait of a Lady* begins as Isabel Archer, an American who is without a father or a mother, goes to England to visit her wealthy uncle, Mr. Touchett. He has encouraged a suitor that he thought would be a good match for her, but the headstrong Isabel turns down his proposal: "I know it seems tasteless, ungrateful. But I can't marry him."

Responds Mr. Touchett, "You didn't find his proposal sufficiently attractive?"

"It was attractive. There was a moment when I would have given my little finger to say yes. But . . . I think I have to begin by getting a general impression of life . . . and there's a light that has to dawn."

To Isabel's surprise, her uncle dies and leaves her his vast estate. As she moves about society in an effort to find herself, she is introduced to Gilbert Osmond, for whom she develops an overpowering infatuation. Her cousin, Ralph Touchett, warns her about the man, but she refuses to listen. Says Isabel: "He has the gentlest, kindest, lightest spirit. You've got hold of a false idea. It's a pity, but I can't help it."

Not long after she marries Osmond, Isabel's life spirals out of control. Much of the movie revolves around a diabolical plot by Osmond and his friend, Madame Serena Merle, to use Isabel's money and her past relationship with Lord Warburton (her former suitor) to entice him into marrying Osmond's daughter.

When the lord leaves the city without proposing marriage, Osmond and Isabel fight over the matter and he slaps her and pushes her to the floor. Subsequently, the child is sent to a convent by her father out of spite and Isabel goes to America to be with her dying cousin. Nicole has a brief nude scene in the movie, but the story is curiously devoid of overt sexuality, perhaps because of Campion's feminist approach to the adaptation.

After production was wrapped up in November, Campion returned to Sydney to edit the film. Nicole and Tom went back to London, where she collapsed. Exhausted, she remained in bed for two weeks, her temperature going as high as 104 degrees. Tom freaked out while trying to locate the Tylenol in their medicine cabinet and she had to remind him that he was supposed to be calming her down.

"I was so angry with myself for getting so sick, just sheer emotionally and physically exhausted, and then I saw the film and thought, 'No wonder,' " she told the *Boston Globe*. "The workload was more than I realized . . . I drove myself. My desire to please Jane and not have her disappointed was so strong, I wanted to live up to her expectations."

Once she recovered, she went to Sydney to put the final touches on the film. By that point, Campion was focusing on overdubbing those portions of the film where the sound quality suffered as a result of unanticipated noise, such as from swishing dresses. Nicole proved to be very demanding, often asking to rerecord parts over and over again.

Campion took Nicole's perfectionism in stride, for by the time she looked over what they had filmed she was convinced they had made a great movie. Going into the project, she was skeptical she would ever cry over anything Nicole did, but at this stage of the project she could not watch portions of the film without weeping.

Nicole felt the same way. Shortly before *The Portrait of a Lady* was released, Nicole told the *Atlanta Journal-Constitution:* "This film means more to me than any other film I've made. And I know it does to Jane, too. Some films you make which you can walk away from. This is one we're very protective of. We're out there feeling that we have to shield the baby. Protect the baby!"

With the arrival of 1996, Nicole won best actress or best performance awards from the Broadcast Film Critics Association, the Southeastern Film Critics Association, and the Golden Globes for her work in *To Die For*. To the surprise of everyone, she was not even nominated for an Academy Award. The Oscar for best actress in 1995 went to Susan Sarandon for her performance in the drama, *Dead Man Walking*. Nicole learned the hard way that the Academy is reluctant to give Oscars to character actors, preferring instead to focus on box-office savvy "movie stars."

Once Nicole finished work on *The Portrait of a Lady*, Tom began work on his next movie, a comedy/drama entitled *Jerry Maguire*. Tom plays a gung-ho sports agent, Jerry Maguire, who has a moral epiphany over his firm's greedy business practices. When he expresses a desire to do the right thing by his clients, he is promptly fired.

The only client who stays with him is National Football League wide receiver Rod Tidwell, played by Cuba Gooding, Jr. Rounding out the cast was Renee Zellweger, who plays Dorothy Boyd, an idealistic woman who leaves a secure job to take a position as Maguire's entire office staff, and soon becomes his love interest as well.

Most of *Jerry Maguire* was filmed in California, which meant that Nicole and the children could be with Tom at their Los Angeles home. They tried to maintain a rhythm in their careers, for the sake of the children, so that they were never making films at the same time. Both Tom and Nicole had become very family-oriented, doting over their children like any other parents. The more time Nicole spent with Isabella and Connor, the more appreciative she became of their talents and idiosyncrasies. She wanted Isabella to learn to play the guitar, but the child showed no interest in it. Connor, to Nicole's surprise, took to the instrument right away. Planning a child's future was more difficult than it looked, she discovered, especially when the child has a mind of his or her own.

In the summer of 1996, once Tom wrapped up work on *Jerry Maguire*, they took the children and went to the Mediterranean island of Capri, where they set up house aboard a 247-foot sailing boat. Early one morning, Nicole was on deck with Connor in her arms, when he began chanting, "Boat, burning, boat burning." Sure enough, there was a boat burning on the horizon (shades of *Dead Calm?*).

At Nicole's urging, Tom went to rescue the boat's five passengers. It was his third act of heroism in six months. Previously, he assisted a hit-and-run victim in California and saved two children from being crushed in a London crowd. He was beginning to feel a little bit like Batman or Superman. Needless to say, Conner was mightily impressed.

Not long after that, Nicole had an adventure of her own. She decided to explore Stromboli, an active volcano off the Italian coast. Wearing chinos and sneakers, she set out with a guide, who apparently got them lost before nightfall. The guide went for help, leaving Nicole stranded on a mountaintop with an injured foot.

It was three A.M. before an aircraft was able to locate her and send skydivers down to save her. Her rescuers took her to a nearby yacht, from which she radioed her frantic husband. When Tom arrived at the yacht, Nicole looked bruised and bedraggled, but she was otherwise in good shape. Before leaving the yacht, Nicole insisted that Tom have coffee with the boat owner, so as not to hurt his feelings. Tom thought it strange, but he accepted the coffee and gulped it down, then made for a hasty exit with Nicole in tow.

It was an eventful summer for the Kidman-Cruise household. That same month, German audiences reacted with hostility toward the opening of *Mission: Impossible*. The protest occurred because of Tom's membership in the Church of Scientology. In Germany, the religion is considered an insidious cult.

In Hamburg, where Scientologists have their German headquarters, the city maintains a full-time investigative agency, whose sole purpose is to keep tabs on Scientologists. Its investigators are so fearful of the organization, according to reports in the *Philadelphia Inquirer*, that they work behind bullet-proof glass in a well-guarded building.

As the protests reached a fever pitch—and politicians urged an outright ban on Scientology—German authorities put some distance between them and the protesters. "We haven't been able to prove that Scientology asks its members to commit crimes," a prosecutor told the *Philadelphia Inquirer*. "About all I can say about Scientology is that I'm glad my kids aren't members, but as far as criminal law goes, we don't have anything against them."

The protests were not the only problem Tom had with Germany. The German magazine *Bunte* published a story that alleged that Tom could not have children because his sperm count was too low. Tom countered with a $60 million defamation lawsuit. Within two weeks, the magazine issued a statement apologizing for the allegations: "*Bunte* has been informed that Tom Cruise is not infertile and that his sperm count is completely normal. *Bunte* apologizes to Tom Cruise and his family for this embarrassing and irritating incident." The publisher blamed the mistake on a writer that it promised would never work for the magazine again. Satisfied, Tom dropped the lawsuit.

In December 1996, after what seemed an eternity to Nicole, *The Portrait of a Lady* was released. The reviews were harsh. Under a headline that read AN UNFLATTERING 'PORTRAIT,' *Washington Post* writer Desson Howe wrote that his opinion of the movie had remained unchanged after two viewings—the acting was solid, but the overall film was lacking in energy: "*Portrait* feels like an elegant party, full of attractive people, beautiful finery and tremendous music, yet no excitement. And no matter how many times you revisit the place, it never gets better."

Writing in the *Los Angeles Times*, Kenneth Turan offered his opinion that "Though *Portrait*'s satisfactions don't have much to do with surprise, the argument could be made that the performances of the two leads could use some fine-tuning. Kidman is the picture of clarity, purpose and single-minded intelligence as Isabel, but also colder than she perhaps needs to be."

Barbara Shulgasser, movie critic for the *San Francisco Examiner*, described the film as a romantic horror story. "We never have even a suggestion of what so many men find irresistible about Isabel," she wrote. "Here, Kidman's uncanny resemblance to Elizabeth Montgomery in 'Bewitched' makes taking her seriously a real chore."

Nicole hardly deserved the criticism she received. If she had offered a more glamorous Isabel, she would have been castigated for fluffing up the role. And what does *Bewitched* have to do with all the hard work she put into the role?

Of course, Nicole did have her admirers. David Sterritt, writing in the *Christian Science Monitor*, declared her performance first-rate: "Nicole Kidman, quickly becoming one of her generation's most versatile actresses, gives Isabel a blend of high intentions and unshakable naiveté that James might well have applauded."

The same month that *The Portrait of a Lady* was released, bringing in only $134,805 on opening weekend, *Jerry Maguire* was released with an opening weekend take of $17 million. Turan, the same critic who was less than enthusiastic about *The Portrait of a Lady*, was much more generous to Tom's movie. Wrote Turan: "As loved by the camera as any actor of his generation, Cruise starts with the familiar but expands to show his character in extremis, with the self-confident grin pushed to the cracking point."

Nicole took the slam-dunk competition with good grace, but she would surely have been forgiven if she wondered why she sometimes bothered to get out of bed.


Nicole's next film, *The Leading Man*, is hardly ever mentioned in her press biographies, primarily because she played only a small role, but also because it is an "arty" film that deals, among other things, with interracial romance.

Nicole agreed to appear in the film because she had worked in the early 1990s with Australian director John Duigan on *Flirting*—and she was loath to say no to any Australian filmmaker, for who knew when the American bubble could burst?—and because she had worked on the same film with black actress Thandie Newton, for whom she had a lot of respect.

*The Leading Man* takes place in modern-day London and is about a successful English playwright, Felix Webb (played by Lambert Newton) who has a new play, *The Hit Man*, in rehearsal. Everything is going well, except for his personal life. He is in love with Hilary Rule (played by Thandie Newton), the star of his play, a complication since he is married to Elena (played by Anna Galiena), whom he loves as well. His solution is to ask his leading man, Robin Grange (played by ex-rocker Jon Bon Jovi) to seduce his wife as a means of taking pressure off of him. Elena knows about Felix's affair with Hilary and has been tormenting him with passive-aggressive acts such as butchering his hair while he is asleep and cutting his neckties in half when he is away.

This was not Jon Bon Jovi's first film—he played himself in *The Return of Bruno*, a painter in *Moonlight and Valentino*, and a prison inmate who gets shot in *Young Guns II*—but it was his first attempt at a leading role and he handled it remarkably well.

Thandie Newton had made five films since costarring with Nicole in *Flirting*—among them, *Jefferson in Paris* and *Interview with the Vampire*, with Tom Cruise—and had made quite a name for herself. One critic saw Audrey Hepburn–like qualities in her appearance and gestures. Certainly, director John Duigan would have agreed, for he had long been linked romantically with Newton.

In the film, when Newton's Robin won an Oscar for best actress, it was Nicole who presented it to her. It was Nicole's only involvement in the film and her dialogue consisted of five lines. How ironic that Oscar-hungry Nicole would present a pretend Oscar to Newton, who was making a name for herself as a serious actress!

*The Leading Man* was first shown in September 1996 at the Toronto Film Festival, but it was not released until May 1997 in Australia and in March 1998 in the United States. Duigan was slow to line up international distributors for the film, but whether that was due to its interracial subject matter or because it has a thoughtful, slow-moving pace is unknown.

American reviews were generally good. *Los Angeles Times* critic Kevin Thomas described it as a "handsome, polished effort" and a "sly, traditional-style delight." *Chicago Sun-Times* critic Roger Ebert enjoyed the film, but felt the climax was lacking. "Hitchcock, having brought the gun and the matching love triangles onstage, would have delivered. Still, Duigan keeps us interested right up to the overwrought final developments, and his portrait of the London theater world is wry and perceptive."

*London Standard* critic Alexander Walker thought the film was not British enough. "Indeed, there's the feeling of a foreign hand somewhere in the whole set-up: as if it had all been done on studio sets in Paris," he wrote. "Not so much a Europudding event, more a Eurostar excursion."

Early 1997 was filled with ups and downs for Nicole. Word had trickled out that Tom and Nicole's second child, Connor, had African American parents. That did not go down too well with some people. Why would America's most glamorous Hollywood couple adopt a black child? The feedback they got over the adoption was not always supportive. Once, while walking on the streets of London with Connor, they were subjected to hurtful racial epithets.

Nicole never explained their reasons for adopting a black child, other than saying, "It was our choice." She has steadfastly refused to answer questions about the children's birth mothers or to give details about the adoptions. "I don't want them, when they're older, reading stuff that I've said, or their father's said, and have them say, 'What is this?'" she explained to Australia's *Good Weekend*. "I think it's really important for them to define themselves before we define who they are."

Nicole's expectations as a parent were still evolving at this point, but one thing she had decided most emphatically and that was that she hoped both children would be able to be educated in both Australia and America. She was not sure yet how that would be possible, with their careers the way they were, but it was her dream for the children.

Nicole battled more press reports about Tom's alleged homosexuality—it was beginning to get oh so tiring to her—and she waxed eloquently about her marriage, saying that she and Tom were closer than she ever imagined would be possible.

Lately, she had found herself becoming a worrier, something she had never done until they adopted the children. She worried about the children, about whether they were healthy and happy, and whether their needs were being met. And she worried about Tom, about whether his airplanes would crash or some other disaster would take place.

Oddly, despite the worrying, she was beginning to sleep somewhat better.

For years, she had had a difficult time sleeping through the night. Why she would sleep better now that she had children, with more stuff to worry about, baffled her. On a slow day, she might worry about why she was not worrying about sleeping better.

It was during this time that she withdrew earlier pronouncements that she was a Scientologist. Although Tom remained a member, she said she was just "who I am"—a mixture of religious influences. She credited her parents, Janelle and Antony, for shaping her into the person she had become. She made it clear that Tom did his thing and she did her own thing. She had nothing negative to say about Scientology; she simply put distance between her and the religion.

When the Academy of Motion Picture Arts and Sciences announced its Oscar nominations for 1996, Nicole was disappointed that she was not included for her work in *Portrait of a Lady*, but she was delighted that Tom's *Jerry Maguire* received five nominations, including one for best actor. Five nominations were impressive, but not so impressive as the seven nominations that went to *Fargo* and *Shine*.

Nicole and Tom attended the ceremony together—and Nicole served as a presenter, something that was always difficult for her because of her shyness—but unfortunately they left empty-handed. In the best actor category, Tom was passed over for Geoffrey Rush for his portrayal of an Australian concert pianist in *Shine*. The award for best actress went to Frances McDormand for her role in *Fargo*. The only award that *Jerry Maguire* received was the one for best supporting actor that Cuba Gooding, Jr., received. The big winner of the evening was *The English Patient*, which took home nine Oscars, the most since *The Last Emperor* won nine awards in 1987.

Nicole's next movie was *The Peacemaker*, a suspense story about an American Army colonel, played by George Clooney, and his boss, a nuclear scientist played by Nicole, who must track down stolen Russian nuclear weapons before they are used by terrorists to strike against an American target.

When the film was announced, people were shocked to see Nicole in another slick Hollywood role. Months earlier she had made a big deal about wanting to play only interesting and complex women in independent films. Now she was again playing a one-dimensional "girlfriend" role in another would-be blockbuster, though she would probably argue that her character was a scientist and not the girlfriend. She never explained why she did it, leaving observers to ponder the mystery of the woman herself. One reason may have been because it was the first feature film for director Mimi Leder, who had built a splendid television career with series such as *ER* and *L.A. Law*. Nicole was not, strictly speaking a hard-core feminist, but she did have a preference for working with strong, creative women like her mother.

*The Peacemaker* begins with an assassination, after which occurs a train wreck from which nuclear devices are stolen for sinister purposes. Nicole, who plays scientist Julia Kelly, head of the White House Nuclear Smuggling Group, makes her first appearance in the film in a one-piece swimsuit, when she is summoned from a swimming pool to deal with the potentially disastrous situation.

Once they get a handle on what has happened, Julia and Lt. Col. Thomas Devoe, played by Clooney, are sent to Vienna to devise a plan to recover the nukes. There they strong-arm a trucking executive to get information from his computer and then become involved in a car chase as they try to escape.

When they locate, via satellite, the truck carrying the nukes, Thomas dashes off to intersect them. She rushes after him, urging him to use caution. She cautions him not to "take action without authorization."

"What do you think I am?" he responds. "Some gung-ho, stupid son of a bitch?"

"No, I don't think you're stupid. I think you're a talented soldier with sloppy impulse control."

They intercept all the nukes, except for one, which makes it way to New York City. At that point, the story revolves around whether Julia and Thomas can locate the nuke before it can be detonated. Nicole does not have any memorable lines in the movie, but she did undertake her most physical role to date—running, jumping, leaping, and being blown through the air by a bomb blast.

Most of the movie was filmed in Bratislava, a Slovakian city near the Austrian and Hungarian border. There was not much to do after hours in Bratislava, so Nicole, Clooney, and various members of the crew frequented the local pubs. Once they had enough gin, they would pile into a cab and, on the drive home, call London-bound Tom on a cell phone and laughingly tell him, "Wish you were here!"

When she first arrived on the set, Nicole—who had heard horror stories about Clooney's penchant for practical jokes—begged him to spare her any such indignities. Clooney reluctantly agreed to a truce and he stuck to it. But once the production wrapped, he told a writer for *US* magazine that the truce had been lifted. Put this in your magazine, he told the writer: "George is working on a prank for her right now! When she reads that, it'll make her sweat like a pig."

Once, several years before filming began on *The Peacemaker,* Nicole and Michelle Pfeiffer each bet Clooney $10,000 that he would be married and a father by the age of forty. When that magical day arrived on May 6, 2001— without the prophecy being realized—Nicole sent him a check for $10,000. Clooney returned the check and offered her double or nothing on his fiftieth birthday.

When *The Peacemaker* was released, no one, least of all Nicole, expected an Oscar buzz. It was not that kind of movie. Movie critics, for the most part, were generous in their assessments of the film. Writing in the *Los Angeles Times,* Kenneth Turan said: "Both Kidman and Clooney give dependable, movie-star performances in these James Bond-ish roles. While Kidman's Dr. Kelly is too much the clichéd frazzled female at times, the script balances that with scenes of strength and competence."

"Against all odds, Kidman makes the audience forget the absurdity of the role she's playing," wrote Mick LaSalle in the *San Francisco Chronicle.* "Choosing to pay Dr. Kelly as a harried, ambitious young executive, Kidman becomes quite sympathetic. She also looks more striking than ever. Her face is now taking on a sharp, classic look, at least before she starts outrunning fireballs."

Nicole was always grateful for good reviews, but she couldn't help but wonder how long critics would focus on her looks first and her acting second. Why were the critics not constantly saying Tom was "more handsome than ever"?

# CHAPTER SEVEN

# The Making of
# Eyes Wide Shut

For several years, Tom Cruise and director Stanley Kubrick had exchanged faxes on a wide variety of subjects of mutual interest, including cameras and airplanes. Kubrick was a well-known recluse who did not like to leave his home—rumors abounded that he refused to fly, refused to be driven in a car traveling over thirty miles per hour, and so on—but he was not hesitant to use modern technology to reach out to individuals that his instincts told him he could trust. Tom was such a person.

One day, Nicole and Tom each received simultaneous faxes from Kubrick. The faxes said simply that he was going to do a film titled *Eyes Wide Shut* and he wondered if they would be interested. To Nicole, he wrote: "I want you in my movie—please play Alice." They were speechless. They both considered the eccentric director to be one of the best in the business. They responded that yes, of course, they would be interested. Kubrick faxed them no more details about the film but said that he would send them a script as soon as work on it was finished.

After the failures of *Days of Thunder* and *Far and Away,* Nicole and Tom had vowed to do no more films together since joint ventures seemed to dilute the drawing power that each had with moviegoers. But was that a good enough reason to turn down the great Kubrick's offer? No, they concluded—whatever Kubrick had in mind would be strong enough to override the previous bad luck they had experienced working together.

Meanwhile, Kubrick worked feverishly to complete the script. On this particular project, his heralded perfectionism had gelled into an obsession. He had been working on the script for two years with noted screenwriter Frederic Raphael—of *Daisy Miller, Darling,* and *Far From the Madding Crowd* fame—and he was close to being able to admit to himself that it was as good as it was going to get.

For Raphael, the two-year project had been both joyful and exasperating. It had begun in the spring and summer of 1994, when his agent at the William Morris Agency started receiving mysterious calls from Warner Bros. inquiring as to whether he was available—for what they didn't say.

The inquiries were made on behalf of Stanley Kubrick, who subsequently sent Raphael photocopies from a published novella, from which the title and author's name had been removed. Raphael later found out that the material was from *Dream Story* by Arthur Schnitzler, but at that point he did not have a clue about who had written it. Kubrick, who trusted no one, clearly wanted to keep that information a secret until he had an understanding with Raphael.

Kubrick was so different—so, well, odd—that many people thought he was a product of some darkly secretive European nation that changed its name from decade to decade. Not so. Kubrick was born in Manhattan, New York, during the Great Depression. Because he did poorly in school, his physician father sent him at a young age to California to live with his uncle, hoping that a change in scenery would inspire a more acceptable academic performance. That didn't happen. When he returned to New York, he was just as uninterested in school as he was when he left.

Kubrick's father tried to interest him in hobbies, but nothing really caught hold until he presented him with his first camera. From that point on, Kubrick was hooked on photography. With time, he became very good. He sold a photograph to *Look* magazine and by the age of seventeen he had landed a job with the magazine as an apprentice photographer. It was while he was going out on assignment for *Look* that he came into contact with Hollywood celebrities and developed a voracious appetite for movies. In 1950, he sank all his savings into a documentary titled *Day of the Fight.*

Kubrick made a couple of commissioned documentaries before he was able to raise enough financing to do his first feature film, *Fear and Desire* (1953). For the remainder of the 1950s, he toiled in obscurity, making films that attracted little or no attention at the box office or with critics.

Then, in 1960, his luck changed with *Spartacus* and two years later with *Lolita*. With the 1964 release of the dark comedy *Dr. Strangelove or: How I Learned to Stop Worrying and Love the Bomb*, his career soared. He followed that up with the rhapsodic *2001: A Space Odyssey* in 1968 and the deeply disturbing *A Clockwork Orange* in 1971. He fell into obscurity throughout most of the 1970s, then roared back in 1980 with *The Shining* and in 1987 with the Vietnam-era film, *Full Metal Jacket*.

Kubrick had not made a film in more than a decade, a fact that only peaked the interest of Nicole, Tom, and Frederic Raphael, all of whom considered Kubrick a cinematic genius who probably had not yet done his best work. By the mid-1990s, receiving an unsolicited fax from Kubrick, in some circles at least, was like receiving a fax from *God* and it generated the same uncertainty and fear!

Raphael was no different from anyone else. He was in awe of Kubrick and he wanted to work with him, yet he feared he might lose a part of himself in the process and that fear served to keep him on his toes. After he read the photocopied material Kubrick sent, he told the director he was eager to work on the project. Kubrick telephoned his agent and worked out a verbal agreement for the cost of his services as a screenwriter.

As the lawyers haggled, all that remained for Raphael was to have a face-to-face meeting with Kubrick at his Victorian home located outside London. After traveling in a cab through a series of locked gates, Raphael was deposited outside a rather large house. To his surprise, Kubrick opened the front door.

"He was wearing a blue overall with black buttons," Raphael wrote in his memoir. "He might have been a minor employee of the French railways. He was a smallish, rounded man (no belt) with a beard which less defined than blurred his features...He spoke as if unused to speech and not comfortable with company, even when he had invited it."

It was during that first meeting, which was lubricated somewhat with wine from New Zealand, that the writer and the director tried to come to terms on the direction of the script. They talked about transferring the location of the story to New York and they talked about specific scenes, such as the girl passing out at the party and the orgy that becomes the centerpiece of the story.

Raphael said that he thought the entire story was meant to be experienced as a dream. Kubrick did not like that approach at all. He told him that it

could not all be a dream, for without reality they had no movie. Before they parted company, they agreed on a work schedule. Kubrick asked, almost apologetically, if Raphael would send him chunks of the screenplay as he
completed them. To a writer, such a request is a sacrilege, but Raphael agreed,
against his better judgment. He told Kubrick that he was the only director in
the world that he would consider doing that for.

After he left Kubrick's house that day, Raphael wrote in his notebook: "He
is, I begin to suspect, a movie director who happens to be a genius rather than
a genius who happens to be a movie director. My difficulty with him will be
to guess what he really wants of me."

The process would prove to be grueling for Raphael—he would turn in
scores of first drafts, hundreds and hundreds of pages, only to have Kubrick
suggest changes—but he stuck with it for two years. Finally, he finished the
script and sent it off to Kubrick. He could not imagine it being rejected, for
they had debated every scene, almost every word, in the script. Still, weeks
went by, then months, with no word from Kubrick. What Raphael did not
know was that Kubrick had sent the script to Nicole and Tom.

Tom read the script first and "flipped" over it; then Nicole read it and had
much the same response. No question about it, they wanted to do the movie.
Nicole later said she would have agreed to do the film, without ever reading
the script. She was *that* enthusiastic about working with Kubrick.

When they telephoned Kubrick and told him that they were eager to discuss the project further, he invited them to have dinner with him and his
wife, Christiane, at their house. Kubrick was delighted by their interest, but
being the person that he was, he asked them to please return the script for security reasons. They understood.

A short time later, Nicole and Tom flew to London. They arrived at the
Kubrick home by helicopter, according to Raphael, who wrote in his mem-
oirs that Kubrick described them as holding hands. "It was sweet," said
Kubrick. "Now and again they'd kinda consult together. He'd look at her,
she'd look at him and he'd say, 'Okay, Nic?' and she'd say 'If it is with you.'
They're a truly married couple. It was kinda touching."

Kubrick told Raphael that Nicole had promised him a couple of days for the
nude scenes and he told the screenwriter that it might be a good time for him
to visit the studio. The writer was tempted by the prospect of seeing Nicole
naked, but he declined, feeling that it would be taking advantage of the actress.

After the meeting, they made arrangements for the lawyers to go over the necessary contracts. Nicole was thrilled, but felt unsure of herself. Deep down inside, she later confessed, she worried that Kubrick would hate her style of acting. One of the things they talked about at his house was her shyness, her reluctance to have other people watch her work. He agreed with her that the rehearsal process would be a good opportunity for her to overcome those fears.

In mid-December 1995, Kubrick sent a fax to the still-waiting Raphael, notifying him that he had completed work on the script, made a deal with Warner Bros. and cast Tom and Nicole for the lead roles. Raphael could finally stop worrying about it; his script would indeed be made into a movie starring two of the biggest stars on the planet. On top of the good news, Kubrick reminded Raphael that he must remain mum about the title of the book on which the movie was based.

Tom and Nicole were also sworn to secrecy. They didn't mind. Everyone knew that Kubrick was queer that way, and if cloak-and-dagger intrigue made him happy, so be it. Certainly, there were directors with worse afflictions than compulsive distrust.

Later, when asked about the secrecy by the *Boston Globe*, Nicole replied: "If I say anything, Stanley will get upset. He's not tyrannical. He really believes 'Let's not talk about the film, and let's put all our energy into making it instead of talking about it. And once it's made we can go out there and talk about it as it exists.' Which is right."


*Eyes Wide Shut* production began in November 1996. Kubrick said he thought it would take about twelve weeks to shoot the film, one of the biggest underestimates in film history, for it ended up being a three-year project. Well, perhaps not the biggest underestimate, since his *2001: A Space Odyssey* took four years to complete; before that project was over, anxious studio executives were asking Kubrick if 2001 was going to be the title or the completion date.

At this stage, everyone was optimistic it would be a twelve-week project, but a cautious Nicole and Tom cleared their calendar to spend about five months in London. There were no futuristic, technical components involved in production, no wild car chases or exploding buildings; it was a simple story about not-so-simple human relationships. They didn't see how a character-driven production could possibly be stretched out longer than five months.

Almost all of the filming was done on sets at Pinewood Studios outside London, one of the most respected filmmaking facilities in the world, which features state-of-the-art sound stages, viewing theaters, cutting rooms, and sophisticated lighting systems. The apartment that Nicole and Tom lived in as the movie couple was modeled after one Kubrick once occupied in New York. However, Nicole took one look at the apartment set and—seeing too much of a masculine influence—changed the color of the window shades and picked out an assortment of books to line the shelves. But she didn't stop there. She also put change on the bedside table, just the way Tom did at home, and she brought some of her own makeup to put in the bathroom and she brought some of her clothes to toss about on the floor, to give the apartment the "messy" look she and Tom were accustomed to at home. A couple of times she and Tom slept in the bed, staying overnight on the set, just to increase their comfort level with the furnishings.

Almost from day one, Nicole, Tom, and Kubrick were inseparable. When they were rehearsing or shooting, they got together in his office or some other private place and talked—and talked and talked and talked. Sometimes Tom made pasta and salad for the director. Sometimes Nicole sat around for hours in Kubrick's office, wearing her bathrobe, drinking coffee and asking him questions.

During those private moments, Kubrick probed the couple for every detail about their relationship and how they interacted and resolved conflicts. For Nicole and Tom, it was a little bit like undergoing psychoanalysis. Although the questions were personal and intrusive, neither of them hesitated to share his or her innermost secrets with the director.

"He was always encouraging about me as an actor and as a woman," Nicole told Nancy Collins for *Rolling Stone*. "The shock for Tom and me is that nobody knew us the way Stanley did. Not even my mom and dad. Nobody. It was three years with just the three of us. He *knew* us."

Once, after overhearing interchanges between them, Kubrick chastised Nicole for the way she talked to Tom. He told her that he had been married a long time and he felt that there were things within a marriage that a woman could not say to a man. He encouraged her to consider the impact of her words.

During filming, Nicole effectively reversed that father-daughter relationship by telling the director that he was off base in some of the scenes he had planned for her character. She told him that some of the dialogue did not ring true, in the sense that it did not seem to be something a woman would say to a man. With time, Kubrick became baffled by Nicole's character. Sometimes after conversations with Nicole he would disappear for a short time into his office, then return with a better idea.

The biggest shock of working with Kubrick hit them early on, in the pre-production. The director was famous for doing many takes on each scene. What Nicole and Tom did not realize was that he had the same insecurities about rehearsals. They didn't just go over scenes two or three times, they went over each scene twenty or thirty times, until Kubrick felt every phrase and nuance was in its proper place.

Sometimes Nicole had interesting reactions to that routine. Once, while they were rehearsing the opening scene in the movie—a party that Nicole's character attends with her husband—Nicole got so weary after twenty or thirty attempts that she slipped away during a break and returned with a glass of champagne.

Kubrick, who never seemed to take his eyes off of Nicole when they were rehearsing, saw what happened with the champagne and thought it would be good to have Nicole's character get drunk at the party. So he wrote it into the script. What moviegoers saw in the finished product was a prime example of art imitating life. The most existentialist director in movie history proved himself to be a realist when it came to satisfying the creative bottom line.

That was a quality that Nicole appreciated in Kubrick. The most identifiable scene in the movie is the one in which Nicole and Tom share an erotic interlude in front of a mirror. That one scene—and the music that played in the background, Chris Isaak's "Baby Did a Bad Bad Thing"—was used in the trailer and came to symbolize the spirit of the film. So who was the genius that paired the music with the scene? It wasn't Kubrick. Before shooting the scene, the director asked Nicole to pick out a sexy CD from her collection and play it for the background music. She chose "Baby Did a Bad Bad Thing."

Interestingly, Kubrick treated Nicole differently than he treated Tom or any of the other actors. He allowed her more creative freedom and he encouraged her to ad-lib. When she was clever or insightful, he invariably excused himself to go to his office so that he could write her ad-libs into the script. If he was not smitten in the romantic sense (what are the odds there?), he certainly was smitten by her creative energy.

Even so, he cut her no slack when it came to retakes. Sometimes they nailed a scene in one take, but it was not unusual for him to ask Nicole to repeat a scene dozens of times, until she was exhausted by the sheer physical effort needed to read lines over and over again. Sometimes she surprised Kubrick. Just when he thought she was out for the count, when her head seemed to be drooping, she would roll her icy-blue eyes in his direction and say, "Let's do it one more time!"

It was the same thing for Tom, who was not used to redoing scenes over and over again at that point in his career. Incredibly, he kept his ego in check and never faulted Kubrick for his relentless perfectionism.

Not everyone felt that way. Veteran actor Harvey Keitel was replaced with Sydney Pollack, allegedly after he came into conflict with Kubrick, and actress Jennifer Jason Leigh was replaced when she apparently balked at returning for additional filming.

For less experienced actresses like Vinessa Shaw, who played a hooker, the hard work seemed like a reasonable price to pay to be in the movie. "I remember one time, around three in the morning, I did my sixty-ninth take of a scene," she told *Entertainment Weekly*. "I heard somebody say, 'Wow! That must be a record.' And then I ended up doing twenty more takes." It gave her a sense of freedom, she said, because it gave her an opportunity to explore her character.

In the film, Tom and Nicole play Bill and Alice Harford, a New York couple whose lives appear fairly ordinary in the beginning. In an early scene, they go to a party given by Tom's friend Victor Ziegler (played first by Harvey Keitel, then subsequently by noted director Sydney Pollack). Bill, a physician, is called upstairs to a bathroom by Ziegler, who has a problem. A hooker he invited to the party, ostensibly to service him in the bathroom, has taken a drug overdose and appears to be near death. Bill examines her and tells Ziegler that he has dodged a bullet—the girl will recover.

Later, at the party, Bill meets a former medical school classmate, Nick Nightingale (played by Todd Field), who dropped out of school to become a jazz musician. On that night, he is playing with the dance band, not exactly the type of music that he had in mind when he left medical school. He gives Bill the name of an after-hours club where he performs real jazz and encourages him to drop by.

When Bill and Alice return home after the party, they do the well-publicized nude scene with "Baby Did a Bad Bad Thing" playing in the background. Although the script did not call for them to kiss like strangers, that is the way the scene is played. There is a sense of awkwardness in which there is no visible chemistry between the two actors. Bill caresses her breast as she glances disinterestedly into the mirror. As the passion increases, Bill squeezes her on the neck, a little too hard it seems. She seems bored and he seems, at the very least, angry.

Later, as they lie in bed smoking pot, she confesses that she once had a desire to sleep with a naval officer she met in the lobby of a hotel. She tells him that she was so attracted that she was prepared to give up everything—their marriage, their daughter, everything—to spend a single night with him.

Bill is stunned by her disclosure, but before the conflict can be resolved, he is called out of the house to administer to the family of one of his elderly patients, who has just passed away. On the way over to their house, he fantasizes about Alice and the naval officer making love.

After leaving the dead patient's home, he decides to drop by and see his musician friend. While they are chatting, the musician receives a telephone call instructing him where to go for a super-secret private party. He confides that he has done parties for these people before. They blindfold him when he arrives and he is asked to play the piano.

Bill is intrigued and asks for directions. The musician is reluctant at first, but soon caves in to his friend's request. He tells him he must go in costume and he must give a certain password when he arrives at the house.

On the way to the party, Bill experiences another fantasy about Alice and the naval officer. It is clear that he is becoming obsessed with her disclosure. She was not actually unfaithful to him, but the admission that she thought about it was just as damaging in his eyes. She was the mother of his child. He had trusted her.

The party turns out to be a massive orgy, during which all wear masks to conceal their identities. Not long after he arrives, Bill's deception is exposed. He is brought before the entire group and ordered to remove his mask. Clearly, he is in serious trouble, but before the group can issue a punishment, a girl cries out from an overhead passageway that she is willing to take responsibility for his actions.

Satisfied that someone will be punished, the group allows Bill to leave the house, but not before threatening him with dire consequences if he ever tells a soul anything he has seen at the house. The remainder of the movie deals with the consequences of that night (the woman who helps him eventually ends up in the morgue) and with the effect of Alice's fantasy disclosure on their marriage.

Throughout the film, Bill's continuing fantasizes about Alice and the naval officer, all filmed in black and white, provide the story's most erotic moments and the film's most visible chemistry.


During the summer of 1997, Gary Goba was living in London, England, where he worked as a model. Because he was tall and handsome, with Robert Redford–like features, his agency liked to pitch him to potential clients as a stereotypical all-American type. Presentation photos sometimes showed him dressed like a cowboy.

But Goba did not get his rugged good looks from growing up in the American West. Born in Montreal, Canada, he grew up in Ottawa, Ontario, and attended the University of Toronto, where he majored in psychology and French. Part-time modeling assignments led to a full-time career after he realized that it offered greater financial opportunities than a degree in psychology offered.

So it was in London, where he had been working for the past several years, that the twenty-nine-year-old model received a telephone call from his agent, who excitedly told him that he was booked for an audition with Warner Bros. for a movie that starred Nicole Kidman. He was told nothing else about the project, neither the title of the movie nor the director's name. That type of audition was unusual for him because he had never appeared in a movie. All of his modeling work had been for print and television.

When he arrived at the audition, he found a line of men already there, all of them models. "I waited my turn and walked through the door into a small conference room that would have seated maybe thirty people, but there was no table or chair, just an empty room," he says. "I didn't see anybody, but I spotted a small piece of tape on the floor and I knew to walk to the tape and stop. As I did that, I noticed a guy in the corner coming out from behind a camera and walking toward me."

The man was Leon Vitali, Stanley Kubrick's special assistant. Introducing himself to Goba but not telling him his employer's name, he shook Goba's hand and asked him what he was doing in London. When Goba told him that he was living with his girlfriend while working as a model, Vitali observed that he didn't sound British. That's when Goba explained that he had grown up in Canada. As they talked, Vitali asked him to please remove his shirt, which Goba did without thinking anything about it because he was always asked to take off his shirt whenever he auditioned for modeling jobs.

"We chatted about ten minutes and he slowly, slowly backed up to the camera," Goba says. "I thought that after that little chat he was going to turn that thing on and we'd do the formal audition, whatever that was going to be. Instead, he turned the camera off and said, 'That's it.' So that's when I realized that the audition was just more getting a feeling for the guy, rather than finding out his talents as an actor."

During the audition, Goba asked about the part for which he was auditioning and he was told that it was as a United States naval officer. He figured he would be an extra on a ship and would probably salute or something as Nicole Kidman walked past. His expectations were not high because he had never been in a movie. Why would Warner Bros. want him to be anything other than an extra?

Vitali told him that shooting for the part would begin in a couple of weeks and he would get back in touch with him soon to let him know if he had the job. After the audition, Goba waited around London for several weeks. Finally, with no word from Vitali, he figured that the part probably had gone to someone else, so he moved to Switzerland, where his mother and her family lived (Goba says with pride that he is half Swiss). It was then that the telephone calls began. Every week, he says, Vitali, or someone from his office, called him and told him that he would hear something soon.

That went on for several months. Finally, in December 1997, Vitali called and told Goba that they were ready, at last, to shoot his scenes. He told Goba that they had already made arrangements for his flight back to London and his driver would be waiting for him when he arrived. Driver? Goba was impressed.

As he was hanging up the phone, Goba thought he heard Vitali say something. He yanked the telephone back to his ear and said, "Yeah, did you want me?"

"Yes," answered Vitali. "I wanted to run this by you and ask you if you would be okay doing a sex scene with Nicole Kidman."

Goba laughed and said, "Right! Would you have a problem with it?"

"No," answered Vitali.

"Neither would I—not a problem."

"Well, it's not going to happen, so don't worry about it," Vitali continued. "I just wanted to run it past you in case we did decide it would look great— and if you didn't want to be in it, that would be a problem."

"No, no, no," Goba said, stunned that they were even having that conversation. "That will be fine."

The next day, Goba flew back to London, where he made arrangements to stay with his ex-girlfriend and her new fiancé. The first thing Goba did upon his arrival was report to wardrobe, where he spent about four hours being fitted for a naval officer's uniform. The following day, the limo picked him up and drove him twenty miles west of London to Pinewood Studios.

Still in the dark about the title of the film, the director, or his role, Goba arrived earlier than anyone else. "All of a sudden, a car pulled up and Nicole and Tom came out," he says. "Tom was the first one out and he just kinda' ran in and they introduced him to me and he quickly said 'hello' and ran right by me into the make-up room and I never saw him again after that."

Then Nicole made her entrance. "She was more sociable and chatted with people as she came in. She was introduced to me and I guess she knew she was going to be meeting me. She stood there and chatted with me there on the stairs, heading up to make-up, for maybe two minutes or so. She was super sweet, really, really nice and relaxed and said, 'Hi, pleasure to meet you and I'm looking forward to working with you.'

"Then she went up to do make-up. I think she and Tom had a scene together that morning—and then we started in the afternoon. I pretty much sat around all morning until they were done and I didn't see Tom again. He disappeared and went off to negotiate *Mission Impossible II* or something."

Goba waited in his dressing room for someone to call him. By then, he knew that Stanley Kubrick was the film's director and he figured that he and his assistants were busy setting up the scene, whatever it was going to be. He was never given a script and still had no idea what he was going to be doing in the movie, except that it involved Nicole and maybe a sex scene.

Goba was not always alone in the dressing room, for assistants came in and out on a regular basis, mostly to check on the status of his uniform, which had not yet arrived. It was three hours late and the assistants were in a tizzy.

When it finally arrived, it hung on his dressing room door only a few minutes before he got the call to report to the set.

"Okay, I'll just jump into this suit," he replied.

"Oh, no, just throw on the bathrobe," the assistant said.

"I was like, well I guess I'm just going to meet [Kubrick]—right?" he recalls. "So I walked out of my room and Nicole walked out of her room and the assistant director was there to take us down the stairs into the big studio."

Goba and Nicole walked down the stairs and into a drab hallway, then into a gigantic room that housed what they called the Cape Cod suite. It was a beautifully furnished hotel room and the way the lights shone on it made it look even more lavish.

"I saw Stanley [Kubrick] there and chatted with him—super nice guy, completely normal. It was like meeting someone's parents or something—then he said, 'Let's get right to it!' I noticed it was just a bedroom and I thought, 'Well, that's interesting.' Then he mentioned what we would be doing and that's when I realized we were going to have a bloody sex scene."

Kubrick seemed almost clinical as he explained to Goba what he wanted from him. "He's like, okay, what we're going to do here is Nicole will be lying on the bed on her back and you're going to be coming in on top of her and, you know, you're going to be caressing her arms and her dress and maybe give her a kiss and let's get right to it."

Goba was in shock, but he tried not to show it. He kept thinking, *I don't believe this, I don't believe this!* When they entered the room, it was filled with eight or ten people, all working on the lighting or making last-minute changes to the set, but then Nicole asked for a closed set and everyone was asked to leave.

Then it was just the three of them—Goba, Nicole, and Kubrick, who sat in a chair that had been rigged up to a trolley. He planned to operate the camera himself, not a difficult task since he needed only three levers—one to move the chair up and down the trolley, another to pan the camera from side to side, and the third to zoom the lens in and out so that he would get what he needed, anything from tight shots of their faces and hands, to medium distance shots of their entire bodies.

Once everyone but Kubrick was out of the room, Goba and Nicole faced each other and removed their robes, so that within seconds both of them were totally naked. Goba was amazed at how beautiful she was and how easily she showed him her body. But he still couldn't believe it—what strange twist of fate was responsible for him standing before Nicole Kidman buck naked?

Kubrick set the pace with the words, "Just go at it!"

Suddenly, it was as though they were two prized animals at a gladiatorial event, standing at face-off, ready to engage one another in something akin to sexual combat, as Kubrick egged them on from the shadows beyond the lights. She was the very image of physical perfection, with flawless skin so white it appeared blue tinged, and breasts that were small but firm, and a patch of reddish pubic hair that was well-groomed but not shaved—and he, sturdily built, but not muscled-out by steroids, all six feet one of him ready to do his best, his smiling face exuding an innocent schoolboy charm that immediately put Nicole at ease.

For six days, Goba and Nicole engaged in sexual activity, everything short of actual penetration, with Kubrick shouting instructions and encouragement from his trolley, capturing on film every intimate moment they shared. Goba estimates that they probably acted out fifty different sexual positions.

"The three of us got together and tried to come up with different interesting positions," he says. "They were really trying to do things that had never been done in movies before. They were going to do the going-down-on-me thing, but that wasn't even an option. We didn't even film a blow job scenario because it had been and done well. We did a bathtub scene, where I'm sitting on the side of the tub with my feet in it (there was no water) and she was straddling around me, kind of facing me. We just tried to do stuff that we had never ever seen before in movies. Sometimes she would come up with an idea or I would or Stanley would."

The most intimate scene never made it into the film. In that one, Kubrick had Nicole stand nude against a wall, one foot propped up onto a tabletop and her leg flared open so that everything was exposed. Then, he instructed Goba to go down on her.

"They wig-glued on this patch over her private parts and I had to actually put my face right on it and, Stanley, I think he was having fun with it in a joking way because he really wanted me to go for it," Goba says. "I did—and he was like, 'You've got to really push in there and really move your head around,' and I'd see him laughing and she would be like, 'Oh, God, Stanley!' So I was really grinding away in there, with my mouth on her patch—and there was hair in my mouth, too, and I'd be pulling one out."

The second most intimate scene actually made it into the movie, but viewers were treated to a sleight-of-hand that suggested much less on-screen than was actually being delivered during filming. Goba remembers it this way: "She's lying on the bed on her back in a summer dress, with her legs up in the air a little bit, and he's shooting the profile from the side—and I'm coming from the other side, leaning over her.

"The way he directed it was to tell me to obviously kiss her, run [my] hands down her body, like down the dress, and grab the bottom of the dress and pull it up all the way over her breasts—and he's like, 'leave it up there and have those hands continue on down and, like, grab her tits, kiss them if you want, hands all the way down her body and end up between her legs."

Goba was shocked at the specificity Kubrick used to direct his movements. The director spoke to him as if Nicole were not even in the room. If Nicole heard directions that she did not like, she chastised Kubrick for suggesting them, but she never said no to anything that he suggested, no matter how explicit.

After hearing the above detailed instructions, Goba thought *Oh, God— and she's not wearing anything*, but, like Nicole, he did what he was told by the famous director.

"Let's get right to it—no trial or anything," Kubrick barked.

"My hand ended up between her legs, but I thought I could, out of respect, rest it on the inside of her thigh," Goba says. "He was filming from the side. I figured her other leg would block what my hand was really doing, which was just touching her inner thigh."

Suddenly, Kubrick leaned from behind the camera and shouted, "Whoa! Whoa! Gary, you've got to get right in there!"

Goba repeated the entire routine, starting at her breasts, moving his hands down her body, finally stopping between her legs. "So, take two, my hand ended up right on her and he wouldn't stop filming. He just kept going. The music is playing and we have to continue like we're into it and my hand is on her basically moving around.

"I couldn't believe it! I just couldn't believe it! I think he was having fun with it. It was a joke for him, but I think it went a little far for her because as the days went on, she would be, like, 'Okay cut!' Like this is getting too intimate, but he just let it go. It was like he was trying to have things done to piss her off—or the opposite. It was weird. He was laughing. He thought it was *so* funny."

*Practical Magic* begins with Gilly-Bean running off with a man. "I hate it here," she says. "I'm going to go where no one has ever heard of us."

"I feel like I'm never gonna see you again," responds Sal.

"Of course, you're going to see me again. We're going to grow old together. It's going to be you and me living in a big house, those two old biddies with all these cats. We'll probably even die on the same day."

"Do you swear?" asks Sal.

Several years later—in the interim, Sal has married and given birth to two daughters—Sal's husband is killed in a freak accident, making it necessary for Gilly-Bean to return home to comfort her grieving sister. Although she is suitably saddened by her brother-in-law's death, she cannot resist telling Sal all about her new man. "He's from somewhere near Transylvania," she explains. "He has this whole, ah, Dracula cowboy thing about him. He's just so intense. He talks about our relationship in terms of centuries. Sometimes we just stay up all night worshipping each other."

When Gilly-Bean returns to Florida to be with her new love interest, Sal attempts to go on with her life. Everyone in town knows that the sisters are witches and that sometimes causes problem for her daughters, who get teased and tormented about it, but it is the burden Sal has learned to live with and she copes the best she can.

One day Gilly-Bean calls Sal and tells her she needs help. Of course, Sal drops everything and rushes to her aid (what are sisters for, if not that?). Gilly-Bean tells her about the physical abuse she has endured, but before they can resolve that matter they are both kidnapped by the boyfriend. They drug his drink, using too potent a mixture, and he dies, leaving them in a quandary. While it is true that he kidnapped them, it is equally true that they killed him, and if they report the incident to the police they will have to take their chances with a jury—not an appealing prospect to two witches.

Instead, they take him home with them, where they hope to cast a spell and bring him back to life. Successful at that, they suffer the consequences when he lunges to choke Gilly-Bean and Sal hits him over the head with a frying pan, killing him yet again. This time, they just say to heck with it, and they bury him outside the house.

Later, a cop shows up to investigate the man's disappearance. It turns out he was a very bad man indeed, wanted for murder. The cop learns about the sisters' curse from the townspeople and digs deeper for information about the missing man.

Meanwhile, Sal falls in love with the cop, thus complicating the deception, a situation that becomes critical when the boyfriend's evil spirit returns and possesses Gilly-Bean's body. Not only must Sal hang on to her new romance, she must devise a way to drive the evil spirit out of her sister's body. She settles on a witch's party.

The cop eventually completes his investigation and leaves town. A short time later, Sal receives a letter from him that notifies her of his official finding in the case of the missing boyfriend. After reading the letter, Sal peers into the envelope as if looking for the man.

"I don't think he's in there, Sal," says Gilly-Bean.

"What would you do, Gilly?"

"What wouldn't I do for the right guy?"

For whatever reason, Nicole and Bullock never gelled as sisters or girlfriends or even as polite strangers on a commuter train to nowhere. There was simply no chemistry between the two women, an essential ingredient for any chick flick.

After the film wrapped, Nicole and Tom both felt battered. The sex scenes with Gary Goba had taken a lot out of her, as had the surgery to remove the cyst. Tom was in no better condition. The stress involved with making *Eyes Wide Shut*—not to mention the uncertainty of putting his career on hold for nearly two years—had taken its toll. Tom had developed a stomach ulcer during the final weeks of production and it had left him against the ropes, both emotionally and physically.

Nicole and Tom planned to take some time off to recuperate, but then to their disbelief, Kubrick contacted them in May and told them that he needed Tom to return to London to reshoot several scenes. At that point, he had no choice but to comply, but clearly his enthusiasm for the seemingly endless project was beginning to wan. Visitors to the set said that Tom still seemed excited about the project, but displayed less energy than on previous occasions. Who could blame him? The dream had assumed all the markings of a never-ending nightmare.

Added to that stress were the constant media reports that suggested that Tom was homosexual. When a British newspaper, the *Express*, published a story that alleged that his marriage was a sham, entered into as a business

The Kidman Family (left to right): sister Antonia, mother Janelle, father Tony, and Nicole. *(Rex Features)*

Nicole with her first serious love, Tom Burlinson. *(Peter Carrette/Rex Features)*

(TOP, OPPOSITE) With Thandie Newton in *Flirting*. *(Photofest)*

(BOTTOM, OPPOSITE) Nicole deals with a menacing Billy Zane in *Dead Calm*. *(Photofest)*

(THIS PAGE) Tom Cruise and Nicole, *Days of Thunder*. *(Photofest)*

Tom gets the traditional star treatment; here, he's about to set his footprints in cement at Mann's Chinese Theatre in Los Angeles. *(Steve Starr/Corbis)*

The Cruise Family: Nicole holding Connor and Tom carrying Isabella, in Britain, 1995. *(Rex Features)*

(OPPOSITE, TOP TO BOTTOM)

Dustin Hoffman as Dutch Schultz and Nicole as Drew Preston in Robert Benton's film version of E. L. Doctorow's *Billy Bathgate*. *(Photofest)*

Working with Tom again, in *Far and Away*, directed by Ron Howard. *(Photofest)*

Alec Baldwin costarred with Nicole in the twist-filled thriller *Malice*. *(Photofest)*

(OPPPOSITE) Pretty sultry for a psychologist—in *Batman Forever*. (*Photofest*)

(ABOVE AND LEFT) In *To Die For*, Matt Dillon plays the husband Nicole wants to shed—so she can become a media superstar. (*Photofest*)

(RIGHT) Isabel Archer in Henry James's *The Portrait of a Lady*, directed by Nicole's friend, Jane Campion. (*Photofest*)

(ABOVE AND LEFT) Nicole's appearance (including her brief nudity) in the play *The Blue Room* with Iain Glen caused box office stampedes in both London and New York. (*Photofest*)

(BELOW) Sisters and witches: Sandra Bullock and Nicole in *Practical Magic*. (*Photofest*)

Nicole and Tom found enormous professional—and personal—challenges making Stanley Kubrick's final film, the controversial *Eyes Wide Shut*. (*Photofest*)

Promoting *Eyes Wide Shut*,
Tom and Nicole seemed
the picture of contentment,
at the Venice Film Festival
*(Rufus F. Folkks/Corbis)*,
and at the UK premiere.
*(Reuters NewMedia,
Inc./Corbis)*

(OVERLEAF AND ABOVE) The irresistible Satine of Baz Luhrmann's *Moulin Rouge*. (*Photofest*)

With *Moulin Rouge* director Luhrmann and costar Ewan McGregor at the Cannes Film Festival. *(Reuters NewMedia, Inc./ Corbis)*

Nicole chats with Harrison Ford, after receiving the Actress of the Year award at the Hollywood Film Festival. *(Reuters NewMedia, Inc./Corbis)*

(OPPOSITE, TOP) In *The Others*, Nicole's role is Grace Stewart, a young mother who is overprotective and possibly paranoid—with good reason? (*Photofest*)

(OPPOSITE, BOTTOM) In the midst of divorce turmoil, Nicole poses with the director of *The Others*, Alejandro Amenabar. (*AFP/Corbis*)

(ABOVE) A change of pace— Nicole as the not-what-she-seems mail-order bride Nadia, in *Birthday Girl*, with Ben Chaplin. (*Photofest*)

(RIGHT) Russell Crowe is only one of the men with whom Nicole has been linked; here they are at the 2002 Sundance Film Festival. (*Rex Features*)

She may not have won Best Actress, but Nicole dazzled at the 2002 Academy Awards ceremony. (*Rufus F. Folkks/Corbis*)

arrangement or on order of the Church of Scientology, or as a cover-up for his and Nicole's homosexuality, he filed a libel lawsuit against the newspaper's publishers.

On October 1998, Tom stood on the steps of the High Court in London and announced that he had accepted a settlement from the newspaper. It was a major victory which also called for the newspaper to issue an apology (which it did in the courtroom).

"I really don't take a lot of pleasure in being here today," Tom told reporters who had gathered outside the court. "This is the final recourse against those who have printed vicious lies about me and my family. I have to protect my family."

That same month, *Practical Magic* was released. The critics were not kind. Jay Carr, writing for the *Boston Globe*, said that Nicole was "amusing and convincing," but had allowed herself to fall into a "one-note rut." He continued with, "On-screen, it's a patchwork of disconnected segments in search of a tone, unable to blend the earthy and occult." Under the headline HEX EDU-CATION, *Entertainment Weekly* described the movie as "so slapdash, plodding, and muddled it seems to have had a hex put on it." Falling in step was *USA Today*, with its description of the film as "witchy-washy."


On the very day that Tom stood on the courthouse steps defending his family's honor, Nicole embarked on a new acting adventure that left her totally naked on a London stage, much to the delight of British theatergoers. It was one thing to see Nicole naked on a movie screen, but to see her naked in the flesh, talking, walking, and making eye contact, was an experience many Londoners did not want to miss.

The play, Sir David Hare's *The Blue Room*, is based on Arthur Schnitzler's shocking 1912 play, *La Ronde*. Its centerpiece is a sexual relay race in which a series of encounters are observed, with one individual from the previous encounter moving on to participate in the next encounter. Nicole played five different women who bared their souls in separate affairs. She played opposite Scottish actor Iain Glen, with whom—shades of Gary Goba—she simulated lovemaking on five different occasions during the hour-and-half play. To do that, Nicole appeared totally nude onstage.

London theatergoers were shocked by her performance. Why, they wondered, would an actress of Nicole's reputation perform nude on stage for two hundred and fifty pounds a week? Some said it was because the play's author had written the book on which *Eyes Wide Shut* had been based and she felt some strange connection to him and his work. Others said it was because she had become a regular visitor to the theater while they lived in London and had found an offer to return to the stage for the first time in over a decade too attractive to turn down.

By her own admission, Nicole's management agency was horrified by her acceptance of the role. "My agent went 'You're doing what? For how long?'" Nicole told the *London Telegraph*. "No doubt they were rapidly working out their percentage of 250 pounds a week. They used to try to tell me what to do but now they've given up. I'm a lost cause. I usually call and tell them what I'm doing."

Nicole's after-the-fact bravado aside, she almost backed out of the play before opening night. She had a panic attack and telephoned her father, Antony, and told him that she was terrified of failing in the play. She said there was no way she could learn five different accents and play five different characters.

Antony allowed the psychologist in him to talk her through the crisis. After about forty-five minutes of long-distance therapy, she was able to calm down and see the situation more realistically. She hung up the telephone and took a deep breath. Of course, she could play five different characters—a coked-up fashion model, a stage diva, a teenage hooker, a politician's wife, and a French au pair. And, of course, she could be convincing using five different accents; she had played so many different movie roles that she no longer even knew what her own Australian accent sounded like.

When the play opened, London critics fell all over each other in praising her performance. Charles Spencer, writing in the *Daily Telegraph*, described Nicole as "pure theatrical Viagra." One critic called her "achingly beautiful" and another wrote, "She is not just a star, she delivers the goods."

Nicole was totally disarmed by the extravagant reviews. She had not received good reviews like that since she left Australia. The response was so good in London that she agreed to do the play in New York at Broadway's Cort Theater for a twelve-week run, with the opening set for December 13, 1998.

The advance publicity in New York was just as enthusiastic as it had been in London, helped along perhaps by Spencer's "pure theatrical Viagra" comment. Wrote Clyde Haberman for the *New York Times:* "In case you have just emerged from an experiment in cryonics, *The Blue Room* may be the hottest theater ticket since Sophocles wrote about some guy bedding his mother and poking his eyes out."

One of the odd things about the media frenzy surrounding the play was the way it transferred to Tom, who was inundated by reporters wanting to know how he felt about his wife appearing nude, about how he felt about her being away from home for so long. To everyone's surprise, he was totally supportive of her Broadway adventure, saying to one reporter, "I never saw her as Mrs. Tom Cruise." He was going on location to film *Mission: Impossible II*, but he vowed to fly to her side once a week to be supportive.

By the time the play opened, it had garnered an advance sale of over $4 million, with all but a handful of tickets spoken for. *Newsweek* ran a very flattering cover story on Nicole, written by Jack Kroll, that bore the headline NICOLE TAKES OFF. Kroll had reviewed the play when it opened in London, warning that "No one country, no one medium, is going to control her energy and daring."

Other magazines ran charts that showed where best to sit to view the flawless body that one giddy London critic had declared totally free of cellulite. Lines outside the theater typically revealed theatergoers with binoculars in hand. Clearly, seeing what Tom Cruise saw in his bedroom had become the Broadway event of the year. Even Tom Cruise flew in to attend the play, perhaps to see what he was *not* seeing in his bedrooms in Los Angeles and London. Never mind that, Tom was generously supportive of Nicole, sometimes showing up to offer advice.

Reviews were predictably positive. Ben Brantley, writing for the *New York Times*, cautioned those who buy tickets expecting the "highbrow equivalent of a blue movie" to look elsewhere. "Ms. Kidman gives a winningly accomplished performance, shifting accents and personae with an assured agility that never stoops to showing off or grandstanding," he wrote. "She also generates the play's only glimmers of real pathos, letting her face fleetingly betray an irritation that shades into despair when her characters realize that the expectation of sex is as good as sex gets."

Writing in the *Philadelphia Inquirer*, Clifford A. Ridley found fault with the play's "antiseptic atmosphere," but he had praise for Nicole, "whose face and form are as near perfection as my poor heart can stand." He goes on to say that the actress "delivers real acting, not merely the star turn that one might expect from word out of London."

*The Blue Room* turned out to be one of Nicole's most satisfying acting experiences in years. After devoting so much of her time to *Eyes Wide Shut*, time that did not bring an immediate audience response, she reveled in the instant attention she received from her stage performances. Actors need approval to survive and she received more than her share in London and New York.

Unfortunately, about ten days before the play was scheduled to close, Nicole developed a bronchial infection and laryngitis, and she was forced to withdraw from the play. "I am truly devastated not to complete the last week of the run and deeply apologize to the people who have planned to attend those performances," she said in a press release.

Yes, she was devastated, but she also was exhausted and in need of rest and relaxation. Little did she know that her much-needed recuperation would be interrupted by traumatic news.


In the months leading up to the release of *Eyes Wide Shut*, rumors swirled around the film with increasing vigor. British newspapers reported there would be scenes in which Tom's character plays a transvestite. There was talk that Nicole would appear dressed as a man. Rumors circulated that Harvey Keitel was bumped from the film because of a sex scene with Nicole that got out of control. Everyone seemed to agree that, whatever the actual details, it would be the most sexually explicit Hollywood movie ever made, almost certain to receive an NC-17 rating.

Nicole didn't know what to think about the rumors, because she really had no idea what was going to be in the film. She had filmed some terribly explicit scenes, especially with Gary Goba, but how much of that would appear in the film was unknown to her.

On March 1, 1999, amid great secrecy, Nicole and Tom previewed the film for the first time in a midtown Manhattan screening room with a handful of studio executives. Kubrick was so paranoid about details leaking out that he sent word for the projectionist to turn away and not watch the film.

Nicole and Tom watched the film in silence (she couldn't speak anyway since she had totally lost her voice) and then they watched it a second time, scribbling and passing notes to each other in the darkened theater. They were dumbfounded by what they saw. Nicole later said it had a hypnotic effect on her. "The first time, we were in shock," Nicole later told *Time* magazine. "The second time, I thought, 'Wow!' It's going to be controversial. I'm proud of the film and that period of my life. It was my obsession, *our* obsession, for two or three years."

Tom's strongest reaction was to the scenes Nicole did with Gary Goba. "Yeah, who the fuck was that guy?" he later joked to *USA Today* (the newspaper edited the expletive). "You know, I trust Nic. And she is very good about making me feel okay about it. I have scenes that I do also in other movies, and scenes in this movie, and it's something that is part of what we do as actors. There are moments where you feel a tinge of jealousy. But there's a trust there."

Immediately after viewing the film, Tom telephoned Kubrick to tell him how much they liked it, then caught a flight to Australia where he was working on *Mission: Impossible II*. Nicole remained in New York with the children. Unable to speak, she faxed the director a letter that shared her thoughts about the film. Not talking to him was tough on her, especially during that emotional time, for she had become used to speaking to him three or four times a week.

On March 6, Kubrick left Nicole a voice mail: "Nicole, call me. Can't wait to talk to you." The message left a smile on Nicole's face. Her voice had returned by that time and she was looking forward to talking to Kubrick again.

When she awoke the next morning, she thought about calling Kubrick right away, but she put it off a couple of hours so that she could take care of the children. She had just finished baking chocolate croissants for the children when the telephone rang. It was Kubrick's assistant, Leon. He told her that he had some bad news: Kubrick had died in his sleep from a heart attack. He was seventy years of age.

Nicole called Tom immediately and told him the news. Amid cries of "No, no, no," they cried and cried and then cried some more. Tom caught the next flight for New York (a twenty-four-hour journey) and that night Nicole went alone to St. Patrick's Cathedral to light a candle for Kubrick.

When Tom arrived the next day, they immediately caught a flight to London so that they could attend the funeral. Nicole was an emotional wreck and sobbed all the way across the Atlantic. At the funeral, they comforted Kubrick's wife, Christiane, and their daughters. His death was such a shock to everyone; he was not known to have any serious health problems.

At the funeral, all Nicole could think about was how much Kubrick hated funerals. "I'm surprised he didn't will himself out of [his own]," Nicole told *Rolling Stone*. "But it was really for Christiane and the girls. I found it quite traumatic. I went to Princess Di's funeral—Tom knew her; I'd only met her a few times—but I'd never been to a very intimate, private funeral."

After Kubrick was laid to rest, Nicole returned to America, where she tried to prepare herself for the release of *Eyes Wide Shut*. Before his death, Kubrick had told Nicole about the piece of film that he was going to release for the movie's trailer. It was the scene in which she stands nude at a mirror as Tom makes love to her as Chris Isaak's song, "Baby Did a Bad Bad Thing," plays in the background.

She wondered what people would think. She was so lost in the character at the time they filmed it that she lost all perspective. Making love in front of a mirror was something the characters did. Now she had to face the fact that millions of people would see Tom touch her breast, and, because it was only a brief piece of film, the people that saw it would see *them*—Tom and Nicole— making love because they had not yet been exposed to the characters. How would theatergoers react to that?

In April 1999, before the trailer was released, *Star* magazine published a story alleging that two British sex therapists, Wendy and Tony Duffield, were paid to teach Tom and Nicole how to make love in front of the cameras. According to the published story, Kubrick sought professional advice from the therapists after Tom and Nicole were unable to make some scenes look realistic enough for Kubrick.

Tom and Nicole, who vehemently denied working with the therapists, responded to the story with a lawsuit. Said *Star* editor Phil Bunton to the London *Daily Telegraph*: "If Tom and Nicole want to sue over this it means they are leaving themselves open to be questioned in court about extremely intimate details of their marriage. I can't imagine why they want to pursue this unless there is some hidden Scientology agenda I am not aware of. Scientologists are against psychotherapy—and presumably sex therapy, too— so maybe that has something to do with it." The lawsuit was later dismissed, with both Tom and Nicole and the magazine cooling their jets over the controversial story. It quickly became a non-issue, with both parties moving on to other things.

By June, Nicole and Tom were so frustrated over tabloid intrusions into their lives that they told reporters they might retire from acting to pursue personal and family interests. Nicole said that a trip to the beach with the children was looking good to her.

With the death of Stanely Kubrick came a reassessment of his career. Was he a genius with a unique vision of life? Or was he simply a good photographer with extraordinarily good luck and a convincing bluff? Inquiring minds were stumped.

Ty Burr, writing for *Entertainment Weekly*, saw Kubrick as "America's most prominent contribution to the ranks of visionary postwar directors, on equal footing with Bergman and Kurosawa, Godard and Fellini." That seemed to be the consensus among thoughtful observers, although when *Eyes Wide Shut* was released on July 16, 1999, reviews were mixed and Kubrick was treated as a filmmaker, not a saint.

*Movieline*'s Michael Atkinson threw down the gauntlet with the questions: "Is it a masterpiece or a boondoggle? Fascinating or laughable? Des-tined to be venerated in years hence, like most Stanley Kubrick movies, or shrugged off for eternity?"

Under the headline SHUT YOUR EYES: KUBRICK'S FINAL FILM LONG, DULL, SUPPORTING ACTORS SHINE, BUT CRUISE AND KIDMAN ARE UNCONVINCING AND UNEROTIC, *Philadelphia Inquirer* critic Steven Rea wrote: "Long and dull, despite the sumptuous production design and light-shimmering photography (and the orgy), Kubrick's thirteenth and final film is a study of fidelity, infidelity, and how easily impressed people still get when somebody identifies himself as a doctor."

The *Boston Globe*'s Ed Siegel could not have disagreed more. He found the film to be a "near-perfect coda to a most brilliant career" and viewed the success of the film as existing in the eye of the beholder. "I was with Cruise every step of the way in what has to be his best piece of acting," wrote Siegel. "(Kidman continues to be an impressive actress). However many takes it took, the simultaneous expressivity and ambiguity on his and Kidman's faces are worth it."

With critics slugging it out over the importance of the film, it was inevitable that Nicole and Tom would join in the debate. "People were expecting it to be *A Clockwork Orange* with sex, which it's not," Nicole told the *Miami Herald*. "The first time I saw it, I kept saying to Tom, 'This is so elegant!' It's a disturbing film, but it has great subtlety. I've used the word 'Kubrickian' to describe it, and some people look at me funny. They ask me to define it, and I say, 'Why define it? Don't you just know what I mean?'"

As the initial shock of the film wore off, questions were raised about the relationship between the film and Nicole and Tom's marriage. Did they adapt to the film or did the film adapt to them? Did Kubrick help them understand their marriage better or did he initiate an irreparable split in their relationship? Was *Eyes Wide Shut* fiction or was it the ultimate documentary on the breakup of a marriage?

One of the aspects of the film that attracted attention was the different level of interest and passion that Nicole showed in her sex scenes. With Tom, she was cool and distant, almost passionless—and there seemed little physical chemistry between them. With Gary Goba, she was just the opposite—passionate, totally engaged in the encounter, oozing with hot-blooded sexuality.

Some observers attribute those differences to different directions in the script. Perhaps Kubrick wanted her to be passionate with Goba and cool to Tom's advances. That's possible, but the script gives no indication of that. The script instructs her to "respond to his caresses by taking her glasses off and putting her arms around him."

Goba's friends joked with him about it. Asked to compare Tom's encounter with Nicole to his own encounter, Goba was too much the gentleman to offer an analysis. All he could say about it was that it was "a surreal experience."

After the film was released, Nicole and Tom remained staunch supporters of Kubrick's vision and tactics, even though both their health and their marriage had been affected by the long ordeal involved with making the film. The issues that Bill and Alice dealt with in the movie were some of the same issues that Tom and Nicole were struggling to deal with—jealousy, marital independence, the demands of career, sexual communication within a marriage, and fantasy versus reality.

Kubrick worked with Tom and Nicole separately and forbade them to compare notes or to discuss the movie when they were alone. Nicole understood the reason for that to be because he feared that in a three-way situation—which is what it had come down to in their working relationship—two members would find it irresistible to gang up on the third member, perhaps without even meaning to.

Kubrick was a control freak, obsessive and at times paranoid, there is no doubt about that, so Nicole's explanation is certainly plausible. However, since the director's tactic of isolating Tom and Nicole and then working with them separately is a well-known mind-control technique, some weight must be given to the possibility that he had a less laudable goal in mind—namely, to experiment with their marriage, for the sake of the movie, the way a researcher would do in a laboratory setting. It is almost as if he was asking Tom and Nicole to examine their own sex lives within the confines of the film, and then to discern between reality and dream.

The most damning evidence against Kubrick lies in the relentless manner in which he pursued the sex scenes between Nicole and Gary Goba. He asked Nicole to do things that he knew damned well would never make it onto film. It was abusive behavior cloaked in a mantle of professional necessity.

"Every time he set up a scene, he said in a teasing voice, 'What about this, Nicole—we'll put you underneath him, eh?'" recalls Goba. "He was doing stuff like that, antagonizing her. He got a rise out of her for sure. She would say, 'All right, Stanley, that's enough.' She loved him, but he was trying to piss her off in a fun way, but who knows..."

In the film, Nicole's sexual encounters with Goba were only a fantasy, but Tom's character obsessed over them as if they were real; in real life, Nicole's encounters with Goba were actual, insofar as intimate touching was concerned, but Tom viewed them as fantasy. Tom had no idea how intimate those sex scenes were, primarily because of Kubrick's dictum that the couple must refrain from exchanging information—and to this day, Tom is still in the dark about the explicitness of the scenes.

Was it Kubrick's intent to push Nicole and Tom to the point where they no longer could discern reality from fantasy—and then to document that cinematic experiment for posterity? From that perspective, *Eyes Wide Shut* can be viewed as a documentary on the dissolution of a Hollywood marriage. Diabolically brilliant, if true—but the question remains, was Kubrick clever enough to bring it off?

\* \* \*

The same month that *Eyes Wide Shut* was released, *Esquire* published a feature story about Nicole that painted a picture of the actress that was devastatingly unflattering. Tom Junod, a Georgia-based feature writer who went to Australia to interview Nicole for the article, walked away with a story that was kinky enough to ensure his own celebrity.

Nicole was most generous with her time, giving the writer a tour of the bridge that her grandfather helped build, drinking with him at a colorful pub called the Glenmore Hotel, and dining with him at a Japanese restaurant. The way Junod told it, Nicole had a bit too much to drink and got a wee bit tipsy...well, drunk.

On Junod's last night in Sydney. Nicole insisted on dropping by his hotel to tell him good-bye. According to Junod, when she arrived at his room she glanced at his computer screen and then climbed into his bed to get "comfortable." No sooner had he climbed into the bed to lie beside her, than the telephone rang—it was Tom and he was looking for his wife, since he and the children were waiting for her at a Chinese restaurant and everyone was getting hungry.

"Yeah, Tom," Junod answered. "She's right here, in my hotel room. In my bed."

There was a pause, according to Junod, and Tom said, "Yeah, in your dreams, buddy."

With that, Junod held the telephone out in Nicole's direction and asked her to confirm that she was, indeed, in his bed. "I'm afraid so, darling," Nicole called out to her husband. "I'm afraid I'm in his bed at this very moment."

If true—and he did seem to suggest that he and Nicole were having an intimate encounter of some kind—it was an odd thing for Junod to write about in his article. So odd, that Junod himself became the subject of media attention. In an interview with *USA Today*, he seemed to back away from suggesting a sexual encounter. He explained it by saying, "The story is and was a flirtation. I was flirting with her, not only when reporting, but when writing. It's that genre of celebrity journalism. And she flirted back. I just think we kind of liked each other. Of course, it was professional."

Nicole was oddly silent about the article. After the stresses that she had undergone making *Eyes Wide Shut*, dealing with the real-life jealousies and insecurities that had crept into her marriage, Junod's article was the last thing she needed in her life, even if it was written in a tongue-in-cheek style. No one knows for certain, since neither she nor Tom has ever discussed the article publicly, but it surely must have caused a rift.

Emotionally, Nicole and Tom were depleted. The publicity surrounding *Eyes Wide Shut* was nearly as draining as making the film itself. The marriage of Hollywood's most perfect couple was headed for trouble, not because of the article, but because of an accumulation of marital stresses. The article merely demonstrated how truly needy Nicole was at that time in her life.

Even before the release of Kubrick's work, Tom had retreated into another film—this time into a comic drama titled *Magnolia*. Written and directed by Paul Thomas Anderson, the film examines nine lives in the course of one day, all taking place in the San Fernando Valley, California. Tom took the supporting role of Frank T. J. Mackey, the leader of a cultish self-help group of macho womanizers who want to improve their game. Mackey's advice is to "seduce and destroy."

When the film was released in December 1999, Tom received rave reviews for the manner in which he had developed the character (was he listening more and more to Nicole?). Writing in the *San Francisco Chronicle*, Bob Graham had praise for the actor: "The role of Frank T. J. Mackey demands a mesmerizing performance, and Cruise delivers one." Agreeing with that assessment was the Academy of Motion Picture Arts and Sciences, which nominated him for an Oscar (he didn't win).

# CHAPTER EIGHT

# A Gamble on
# Moulin Rouge

W hen Nicole first read the script for *Birthday Girl*, what most impressed her was the fact that she was unable to predict what was
going to happen on the next page. She saw the story as being
character-driven, one in which she could lose herself and adopt a new persona: in this case, as a Russian mail-order bride. What also impressed her about
the project was that it initially would be filmed in Sydney, which meant that
she could take the children and join Tom while he was shooting *Mission:
Impossible II*.

Nicole did have one reservation about making the film: it would require
her to learn Russian, at least enough to make her character convincing, and
she was not certain she could bring that off. Even so, she threw herself into it,
learning not only the Russian language, but the Russian attitude as well,
even though she was still physically exhausted by the emotional investment
she had put into *Eyes Wide Shut* and *The Blue Room*.

There was also another reason for her to undertake another taxing project.
It would take her mind off of her faltering marriage. She did what men have
done for centuries when their marriages take a turn for the worse: she became
a workaholic.

Not unhappy with that attitude was London-born director Jez Butterworth,
who had directed only one other film before signing on to do *Birthday Girl*. The
fact that he had written the script would help him with his duties as a director,

but what he needed most of all was an experienced lead actress who would push herself to the max. Despite her glamorous image outside the movie industry, within the industry Nicole was known for her obsessive attention to detail and her willingness to put pressure on herself that no self-respecting director (Stanley Kubrick, the only exception) would ever inflict upon her.

Starring opposite Nicole was British actor, Ben Chaplin, who plays a lonely bank teller named John who attempts to put some excitement into his drab life by ordering a Russian bride from an Internet dating service called "From Russia With Love."

The movie begins with John arriving at the airport to pick up his new bride, a dark-haired woman with excessive eye makeup who goes by the name of Nadia. To John, a seasoned introvert, Nadia seems shy and forlorn, perhaps even homesick, so as he drives her to his suburban home, he tries to make polite conversation with her.

John soon becomes suspicious after she answers yes to every question and he asks her, as a test, if she is a giraffe, to which she gleefully answers yes. Minutes later, she hangs her head out the car window and vomits.

When they arrive at his house, the first thing he does is place a telephone call to the dating service to tell them that they have made a terrible mistake. He had ordered an English-speaking bride and they had sent the wrong order. Since no one answers the telephone, he leaves a voice mail plea for someone to call him. It was, he explains in a desperate voice, an emergency.

No one with the dating service ever returns his calls, so he settles into sort of a routine with Nadia. He gives her a Russian-English dictionary and tries to make the most of what he sees as a bad situation. She responds by giving him sex of such intensity and variety that he soon forgets his reservations about having her in his home.

Not long after Nadia arrives, her cousin Alexei (played by Vincent Cassel) shows up with his friend Yuri (played by Mathieu Kassovitz). Things go well for a while, but when John asks them to leave, Yuri goes berserk and threatens to hurt Nadia if John does not pay him money. To get the money, John robs his own bank, carting out bundles of bills in two guitar cases. Once Yuri has the money, Nadia starts speaking English and showing affection for Yuri. As it turns out, John's relationship with Nadia was all part of a money-making scam. Of course, the money soon becomes secondary to resolving the conflict of who gets the girl—and therein lies the heart of the drama.

Making the movie was physically less demanding on Nicole than other movies she had made, but emotionally it was a challenge, for to do it properly she knew she had to not only change her appearance, but she also had to change her speech.

During rehearsals, she showed up each morning with the same comment: "Oh, shit! I can't do this!" Cassel and Kassovitz were in much the same position. Both men were born in France and they had to learn Russian the same way Nicole did.

On their first day of rehearsals, the two men showed up together and asked Nicole, half jokingly, if she had learned her lines in Russian yet.

"Oh, yes," she later told *Interview*. "I've learned all my Russian. I have an accent which is from the suburbs to the south of Moscow."

The two men turned pale and looked at each other, one saying to the other, "Shit! We're in trouble!"

Ben Chaplin had problems of his own starring opposite Nicole, for it meant sitting around naked with her for long periods of time between takes. Recounted Chaplin: "Nicole and I would look at each other and say the most God-awful, stupid things like, 'Can you believe this weather?' 'Do you think they'll serve the good fish for lunch?' It's almost like being in a doctor's office. You can't wait until it's over, even if it is Nicole Kidman across a bed from you."


Even before Nicole threw herself into *Birthday Girl*, she was obsessing about another movie named *Moulin Rouge*. One evening, during the New York production of *The Blue Room*, a bouquet of long-stemmed red roses with Nicole's name on it was delivered backstage. The roses caught her attention because, believe it or not, no one had ever given her long-stemmed red roses. *Were they from Tom, a reaffirmation of his love for her?* No, they were from Australian movie director Baz Luhrmann, who wanted something from her. The note attached to the flowers read: "I have this great character. She sings, she dances, and then she dies."

In a strange sort of way, *that* was the way Nicole saw her own life, so how could she not respond in a favorable manner to Luhrmann's teaser? She knew him, but not very well (a decade ago they had worked together guest editing the Australian edition of *Vogue*), so she called him and asked to see the script.

There was no script, Luhrmann explained, merely a booklet composed of photographs, drawings, and captions. There was one other bit of information she should be aware of before accepting his offer, he explained—the movie was a musical and she would be asked to actually sing, not lip-snych to another woman's voice.

Nicole liked to sing. She sang to her children all the time, although they usually asked her to stop. But she had no idea if she would be able to sing professionally. Nonetheless, she readily said yes, figuring that she would simply rely on her innate ability to mimic with deadly accuracy, only to be told the second surprise of the conversation—namely, that all the actors chosen for the movie would be asked to go to Sydney, without compensation, to rehearse for three to four months at his headquarters, a former insane asylum. How could Nicole possibly resist an offer like that?

Luhrmann was not so much eccentric as he was headstrong to re-create the vision he had for the movie. He first got the idea while visiting India in 1994 to research an opera. He went to see a locally produced movie and was fascinated at the way in which the director had blended corny comedy with drama and then set it off with music. It was totally off the wall, but everyone in the theater, himself included, was riveted to the screen, wondering what outlandish event would next appear.

When he returned to Sydney, he told his staff that he planned to do a movie unlike any other ever done. It would be a musical with a serious plot line, and the characters would all be larger-than-life caricatures that would be surrounded by lavish sets bathed in vibrant hues of red and blue. He didn't have a plot in mind yet, but he already knew that he wanted the actors to sing live onstage—and he wanted them to sing popular contemporary songs that would be recognizable to the public. It would be a musical unlike anything Hollywood had ever envisioned.

No one doubted Luhrmann's ability to bring the idea to life. His 1996 production of *Romeo and Juliet* had been universally hailed and had established him as a serious filmmaker with a grand vision, who could reshape the familiar into something new and extraordinary.

Once he decided to make the movie, Luhrmann had to decide on a story line. "I wanted to deal with the Orphean myth: 'Idealistic young man with a gift descends into the underworld looking for idealistic perfect love, finds her, tries to rescue her from that underworld. He makes a very human mistake, loses that love forever and is scarred,'" he explained to *Movieline*. "That myth is about that moment that comes for us all when you realize that some relationships, no matter how perfect, cannot be. People die. Doors close. You won't always be young. You go through that journey, and in place of the gifts of youth come the gifts of spiritual growth. You're bigger inside."

Where better for that vision to take place than in a nineteenth-century Parisian nightclub, where money could buy literally anything, including love, for a reasonable price. Once Luhrmann had the vision and the setting for his motion picture, which he decided to call *Moulin Rouge*, all that remained was to people his fantasy with actors who could make his characters come to life.

To do that, he spent three months going door to door, looking for just the right actors. For the role of Harold Zidler, the nightclub owner, he chose veteran character actor Jim Broadbent. John Leguizamo was asked to play Toulouse-Lautrec, and Richard Roxburgh was tapped for the role of the womanizing Duke of Monroth.

The male and female leads were the last cast. He pretty much considered every male and female actor that was available. Catherine Zeta-Jones was high on his list to play Satine, the ambitious courtesan torn between getting ahead in life and finding true love, primarily because Jones had enjoyed a successful career in musical comedy in London, but, after pondering every angle, he ended up passing over her because he felt that she was not emotionally eccentric enough to be convincing. Nicole attracted his attention because he felt she had both a girl-next-door quality and a dangerous, unpredictable quality about her. When he saw her electric performance in *The Blue Room*, he was certain she was perfect for the role of Satine.

Heath Ledger was the front-runner for a long time for the role of Christian, the penniless writer, but, in the end, Luharmann decided that the nineteen-year-old was simply too young to do the character justice. Instead, he went with Ewan McGregor, whom he had auditioned in the mid-1990s to play Mercutio in *Romeo and Juliet*.

Luhrmann's preference was to select his male and female leads and then bring them together to see if there would be any chemistry, but he soon realized that would be impractical with the two actors he had in mind, so he invited everyone to Sydney for rehearsals. If any of the principals failed to live up to his expectations, insofar as the singing and dancing was concerned, then they would be replaced. Everyone knew that and considered it an acceptable risk.

To Luhrmann's delight, when Nicole and Ewan arrived for rehearsals, there seemed to be an instant chemistry between the two actors. They were as playful together as cats on a lazy day. Ewan appreciated her daring and her beauty, and she appreciated his youth and optimism, qualities that she—at age thirty-three—yearned to revisit.

Nicole also demonstrated a playful chemistry with Luhrmann. A decade earlier, when they did a photo shoot for the Australian edition of *Vogue*, they met for the first time at a restaurant where the photographs were to be taken. Nicole's first impression of him was of how blatantly "Australian" he was; she was also somewhat taken aback by a loud, hacking cough he seemingly exercised at every opportunity. Despite the cough, she decided then that she hoped she would someday work with him.

Nicole caught Luhrmann's attention because of the loud, boisterous way she interacted with the other people involved in the photo shoot. Years later, he recalled that meeting in a conversation with Nicole for *Interview* magazine: "When I met you, you were like so many of the girls I knew growing up—so crazy, so noisy. I say noisy because I remember you were eating along and suddenly '*Yahh!*'—you let out a big scream. I can't remember if they threw us out, but I think they wanted to."

One week before rehearsals began, Nicole got cold feet and begged Luhrmann to let her go. He refused, telling her she was there for the duration. The rehearsals were filled with surprises. Everyone was shocked at how well Nicole sang and how poorly she danced. She went into rehearsals thinking she could not sing and pretty sure that she was athletic enough to handle the dance routines.

She was wrong on both counts. Her voice was surprisingly engaging and her dancing was the equivalent of two left feet. The dancing was what surprised her the most, for she had always considered herself very athletic, a tomboy in diva's skin. But the deeper they went into rehearsals, the more confident Nicole became in her ability to do the role justice.

All of the actors spent long days doing readings, improvising, and taking singing and dancing lessons. Tom, who was in Sydney filming his *Mission: Impossible* sequel, stopped by Luhrmann's headquarters often to show support for Nicole—or was it because he had heard the same rumors about Nicole and Ewan that everyone else had heard?

"Of course, people said, 'Nicole and Ewan are having an affair. They're inseparable,'" Luhrmann told *Movieline*. "People love stories like that. I'm not surprised by it. It can happen. But as far as I know, there was a line. It just didn't happen. But it was very close. I mean, look, they're two gorgeous-looking people."

On the last night of rehearsals, Luhrmann gave a party for the cast and introduced them to absinthe, a hallucinogenic green substance favored by the bohemian subculture at the turn of the century. Everyone went crazy that night, but, thanks to the drug, no one was able to remember anything the next morning.

When they went from rehearsals to actual filming, the pressure to perform increased dramatically, for their singing and dancing was no longer pretend, it was now for real and the cameras were ready to roll, to capture their every move.

Tragically, on the day production was scheduled to begin Luhrmann received word that his father had died of skin cancer. He left to attend the funeral, and the cast stood about in stunned disbelief, grieving for the director's loss, but also wondering if the entire project would be jinxed.

One week later, on November 1, Luhrmann returned and picked up where he had left off; it was a painful time for him, but the deeper he got into production, the more he was able to put his grief aside, at least temporarily.

*Moulin Rouge* begins with Christian going to Paris to write about love, even though he has never been in love. After befriending Toulouse-Lautrec, he is asked to co-write a musical. He goes to the Moulin Rouge, the most ostentatious performance hall in the city, where the stage is filled with can-can dancers, musicians, and singers.

Satine makes a spectacular entrance on a swing suspended over the audience and sings "Diamonds Are a Girl's Best Friend" and then "Material Girl." She faints during one of her songs and is taken backstage, where she coughs up blood. The duke of Monroth arrives to meet her and she becomes convinced that he will become her patron. She mistakes Christian for the duke, then she has to hide him when the real duke arrives.

After the duke leaves, Christian comes from his hiding place and asks, "Before, when you thought I was the duke, you said that you loved me and I wondered if..."

"If it was just an act?" says Satine, finishing his sentence.

"Yes."

"Of course," she says.

Christian says that it feels real enough to him.

"Christian, I'm a courtesan. I'm paid to make men believe what they want to believe."

"How silly of me. To think that you could fall in love with someone like me."

Of course, Satine has fallen in love with Christian. Her dilemma is whether to pursue true love with Christian or financial security with the duke. The love triangle becomes more complicated when Christian writes a similar romantic predicament into the musical, prompting the duke to pledge to kill Christian if Satine does not do the show the way he wants and, on top of that, sleep with him.

It is at this point that Satine learns that she is dying of consumption. Moulin Rouge owner Harold Zidler tells Satine she must break Christian's heart to save his life. "Hurt him to save him," he advises.

Satine takes his advice and tells Christian that she has decided to go away with the duke. The story ends the only way it possibly could—with Satine dying onstage.

There were times during production when Nicole felt she would die onstage. Early on, she broke her rib during a lift sequence in one of the dance numbers and had to take several weeks off to recover at her home in Sydney. Luckily, Tom was there to take care of her and the children. She used the time to stretch out on her sofa and rehearse her songs for upcoming scenes.

On another occasion, she was walking down the stairs during the "Pink Diamonds" routine, when she stepped on some feathers and missed her footing, falling and tearing the cartilage in her knee. She didn't realize the seriousness of her injury for several days and continued working, denying that she was hurt, even though it was apparent to everyone around her that she was.

When the pain became too much for her, she was taken to a hospital, where she underwent surgery to repair the torn knee cartilage. "The rib wasn't so bad, but the cartilage was a nightmare," she told the *Sydney Morning Herald*. "I didn't really realize the damage I was doing to my body. I just sort of kept going and taking painkillers and getting steroid shots just to get through it. I felt like a footballer."

For the final scenes, Nicole was on crutches or sitting in a wheelchair. Luhrmann was forced to devise creative ways of filming her so that her injury was not apparent; that meant using close-ups where he previously had planned more expansive images and it meant surrounding Nicole with extras to cover up her disability.

On top of her injuries, she had to endure three-hour makeup sessions each day and costumes that inflicted pain whenever she moved. "The corset itself was just a complete nightmare," she explained in an interview that accompanied the video version of the movie. "Doing high kicks in a full corset—forget it. The other girls, the can-can girls, wore it, too. We'd all have bruises and our nerves went numb...not pleasant, but as Baz Luhrmann said, 'Hey, it looks great!' "

Amid all that pain and suffering, Nicole sang her heart out. Many of the songs were done live onstage, with Nicole and Ewan surrounded by hundreds of extras, singing without benefit of the electronic studio "helpers" that recording artists use to make their voices sound better.

Typically, live recording sessions for Hollywood musicals would include an elaborately produced sound track, to which the singers' voice could be added. Luhrmann did it the hard way: he recorded the songs live, then added the orchestra later, gluing the orchestration around the voices. No one had ever done it that way before, but Luhrmann didn't care; he thought it could be done and proved the doubters wrong.

Despite all the chaos surrounding the film, Nicole maintained a normal relationship with her children, Bella and Connor, who stayed on the set the entire time. At lunch, she took the children into her dressing room, where, typically wearing fishnet stockings, a corset, and four-inch stilettos, she cooked their favorite meals. The children thought nothing about seeing their mother dressed that way; to their way of thinking their mother was a circus performer and the funny clothing was just her work uniform.

"Yeah, I would go back in after doing takes to make sure the homework was being done," she told *Interview* magazine. "Then suddenly I'd be doing grade one reading for twenty minutes, and then back on the set. And for their math lesson, they'd be out betting with the crew. Playing poker—now that's how to do mathematics!"

The production was actually wrapped before it was completed. The death of Luhrmann's father and Nicole's injuries had eaten up about six weeks of precious studio time. There was no way to get an extension because the studio had been leased out for Ewan McGregor's next movie, *Star Wars: Episode II*. Within minutes after Luhrmann and company left the studio, wrecking balls were in place to demolish the set.


Luhrmann eventually finished filming in Madrid, Spain, where Nicole and Tom went to film the supernatural thriller, *The Others*, a project for which Tom had signed on as producer. The time that Tom and Nicole spent in Sydney was special in that it allowed them to be together with the children, but it was stressful in a professional sense because of all the problems that plagued both *Moulin Rouge* and *Mission: Impossible II*.

From beginning to end, it took two years to complete work on *Mission: Impossible II*. They were well into production before the screenwriter, Robert Towne, turned in his first lines, long after Tom and director John Woo had worked out the action sequences. It was, after all, a movie that depended on action, not words, for its creative energy.

Woo saw Tom as what he called a "rock star," meaning that when the actor spoke he generated so much energy it was as though he were playing an instrument and dancing. Woo used that energy, he later explained to reporters, to choreograph Tom's action scenes. It was a good thing that Woo, the master of karate flicks, saw those qualities in Tom, for despite all his action movies, the actor had never been in fight scenes in which he delivered karate chops. Woo pretty much "danced" him through those scenes, making it up as he went along.

Tom was his usual charismatic self on the set, enthusiastic and ever ready to offer suggestions on how a scene could be done better, but there was something different about him, something no one could quite put a finger on. He sometimes seemed preoccupied, distracted perhaps by his trips to the *Moulin Rouge* set to check up on his wife and children.

Tom also seemed more aggressive, from a director's point of view, in that he wanted to do some of his own stunts. Was he trying to compete with his high-spirited, daredevil wife? Or was he trying to impress her? She had broken a rib and torn knee cartilage while making a girlie musical, wounds she wore like a badge of honor. What did he have to show for his efforts on the set of a manly action movie? He had suffered no broken bones or bruises, nor did he walk with a limp.

Woo was stunned when Tom told him he wanted to do his own stunt on the "massive gorge" scene (shot in Utah), where supported only by a single cable, he clung to the face of a cliff over two thousand feet in the air. Everyone tried to persuade him not to do it, including Woo and the studio executives—even Tom's mother joined in the don't-do-it chorus and flew to Utah to see for herself—but he insisted, making fun of those who asked him where the nets would be placed (there were no nets or air bags).

Nicole never seemed to be far from his thoughts. He insisted that production on *Mission: Impossible II* begin in Sydney so that he could be there with his wife and children. He went often to the *Moulin Rouge* set, but no one can recall her ever visiting the *Mission: Impossible II* set. There marriage was undergoing a major shift, and no one but Tom and Nicole was aware of what was happening.

In the beginning of their marriage, Nicole had made a major effort to be at Tom's side, offering support, even when it was not needed. Now it was Tom who was making an effort to be at her side, going out of his way to be supportive of her career. People who witnessed his public displays of support and affection toward Nicole sometimes marveled at his dedication to a marriage that Nicole seemed to take for granted.

When he became a producer on *The Others*, he insisted that Nicole be given the starring role. That, in itself, was no big deal because everyone associated with the film thought that she would be perfect for the part.

Tom has always insisted that that casting decision was purely professional, but skeptics might be forgiven for suggesting that it had a personal element as well. Had Nicole not been cast, she surely would have accepted an offer for another film, a decision that would have left Tom alone and isolated in Spain. Besides, he had learned early in the marriage that the best way to keep Nicole happy was to keep her working.

*The Others* was written and directed by Alejandro Amenabar, a Chilean-born filmmaker who fled to Spain in 1973 with his family on the eve of a military coup d'état. He made his first film in 1992 and quickly gained a reputation as one of Spain's hottest new directors and screenwriters. Tom liked his work very much and thought they had a future together.

Nicole was asked to play the part of Grace Stewart, an eccentric mother of two children who lives in a darkened old house located far out in the countryside. When Nicole arrived in Spain and realized that she would be playing a mother who had obsessive thoughts about her children (she had not read the script beforehand), she became distraught and tried to back out of being in the film.

After a week of going back and forth with Tom and the director, she realized that they were not going to release her from the film and she agreed to stay. However, by that time, she was so worked up emotionally that she was in character to play the part. All it took to complete the characterization was a pair of old-lady lace-up shoes.

The movie begins with Grace screaming in bed, obviously the recipient of a bad dream. Her skin is very pale and there is something about her that telegraphs trouble.

After her servants mysteriously disappear, Grace places an ad in the local newspaper for new employees. To her surprise, three would-be servants appear at her front door looking for work. Grace assumes they have come in response to the newspaper ad, but, as it turns out, the postman never picked up the letter containing the information for the ad. They have arrived quite by chance.

Grace hires them on the spot. As she shows them about the house, she says, "You'll notice what I'm doing," at which point she closes a door. "No door must be opened without the previous one being closed first . . . There are fifteen different keys for all of the fifty doors, depending on which area of the house you are in at the time."

She explains that there is no radio, no electricity, no telephone—"Silence is something we pride in this house." In a roundabout way she explains to the servants that her two children are light sensitive and must be kept in the dark at all times. A single ray of sunshine could have a deadly effect on them.

As the story progresses, the little girl says she hears voices, the ramblings of a little boy named Victor. Soon after that, Grace begins to hear voices. "There is something in this house," she says. "Something diabolic. Something that is not at rest."

The housekeeper offers an explanation of her own: "Sometimes the world of the dead gets mixed up with the world of the living." Horrified by that thought, Grace tells the housekeeper that the Lord would never allow such a thing to happen.

Finally, Grace decides to go seek help from a priest in dealing with what she perceives to be demon-related problem. In the fog, she runs into her missing husband who is on his way home from the war. She takes him back to the house and introduces him to the housekeeper. Gradually, it becomes apparent that the servants know something that everyone else doesn't know.

Soon it becomes clear that Grace has issues with her husband over his going off to war. They make love and when she awakens, she discovers that he has disappeared and presumably taken all the curtains in the house with him. Emboldened by the incident—and determined to protect her children—Grace wanders about the house with a loaded shotgun, ready to shoot anything that seems out of place.

From that point on, the story assumes a bone-chilling clarity that makes everything suddenly make sense. No one is who he or she appears to be and nothing that seems certain remains so for long. There is, indeed, a mystery associated with the house, and although the unsettling story appears to end well, it is not without Hitchcockian harbingers of doom.

Nicole delivered a breathtaking performance, the full extent of which was not apparent until the movie ended. How odd it was that Tom would choose this story for Nicole, for, in its own way, it seemed to mirror their marriage, down to the smallest detail. Both Grace and Nicole had two children they sought to protect from "outside" influences, both lived in a household that was never what it seemed, both had a difficult time holding onto servants, both were fastidious about the smallest of details, and both had husbands whose roles in their lives was in question.

Was art imitating life, or was life imitating art? Would Nicole, like Grace, end up raising her two children alone? Had Tom finally proved to Nicole that he was the better actor?

# CHAPTER NINE

# Days Asunder:
# Divorce Hollywood Style

After ten years of marriage, Hollywood's power-glam couple was in trouble, but friends and work associates saw only the glossy exterior they presented to the outside world. They saw Nicole holding Tom's hand and clinging to him in public (when reporters were present he continued to lean over to whisper into her ear, talking her down from her frequent panic attacks), and they saw Tom showing up on her movie sets, glad-handing her associates and praising his wife's acting abilities.

Of course, marriages don't suddenly go bad, not the way milk with last week's expiration date does—it takes a series of events over a long period of time. The earliest sign that Tom and Nicole's marriage might be in trouble was also a sign that some people interpreted as a sign of strength: their adoption of two children.

Seasoned adoption workers know that one of the most common reasons that couples decide to adopt is to bolster a shaky marriage. In such cases, couples view children as a means of cementing a fragile emotional bond or compensating for an inadequate sexual relationship. Social workers can usually weed those couples out in quick order.

For couples with low or moderate incomes, that is usually the end of the story. They eventually separate and divorce, and hopefully find more compatible partners the second time around. For wealthy couples, however, there is a way to skirt the scrutiny of social workers: they can hire attorneys and pursue private adoptions that can be shielded from the prying eyes of social agencies.

None of this is to suggest that Tom and Nicole had ulterior motives for adopting children (couples who apply for children are seldom aware of their reasons for doing so). Tom and Nicole both longed for a family and they have proven to be exemplary parents. However, it is to suggest that professional social workers, given an opportunity, would have spotted the problems in their marriage, even at that very early stage.

In retrospect, signs of marital problems were plentiful. Over the years, perhaps disappointed by her "Mrs. Tom Cruise" label, Nicole spoke, publicly at least, less and less about her husband, while he seemed to toss her name about with greater frequency. It was like a dance: she withdrew, he charged ahead, overcompensating.

When *Days of Thunder* and *Far and Away* did poorly at the box office, it killed any dreams they had of becoming Hollywood's newest Bogart and Bacall incarnation, which meant that they had to pursue separate career opportunities. For two actors, both of whose careers had been built on sex appeal (Tom's more so than Nicole's), that opened the door for temptations and frustrations of a magnitude seldom experienced by ordinary married couples.

For Tom and Nicole, the previous year and a half had been a nightmare. The Kubrick adventure—or was it more of an experiment?—opened the door to a wide range of insecurities in their personal lives. Tom had no idea that his friend the director and Nicole had filmed such sexually explicit scenes; it was not until he saw the finished product that he asked about Gary Goba's role in the film. More than anyone else, he could see the chemistry between Nicole and Goba; it was a chemistry he did not see in his own scenes with her.

For Nicole to step so quickly from *Eyes Wide Shut* into *The Blue Room*, which featured onstage nudity of a explicitness seldom engaged in even by professional strippers, demonstrated, more than anything else, how emotionally needy she was. All of that was followed up by Nicole's embarrassing encounter with the *Esquire* writer, then with rumors of an affair between Nicole and Ewan McGregor. Was Nicole sending Tom a message? Or by her behavior was she medicating her deepest inner needs?

On December 24, 2000, Tom and Nicole celebrated their tenth wedding anniversary in Los Angeles with a small group of friends, away from the prying eyes of the media. Shortly thereafter, Tom returned to New York, where he was filming *Vanilla Sky*, with Penelope Cruz, Cameron Diaz, and Kurt Russell. Written by Alejandro Amenabar, who had directed and written *The Others*, the film was being directed by Cameron Crowe, who also had directed Tom in *Jerry Maguire*.

Early in February 2001, Nicole and Tom separated. Tom had been sleeping on a sofa in the screening room for several days and one day, while Nicole was away from their Pacific Palisades home, he backed a moving van up to the door and loaded all of his personal possessions.

When it became apparent that the *National Enquirer* was going to print a story about their marital problems, Tom and Nicole issued a press release on February 5 that officially announced the split and blamed their difficulties on "divergent careers which constantly kept them apart." The day before the announcement, Tom gathered the cast of *Vanilla Sky* around him and broke the news to them himself.

The breakup of Hollywood's most glamorous power couple was big news around the country, but especially in Los Angeles, where rumors about their marriage had circulated for years. Almost immediately, reports were published that linked Tom to Penelope Cruz, his love interest in *Vanilla Sky*; other reports linked Nicole to Ewan McGregor, George Clooney, and her former boyfriend Marcus Graham.

*USA Today* reported that it was Nicole who initiated the split. Citing sources close to the couple, the *National Enquirer* reported that Tom dumped Nicole because she had cheated on him. Others blamed the problem on Nicole's refusal to embrace Scientology. The media didn't know about the secret sex scenes in *Eyes Wide Shut* or that would have been offered as an explanation as well.

Nicole was two weeks into filming a suspense movie, *The Panic Room*, at the time of the separation and withdrew from the film, citing a new injury to the knee she hurt while making *Moulin Rouge*. Director David Fincher quickly replaced her with Jodie Foster, who, in turn, had to withdraw from her position as president of Cannes International Film Festival. Foster said she was "mortified" at letting down festival organizers and she expressed hope they would understand.

No sooner had the dust settled on the separation, than Tom dropped a bombshell. He filed for divorce on February 7, citing—what else?—irreconcilable differences. He requested joint custody of their two children, Bella, who was eight, and Connor, who was six. Apparently, Nicole was just as surprised as everyone else, especially at the date Tom established as the date of separation—early-to-mid December 2000, just shy of ten years marriage. In court papers, Nicole challenged the date of separation, stating that they had been intimate during the balance of December and well into the new year.

Then she dropped a bombshell of her own: she had become pregnant with Tom's child during that time and had suffered a subsequent miscarriage on March 15. Perhaps anticipating a denial of paternity, she asked doctors to keep DNA samples of the fetus so that she could prove that Tom was the father.

Nicole further stated in court papers that she had protested Tom's intention to dissolve the marriage and had "urged him not to leave but to enter marriage counseling with her or to take other steps to address whatever problems may have existed in their marriage relationship. [Tom] said his decision was final, and he departed the parties' home."

In her response to Tom's lawsuit, Nicole insisted on face-to-face meetings with Tom and said that his request for joint custody was "contingent upon [his] agreement to communicate, consult, and—from time to time—meet directly with [Nicole] as to all important issues affecting the children's general welfare." She also stated her interest in living with the children primarily at her home in Sydney or "elsewhere in the United States."

News of a miscarriage only whetted the appetite of the news media. Tom had been sexually active for almost two decades and had gone through two marriages, all without ever fathering a child. Was it within the bounds of reason that he would suddenly do so in the final weeks of his marriage with Nicole? There was speculation that someone other than Tom had fathered the baby. Why, skeptics argued, would Tom divorce Nicole if she was carrying his child?

Ewan McGregor was so concerned about the finger pointing revolving around the miscarriage and breakup that he issued a statement denying that he had ever had an affair with Nicole: "I don't know anything about it—it wasn't anything to do with me." The other men identified as possible lovers, George Clooney and Marcus Graham, issued similar statements describing the rumors as nonsense.

News reports described Nicole as being shattered by the divorce, distraught enough to lose the baby. Reported the *Star*: "She had tried all these years to get pregnant by Tom and when she finally manages to, he is not here for her. She has absolutely no doubt that it was his treatment of her that caused her to lose the baby. She was up crying night after night after night. She was a complete emotional wreck."

Tom's response to the miscarriage and divorce was markedly different. When news of the miscarriage reached him, he reacted "coolly," according to *People* magazine, which also reported him telling a friend that "Nic knows exactly why we are getting a divorce. But she's the mother of our children and I wish her well."

Immediately after Nicole informed her family about her marital problems, her sister, Antonia, and her mother, Janelle, flew to Los Angeles to be with her and the children. At one point, Nicole was so distraught that she lay on the floor in a fetal position. Janelle's choice of therapy for her daughter was to encourage her to paint. She set an easel up next to a pair of French windows where the light cascaded into the house and she showed her how to work with color on canvas. Nicole quickly learned that she had absolutely no talent as an artist, but just as her mother promised, she found the exercise relaxing.

Antony stayed behind in Australia, but he spoke to Nicole often on the telephone, giving her, we must presume, the advice he offers in his books. "Another myth that keeps coming up in connection with suggested divorce is the belief that because two people once enjoyed life together, there must be a basis for reconciliation," Antony wrote in *Family Life: Adapting to Change*. "This is always worthy of consideration, but to feel that people who were once happy together can inevitably, with sufficient effort, reestablish marital bliss is often unrealistic. Interests, attitudes, activities and goals of people change. To assume that every boy and girl who married in the spring of a youthful romance at twenty-one will find life delightful and interesting together at age forty-one is to believe in fairy tales and magic."

If there were two things that Nicole no longer believed in, they were fairy tales and magic. Thanks to the emotional support she received from her sister and mother, and thanks to the no-nonsense advice she received from her psychologist dad, she was able to rebound from the initial trauma with an attitude that one magazine described as a "textbook example of how to handle a personal crisis."

Nicole dropped her efforts for a reconciliation and focused instead on her children, her career, and her ongoing battle with Tom over how their estimated $250 million estate would be divided up. Tom wasted no time going after the lion's share of the estate and the ferocity of his lawyers' demands at first caught Nicole off guard. She bounced back quickly, however, and hired estate-hungry lawyers of her own.

Los Angeles observers saw the divorce as shaping up to be the celebrity legal battle of the century. Some commentators wondered if the "secrets" of the marriage would somehow slip through the publicity that the couple had in place and find their way into court documents. If so, they would be disappointed, for lawyers on both sides were given strict orders to keep Nicole and Tom out of headlines.

Nicole told the *Sydney Morning Herald* that news coverage of her divorce was very "upsetting" and "invasive" during a period she described as the toughest time of her life. "I understand that people are interested, but it's my life—my personal life," she said. "It's very difficult seeing your life being dragged through the newspapers and the tabloids and your children being dragged through it."

Along with Nicole's name was dragged another name—Penelope Cruz, Tom's love interest in *Vanilla Sky*. Nicole didn't know what to think. Tom denied any involvement with her, but the rumors had just enough credibility in them to make Nicole suspicious. In her own mind, Penelope was the reason for the divorce, at least that's what she confided to friends.

The situation was not helped by a "Legends of Hollywood" *Vanity Fair* cover story. For the cover, photographer Annie Leibovitz shot a group portrait that included, in addition to Nicole, Vanessa Redgrave, Sophia Loren, Meryl Streep, Gwyneth Paltrow, Catherine Deneuve, Kate Winslet, Cate Blanchett, Chloe Sevigny, and—horror of horrors—Penelope Cruz, though why Penelope was chosen was a mystery since her Hollywood presence was almost nonexistent.

The wily Leibovitz posed Nicole on the left corner, hand on hip, smileless with a regal posture, and placed Penelope on the opposite corner, leaning forward, forearms crossed in a pose of feminine submission. Nicole appeared slightly tense, Penelope looked like a deer caught in the headlights, and most of the other stars seemed slightly amused at the high drama into which they had inadvertently stumbled.

Writing about Nicole, *Vanity Fair's* Punch Hutton described her as "flaw-less—and we mean it: we saw her naked during the 1998–1999 London and Broadway runs of *The Blue Room* . . . Yes, Hollywood's most elegant Australian import knows how to create a buzz."

Nicole took it all in stride, for above all else she considered herself a sur-vivor. Despite a constant stream of emotional upheavals, Nicole reached a point at which she felt comfortable sending her mother and sister back to Sydney. She decided to allow her lawyers to fret over the terms of the divorce settlement while she got the children settled into a routine and herself back in touch with her career.

In early April, when Tom took the stage at Los Angeles's Shrine Auditorium on Oscar night, Nicole was not in the audience; she was at the home of a friend, watching the awards show on television. Friends said she was over wanting to get back together with him, but was still puzzled over why he had left her.

In early May, Nicole taped the *Oprah Winfrey Show,* ostensibly to promote the upcoming release of *Moulin Rouge.* Nicole told Oprah that she was fearful that if she didn't deliver on her performance in the movie, she would let a lot of people down.

After a few initial questions about the movie—and the customary head-nodding chitchat—Oprah got right to point: "The message of the movie is it's better to have loved and lost than to never have loved at all. Do you be-lieve that?"

"Definitely."

"Yeah—so how are you?"

"I'm—I'm—I'm good," she answered, then quickly admitted that she was a terrible liar. "Anyone here who has been through a divorce, it's—it's a nightmare. It just is. That's what it is. And you pretend that you're fine and there's days when you're great and there's days when you're not great and I'm kind of in a position now where I have to sit in front of people and answer questions about my life that I never thought I'd be doing."

Nodding sympathetically at each comment, her eyes searching Nicole's face for the slightest sign of emotion, Oprah was her customary consoling self; she did everything but reach out and give Nicole an enormous hug. But, every once in a while, a light would go off somewhere in her consciousness and she would perk up with a question that made Nicole squirm. Out of the blue, she asked the actress: "Do you wish you would get back together?" To which, Nicole, her frantic eyes darting, said, "Shush—Oprah!"

Next up for Nicole was the *Moulin Rouge* roller coaster. On April 18, 2001, she attended a celebrity-packed screening of the film in New York. She was scheduled to participate in additional screenings and press conferences, but the studio canceled them because of the continuing media frenzy over her miscarriage and divorce, which studio executives felt might detract from coverage of the film.

Instead, it was decided to use the film's screening at the Cannes Film Festival on May 9 to kick off the film's media campaign. Surely, by that time, the executives reasoned, Nicole's divorce would be old news.

What *was* making headlines, besides the divorce, were charges made by Nicole's lawyers that a forty-year-old man named Matthew Hooker was stalking her. In papers filed in Los Angeles Superior Court, Nicole alleged that the man had "come to [her] home on numerous occasions" and "threatened to commit acts of violence." It was also charged that the man had posted a message for Nicole on his Web site that accused her publicists and managers of "sabotaging any chance we have of being close."

Nicole's petition further stated that Hooker had showed up at her gated home and tried to lure her out to go to the ballet with him and to take her children to get ice cream. According to the New York *Daily News*, Hooker told her staff that she was "playing hard to get." After he had a run-in with Nicole's security guards, the police were called, causing one officer to proclaim Hooker "mentally unstable."

The *Daily News* further claimed that Hooker had stalked supermodel Claudia Schiffer in April 2000 at her home on the island of Mallorca. According to the newspaper, he was picked up by police after Schiffer said the man was not welcome at her home.

When Hooker was brought before a judge in the Kidman case, he denied being a stalker. He was merely in love with Nicole, he explained. He admitted going to her home to ask her to attend the ballet with him. He admitted asking if he could take her children out to get ice cream. He admitted writing her love poems. But he denied ever stalking the actress.

After the court hearing, at which Nicole won a temporary restraining order,

Hooker told reporters he had no idea why Nicole had told "lies" about him. All he had done, he insisted, was ask her out on a date. "All I know is, I've never been violent—I've never been angry—I've never harassed anyone," he said. "I tried to meet a woman and date a woman and that's all."

Not impressed by Hooker's explanation was the judge, who ordered him to stay at least two hundred and fifty yards away from Nicole, her children, their homes, work, and schools for a period of three years.

In early May, before going to Cannes for the festival, Nicole and director Baz Luhrmann huddled in a small windowless office on the Twentieth Century–Fox lot, where he was still hard at work editing the film. "Let's be honest here," Luhrmann told Nicole, according to the *New York Times*. "It won't be the most gorgeous print in Christendom, but it'll play." To which she responded, "At least you'll have something to show. Ewan and I have been joking that if it's not ready, we're going to have to get up and do some of the scenes and sing a few of the songs—do a medley."

The film was roundly praised after its New York screening, but Luhrmann still felt insecure about it, which was why he continued to tinker with it. Rumors circulated around Hollywood that Fox executives felt the film was too edgy for a mainstream audience and, after spending approximately $50 million on the film, they wanted something that would cruise with ease into Middle America.

Luhrmann did not impress the *New York Times* writer as being especially optimistic—or perhaps, the writer wondered, his subdued manner could be attributed to a lack of sleep, for it was clear he had not slept in a long time. Luhrmann was glum and compared the experience of editing the film to facing the gallows. Nicole was not much more optimistic, telling the writer, "If this doesn't work, nobody will want to touch me."

All that doom and gloom disappeared once they arrived in Cannes. Nicole was the toast of the city as reporters clamored to get close to her. Luhrmann noted, with just a hint of resentment, that the only comment he made that was picked up by the twenty-five or so television cameras there to cover the event was his observations that "Nicole is very strong." None of the other statements he made about the movie was ever aired.

There was a reason for all the media attention around Nicole, of course.

Her life, with all its Hollywood nuances of power and romance, was more in-teresting that any movie scheduled to be shown at the festival. Right before she made her first appearance outside the Palais, she gave her emotions a tight pinch as she walked up the stairs. She reminded herself to enjoy the moment.

As soon as she stepped into view, wearing a black gown slit up the front, with a bow on her left hip, shouts of "Nee-cole! Nee-cole!" rose from the crowd of ten thousand, their excitement creating a wave of sorts. She got so caught up in the excitement that she broke away from Luhrmann and rushed toward the fans who were barricaded behind the stands. She blew kisses and she signed autographs, then pressed even deeper into the crowd, reveling in its embrace. After a few moments of that, she turned and rushed back to the red staircase, pausing at the top to wave to her fans.

Observing her at the festival was *Vanity Fair* writer Dominick Dunne, who noted that the media asked her more questions about Tom than about *Moulin Rouge*. "She looked so beautiful," he later wrote. "It's very difficult for a pub-lic person to have to talk about the intimacies of her life while she's plugging a movie, going to premieres, waving to the crowds, calling home to the kids—and doing all these things well. That's what a star is all about, and hats off to her."

At a press conference, during which McGregor sat next to her and shared a cigarette with her, Nicole said she had developed an "emotional adoration" for her costar during production, especially when he sang to her. Singing about love, she giggled, made it easier to play the love on-screen because it "extends" the emotions: "It lets you get lost in it, particularly when Ewan sang Elton John's 'Your Song,' I must have heard it six hundred times, but every time he did it, it still evoked an immediate emotional adoration of him."

Asked by reporters if her marital problems made it difficult to promote the film, she said, "Obviously this would not be my choice . . . to sit in front of everyone and have questions about my personal life, but I do feel really proud of this film."

After *Moulin Rouge* was presented at the festival—it was one of twenty-three selected for the honor—Nicole and Ewan McGregor were asked to sing a song or two from the film, but they laughingly declined each request, citing a pledge to each other never to let that happen, "no matter how drunk any-one was."

Despite mixed reviews of the film at the festival, Nicole left Cannes convinced they might have a hit on their hands. Exhausted by all the publicity demands, she went home to Sydney to be with her family. There at the airport to greet her private jet was her mother, Janelle, who lovingly planted a kiss on her cheek.

"My mama," Nicole intoned to a reporter for the *Sydney Morning Herald*, her soft voice on the verge of tears. "She gave me the best advice just by who she is. She's seen herself through many tough times. She's a proud woman. I think you hold your head up and you move forward—and every day is another day."

Later, she told an Australian magazine writer that she was just happy to be home where she could curl up in her own bed.

After less than a week's rest and relaxation at her parents' home—her only diversion was a *Moulin Rouge* homecoming premiere and party which drew nearly three thousand guests—Nicole left Sydney to start work on a new film, *The Hours*, which was set to be shot in New York, London, and Fort Lauderdale, Florida.

Directed by British-born director Stephen Daldry, best known for *Billy Elliot*, the film is based on the best-selling novel by Michael Cunningham. Nicole was asked to play the part of literary lesbian Virginia Woolf.

It was exactly the type of role she relished. Not only would she get to play a lesbian, she would be thrust into the world of literary feminism, familiar territory she was fond of exploring with her feminist mother. Nicole also was pleased to share the spotlight with two actresses for whom she had great respect, Meryl Streep and Julianne Moore.

For her role, Nicole used a prosthetic nose and spoke in a deep, rough-edged British accent. It made her practically unrecognizable. Later, when the film was shown to test audiences, several people approached the director and, with a disappointed tone in their voices, told him that they thought that Nicole was supposed to be in the film.

"I think whenever you play somebody, it's not about imitating them," she subsequently explained to *Interview*. "It's about finding their essence, trying to embody them in a certain way...With Virginia, it was smoking those hand-rolled cigarettes. And there was a hankie I carried in my pocket. I don't know why, but this hankie in the pocket of the dress, this sort of housedress, did it. Everyone would look at my face and say, 'You look so different.' But it wasn't the make-up that did it for me; it was the smoking and that handkerchief. Then I changed the way I walked, and suddenly, Virginia was alive."

Nicole did not mind altering her face and her elegant demeanor to play the part, but, to the surprise of everyone associated with the movie, she dug her heels in and refused to do a nude scene. Why would an actress who had disrobed in most of her films, who had stood, night after night, totally naked on stages in New York and London, suddenly decide that nudity was out of the question?

She never explained, but certainly the trauma associated with her divorce would have figured into the equation. Apparently, director Stephen Daldry did not press the issue. Instead, he arranged for a wetsuit manufacturer to custom-make a skintight, skin-colored suit for Nicole that made it appear that she was totally naked. Sometimes Nicole could be devilishly inscrutable—and the nudity issue was one such time.

Before leaving Sydney, Nicole explained to reporters that it was her intention to avoid the mainstream when choosing new films, preferring instead to focus on what she termed "risky projects"—you know, the type of films that Tom shied away from.

Meanwhile, as Nicole set her sights on a new project, *Moulin Rouge* was released to mixed reviews in the United States. *New York Times* critic Elvis Mitchell wrote: "What Mr. Luhrmann has done is take the most thrilling moments in a movie musical—the seconds before the actors are about to burst into song and dance, when every breath they take is heightened—and made an entire picture of such pinnacles. As a result, every moment in the film feels italicized rather than tumescent... This movie is simultaneously stirring and dispiriting."

*Premiere* magazine gave it three and a half out of a possible four stars and declared: "The sweet-voiced Kidman has never been sexier, McGregor could quite creditably sub for Bono if the U2 front man's voice craps out and Broadbent can sell the unlikeliest song imaginable—at one point in the movie, he croons 'Like a Virgin' and actually makes you like it. *Moulin Rouge* is surely the most daring summer movie of the year—it will no doubt be the most daring movie of any season this year."

Writing in the *Los Angeles Times*, Kenneth Turan noted: "Although it showcases excellent work from costars Nicole Kidman and Ewan McGregor as singing star-crossed lovers in turn-of-the-century Paris, *Moulin Rouge* is a film that can't escape the defects of its virtues. Over the top in all things, it's unwilling to differentiate between the delights of being cinematically outrageous and the drawbacks of having a plot that's as simplistic dramatically as the film is complex visually, of characterizations that verges on cartoonish, especially in the minor roles, and of a weakness for the broadest, most exaggerated farce."

The consensus seemed to be that while the film was visually vibrant and grandly decadent, it underplayed the talents of both Nicole and McGregor—and never found its true heart and soul. The big question was whether academy members would deem it powerful or special enough to snag an Oscar.

By the time American moviegoers were queuing up to see *Moulin Rouge*, Nicole was transforming herself into Virginia Woolf and thinking about what she would tell reporters about her next movie, *The Others*. It was a rhythm that seemed to suit her, for it meant that there was always something going on, professionally at least, in her life. She couldn't tolerate "down" time, not when her emotions were dancing so carelessly along the edge of the abyss.

Divorce negotiations did not go as smoothly as she had hoped. She and Tom seemed to be in agreement about the children, but when it came to finances she found him difficult to deal with. Their lawyers huddled, worked out compromises, only to learn that they had compromised away exactly what each partner wanted most.

By June, Tom had his lawyers working double time when he discovered that a Los Angeles man, Michael Davis, was contacting magazines and offering to sell them a secret videotape of Tom having sex with a man. Tom responded with a $100 million defamation lawsuit that claimed that the media pitches by Davis, publisher of *Bold* magazine, were "of the sort calculated to cause [Tom] harm both personally and professionally." Legal documents filed by Tom's attorneys denied that the actor had ever had a homosexual relationship and that such a videotape existed. Such allegations, the court documents asserted, were "unequivocally false."

Tom subsequently dropped the lawsuit after the publisher agreed to a court stipulation that read: "Cruise does not appear on the videotape to which said defendant referred...[He] is not, and never has been, homosexual and has never had a homosexual affair." Under the terms of the settlement, the publisher was required to pay his own legal fees and was prohibited from "issuing or authorizing the issuance of any statement contrary to any of the foregoing findings."

In an unrelated lawsuit, Tom sued porn actor Chad Slater, who was quoted in the French magazine *Actustar* as saying he had a continuing homosexual relationship with Tom during the actor's marriage and that the relationship was discovered by Nicole, who ended the relationship. Tom asked for $100 million in damages. The case never went to trial because the porn actor denied ever making the comments and the magazine agreed to print a retraction. Tom won a $10 million default judgment.

As Tom's July 3 birthday approached, word leaked out that he was planning a big party, one at which he might introduce his new sweetheart, Penelope Cruz. According to news reports, Nicole asked their mutual friends not to attend as a sign of loyalty to her. Some of her friends honored her request, but Tom's longtime friends Emilio Estevez, Rob Lowe, Ben Stiller, and Cuba Gooding, Jr., showed up, along with new friends such as Renee Zellweger and Jim Carrey, who roared up to the door on his Harley-Davidson.

In the days following the party, Tom's publicist confirmed that Tom and Penelope were indeed dating. Nicole heard that bit of news on television, as did their son, six-year-old Connor, and it made her furious. She told friends that she suspected the romance had been going on for quite some time. In the weeks ahead, as publicity about the Cruise-Cruz romance intensified, both Connor and Bella urged Nicole to get a few dates of her own, advice she said she did not take.

In mid-July, Nicole took the children and went to Fiji on her private jet for a vacation. She and Tom had planned the two-week vacation long before their marital separation took place, so they divided the vacation time, with her taking a week and him taking a week. Shortly after Nicole arrived at the exclusive island retreat, longtime friend Russell Crowe was seen arriving at the airport in his private jet. There had been rumors about Nicole and Russell for years, so no one was surprised to see him arrive in her wake.

When Nicole concluded her vacation on the island, she left on a Saturday. The following day Tom arrived with a party of ten, including Cameron Crowe, who directed him in *Jerry Maguire* and his upcoming *Vanilla Sky*, and Crowe's wife, singer Nancy Wilson. Penelope was thought to be included, though Tom's publicist declined to confirm it, saying only she "might be there."

New light was cast on the Cruise-Cruz relationship, when a *Vanity Fair* profile of the actress quoted Cameron Crowe as saying that Penelope possessed a rare quality that enabled audiences to fall in love with her. In describing the on-screen romance between Tom and Penelope, Crowe said: "In this movie we really had to have this intense love story. So Penelope has to truly fall in love. And Tom falls in love with her. They did the rarest thing: they fell in love with someone on-screen. You watch them actually go through that hideous, great, awful, intoxicating moment. Without it, we wouldn't have a movie... The first time we screened the movie—just in-house—it was that situation where at the end you get that reaction of 'Wow! They were really in love!'"

For her part, Penelope handled the stories about her romance with Tom with admirable skill, batting her pretty eyes and slipping deeper into her Spanish accent whenever the questions became too personal. Her stock answer: "It's not true—we're friends." Certainly, fielding such questions was something with which she had experience. Before meeting Tom, she was rumored to have had affairs with Nicolas Cage and Matt Damon. Interestingly, all three men ending longtime relationships—Tom with Nicole, Cage with his wife, Patricia Arquette, and Damon with girlfriend Winona Ryder—after meeting the doe-eyed actress.

Throughout the summer, rumors swirled about Nicole and Tom as their "friends" and employees—the couple had long required employees to sign agreements that required them to pay huge fines if they ever disclosed information to the media—disclosed tantalizing new information about the marriage.

One week, Nicole was painted as an ice queen who had contributed little to the marriage; Tom was depicted as the partner who held everything together and saw that the children were cared for. The next week, Tom was painted as a lout who had gotten his wife pregnant, and then dumped her for Penelope Cruz. If Gallup had taken an opinion poll on the couple, the pollsters would probably have found that the public was evenly divided over who was the cheater in the marriage.

Nicole kept saying that she had no idea why Tom was divorcing her—"What the hell happened?" was her constant refrain—and Tom kept saying that Nicole knew "exactly" why he had filed for divorce. When pressed by reporters, Nicole sometimes said she would probably never tell her side of the story.

Despite their personal difficulties, the couple presented a united front when it came to their business interests. On August 7, 2001, they both attended the premiere of her new movie, *The Others*, although not together. Nicole arrived with director Alejandro Amenabar and two of her close friends, actresses Naomi Watts and Rebecca Rigg.

As she walked up the red carpet outside the screening room, a crowd outside chanted what others had chanted in Cannes: "Nee-cole! Nee-cole!" Wearing a black dress flecked with silver, her hair pulled back into a ponytail, she paused to sign autographs and shake hands with well-wishers before disappearing into the theater.

Fifteen or twenty minutes later, in a well-choreographed move, Tom arrived, wearing black slacks and a white shirt, sleeves rolled up to the elbow. Asked by a reporter how he dealt with the publicity surrounding the divorce, he laughed and said he simply told everyone to mind their own business. He said no one should be surprised that he and Nicole both attended the premiere. "Tonight is a celebration of a picture that we all worked very hard on, and the performance that Nic has given is flawless," he told an Associated Press reporter. With that, he moved quickly into the theater and sat down without saying a word to Nicole.

As always with Nicole's movies, reviews were mixed. *Newsweek*'s Owen Gleiberman wrote that the film featured Nicole at her "icy best," but then he went on to say, "The gimmicks, in the end, are too arbitrary to tie together in a memorably haunting fashion, though they do culminate in a Big Twist, a nifty one that almost—but not quite—makes you want to see the movie again."

Writing in the *Los Angeles Times*, Kenneth Turan described Nicole's performance as "diva-style," delivered as if she were Lady Macbeth. "Though Kidman doesn't hesitate to make Grace high-strung and as tightly wound as they come, she also projects vulnerability and courage when they're called for," he noted. "It's an intense, involving performance, and it dominates and energizes a film that would be lost without it."

Wesley Morris writing in the *San Francisco Chronicle*, said, "Clever as the film is, though, it turns out to be an exercise in narrative withholding that's more headache provoking than suspense laden." He said the real star of the film was not Nicole, but rather her skin: "Has it ever been paler or clammier-looking?"

\* \* \*

On August 7, 2001, one day after Nicole and Tom attended the premiere of *The Others*, the court finalized their divorce and gave them additional time to work out a property settlement. Over the next three months, they met several times in the presence of their lawyers in an effort to iron out the details.

Finally, on November 12, they met one last time in a Los Angeles office building. The couple arrived separately, with Nicole wearing a blue suit and scarf, and Tom wearing a black T-shirt and black slacks. For three hours, they pored over the details of a settlement that divided up their $250 million combined estate.

Nicole took their $4.3 million home in Pacific Palisades and their $4 million Sydney Harbour mansion, while Tom took their 280-acre estate in Telluride, Colorado, and their fleet of airplanes, which included a Beech F90, $100,000 Pitts S-2B, and a $28 million Gulfstream IV jet. Tom agreed on alimony and child support, but the amount was sealed under court order.

The couple agreed on joint legal and physical custody of the children. Under the agreement, the children will live alternately with both parents and—this was important to Nicole—make joint decisions about their lives and religious upbringing. By this stage in the divorce, Nicole was expressing fears to friends that Tom would want to raise the children as Scientologists, something she did not want. She fought for the right to educate them in private schools in Sydney and with private tutors when they were in Los Angeles or on location with either parent.

Nicole and Tom signed the papers before leaving the office that evening and then, avoiding the awkwardness of a handshake, embraced as the friends they once were. "Nicole is relieved that everything is finally over," a friend told *Newsweek*, "and that she and Tom will have some kind of amicable relationship."

Most experts considered the final agreement a victory for Nicole, but since the nonproperty aspects of the settlement were sealed, it is not known how she fared with alimony or child support, or with other aspects of their wealth such as cash, stocks and bonds, and investment properties.

After wrapping up the agreement, Nicole said good-bye to Bella and Connor—it was Tom's turn to have them with him for the remainder of the month at the $45,000-a-month Tudor-style mansion he rented in Beverly Hills—and flew to Sydney to be with her mother and sister, with whom she had invested in a chain of manicure salons.

In an interview with Liz Smith for *Good Housekeeping*, Nicole was asked if she had given any thought to dating again. "No, but everyone keeps telling me I have to," she answered. "Everyone keeps telling me I have to start dating, and I keep saying, 'You've got to be kidding.'"

Smith, sympathetic to her plight, suggested that dating was a horrible concept. "At this moment, it's not horrible," said Nicole. "I look forward to it. I hope that one day I can fall in love again. I mean, I still am a romantic, and I still believe in love. But in terms of right now, I don't have anything to give. That's not fair, to enter into something with somebody when I don't have enough to give them."

Nicole returned to Sydney in early November and appeared on a local television show hosted by Ray Martin. Perhaps lobbying for Nicole to have a romance with Russell Crowe, Martin played a video clip for her of an interview he had done with Crowe.

Said Martin: "There was a quote, in which you said, 'She's not just the most beautiful woman in Hollywood, but the most beautiful woman in the universe.'"

"Did I?" asked Crowe. "Did I say that? If she's watching, yes. Of course I say that about Nicky just about every day."

After seeing the clip, Nicole said, "Now, you've got to ask me about him. Is he the most beautiful man..."

"Is he?" asked Martin.

Nicole laughed. "If he's watching, absolutely!"

Nicole ended 2001 with an unexpected honor. She was chosen "Entertainer of the Year" by *Entertainment Weekly*. "In case anyone missed it—and given her string of provocative, nuanced performances in movies like *To Die For, Portrait of a Lady*, and *Eyes Wide Shut*, we should have been more alert—Kidman has become one of the more interesting actors working in movies," declared the magazine, which rated her above the actors in *Sex and the City*, *The Producers*, singer Alicia Keys, and talk show host Bill O'Reilly. "This year, she gave a pair of performances so fearless and assured that even if she had not owned a half share in the year's most headline-making celebrity split, the 'Mrs. Tom Cruise' label would have been banished permanently."

Not everyone was happy with the magazine's selection. Marilyn Beck and Stacy Jenel Smith, who write the daily "Ask Marilyn" column on *E! Online* took exception to the honor. "Oh, gag us with a spoon—or whatever," they wrote. "The fact that her marriage to Tom Cruise bit the dust is a shame, but the only things that differentiate her from millions of other divorced women is that she'll never have to worry about supporting her children...but we don't see why she should be singled out as a woman of the year for 'making it on her own.'"

"Was it a good year?" Nicole wondered aloud in response to the honor. "It was an interesting year. A strange year. A cathartic year. Creatively, it was very fulfilling, but there were some pretty dark times. If everything had fallen apart—if *Moulin Rouge* and *The Others* had tanked—that would have been too many blows. But somebody was looking out for me."

# CHAPTER TEN

# Heels'-Eye View:
# Life Without Tom

Nicole began 2002 by reading a cover story article about Tom in *Vanity Fair*. In the story, entitled "The Naked Truth," by Evgenia Peretz, the actor once again answered questions about the divorce. "[Nicole] knows why, and I know why," Tom said. "She's the mother of my children, and I wish her well. And I think that you just move on. And I don't say that lightly. I don't say that with anything. Things happen in life, and you do everything you can, and in every possible way, and there's a point at which you just sometimes have to face the brutal reality."

Told by Peretz that his answer would only pique people's curiosity, Tom responded, "I don't care if it piques people's interest. Honestly, people should mind their own damn business. And get a life of their own . . . My personal life isn't here to sell newspapers."

Tom disclosed that he kept in touch with his children by telephone and by satellite television. When they were with him, he said, he used an elaborate chart system, which, in keeping with Scientology doctrine, established a point system of duties and rewards, along with a dialogue about helping each other. If he asks them how they think they can help him—and they say they don't know—he suggests that they can clean up their rooms or put up their plates after meals.

Tom went on to talk about how he and Penelope had enjoyed the company of the children at his home in Telluride. "She's beautiful," he told Peretz.

"She's a very skilled actress, but has an effortless quality about her. You look at Audrey Hepburn. She had that kind of elegance and yet was accessible."

Nicole did not mind him talking about their divorce—he had his opinions and she had hers—nor did she mind him discussing his point system for disciplining the children (it wasn't the way she did it, but she could hardly argue against it), but there was something about him lumping the children in with his and Penelope's activities that annoyed her. Most divorced women feel a certain amount of discomfort when their children are exposed to the father's new love interest and Nicole was no exception.

*Vanity Fair* wrote about *her* children as if she were no longer in the picture. Just when she thought the nightmare that was 2001 was over, new issues arose to aggravate old wounds. Always prone to sudden changes in her health during times of emotional upheaval, Nicole was stunned to learn from her doctor, after a routine office visit, that her Pap smear had come back positive for possible cervical cancer.

According to press reports, a follow-up biopsy came back negative for cancer, but doctors cautioned her that such results can be wrong. She was urged to undergo another test in several months to be certain. The *Star* reported that she was "freaked out" by the news, prompting a friend to say, "She's been praying that everything's okay, but she can't get the fear that she has cancer out of her mind."

The cancer scare proved to be groundless, but it did take its toll on Nicole, leaving her emotionally and perhaps even spiritually bruised and battered by the experience. Because of what had happened to Janelle, *cancer* was the most menacing word in the Kidman vocabulary.

Following on the heels of the cancer scare, Nicole had a fight with Tom, after which, according to news reports, she was taken to the University of California at Los Angeles Medical Center, where she received emergency treatment for what was diagnosed as a panic attack. Witnesses said she was shaking and sobbing, nearly out of control.

Even though she continued to live in a whirlwind of emotions, Nicole pulled herself together and faced the tasks at hand, the most pressing of which was work on a new project, *Dogville*. Written and directed by Lars von Trier, the film was set in an American town in the Rocky Mountains in the 1930s, but it was shot entirely in a studio in Sweden, where the actors all lived in a hotel and dined dormitory style together. To Nicole's delight, she costarred with screen legend Lauren Bacall, James Caan, Blair Brown, and Chloe Sevigny.

With the Golden Globe Awards scheduled for January 20, 2002, she took a week off from shooting *Dogville* to fly to America to attend both that ceremony and the Sundance Film Festival in Park City, Utah, where *Birthday Girl* was set to receive its first screening. The film had been on the shelf for nearly a year and a half, so she was understandably anxious about how it would be received by critics.

At the pre-screening party, she was in the process of challenging a reporter to come closer to smell her pesto breath, when someone rudely stepped between them with a "Sorry, mate" dismissal to the reporter. It was Russell Crowe, who had come to the festival to attend the screening of his documentary entitled *Texas*.

With the reporter sent packing, Crowe planted a big kiss on Nicole's mouth in front of everyone and wrapped his arms around her in a tight embrace as a studio photographer snapped a picture of the two Aussies enjoying each other's company.

The two actors had been friends since the early 1990s. Indeed, some people have interpreted Nicole's famous "sexy hands" comment about guitar players as being traceable back to Russell Crowe. When he heard about her separation from Tom, he was among the first to offer his shoulder for her to cry on.

After leaving Utah, Nicole went to Los Angeles, where the night before the Golden Globe Awards, she was a guest on the *Tonight Show with Jay Leno*. Wearing jeans and a low-cut white blouse beneath a gold jacket, she appeared radiant and a little bit jittery. She wore her hair pulled back, an unfortunate decision because it highlighted her darting eyes.

Since she was nominated for best actress in a comedy or musical for her role in *Moulin Rouge*—and for best actress in a drama for her role in *The Others*—Leno asked her if she preferred one film over the other. She laughed and said she could not pick a favorite. When she learned she had two nominations—a distinct rarity—she said she thought, "I really have to appreciate this because this will never happen again and it's one of those things were you go, 'Wow!'"

What she really wanted to talk about was Sweden, which she found—at minus twenty degrees—to be such a "serious" environment. Inexplicably,

Nicole shifted the conversation to the topic of trolls. She explained that the part of Sweden where she was filming was famous for inventing the troll doll. "We went shopping for the trolls 'cause I wanted to get trolls for my kids, and they all have—it was so strange—they all have genitalia," she exclaimed. "They do! We went into this store. It's weird." She went on describe one troll as having a "huge red penis."

The following night, wearing a black strapless gown that was slit up to her upper thigh, Nicole arrived at the Golden Globes with her father and mother. Before going into the hotel, she introduced her father and mother to a television interviewer and confessed that she was "very nervous" about the event.

Antony was asked if he was proud of his daughter. "Very proud indeed," he said. "We're hoping for a good result tonight."

Inside the hotel, when the award was announced for best actress in a drama, Nicole lost to Sissy Spacek for her performance in *In the Bedroom*. Nicole's luck changed when actor Michael Caine came onstage to present the award for best actress in a musical or comedy. There were five nominations: Thora Birch for *Ghost World*, Cate Blanchett for *Bandits*, Reese Witherspoon for *Legally Blonde*, Renee Zellweger for *Bridget Jones's Diary*, and, of course, Nicole Kidman for *Moulin Rouge*.

When Caine called out Nicole's name, she energetically bounded to the stage. Taking the award from Caine, she said: "Wow! Thank you, Hollywood Foreign Press." Then she acknowledged that her hands were shaking. "This is really, really special," she continued, "because I never thought I would be in a musical, let alone win an award for one. So I have to thank for that Mr. Baz Luhrmann. He believed I could do it. He's innovative and a visionary and his partner Katherine Martin, they're such a powerful creative force and I'm proud to say they are my friends. There is another man I would never have done this without—and that is Ewan McGregor. He's so special. A magnificent person, a magnificent actor and he just makes you better being in a scene with you."

Later in the evening the nominations were announced for best film (musical or comedy). Named were *Bridget Jones's Diary*, *Gosford Park*, *Legally Blonde*, *Shrek*, and *Moulin Rouge*. To no one's surprise, *Moulin Rouge* was declared the winner, vindicating the grand vision of Baz Luhrmann, who went onstage to accept the award.

Backstage, the show's producer, Dick Clark, asked Nicole if she was really all that nervous, to which Nicole responded, "My teeth are chattering." He probably thought she was kidding, but she wasn't. She went on to say that she and Russell Crowe, who was nominated for his role in *Beautiful Mind* (he didn't win), wanted the award committee to seat all the Australian nominees at one table. "But they wouldn't allow us," she said. "Thought we'd be too rowdy."

Nicole and Luhrmann were ebullient over their two awards, for it was the first recognition they had received for *Moulin Rouge*. Besides the obvious benefit of winning the awards, there was the possibility that that they were a precursor to the Academy Awards scheduled for presentation in March. Historically, the Golden Globes have been somewhat accurate indicators of how academy members cast their votes.

Nicole returned to the *Dogville* set, floating on a cloud back to Sweden.

Seemingly following her back to Sweden were a contingent of tabloid reporters and photographers, eager to eavesdrop on her new life without Tom. One evening, they caught her having an "intimate dinner" with Jonas Ohlsson, a twenty-two-year-old production assistant, but when they attempted to take a photograph, the two separated, only to meet up again at Nicole's chauffeur-driven car.

Back on the set of *Dogville* the next day, Nicole resumed the persona of Grace, a woman on the run. Director Lars von Trier based the story on the song "Pirate Jenny" from *The Threepenny Opera* by Bertolt Brecht, which is about a servant girl, a newcomer to a village where she is treated as an outsider, only to become the only survivor of an attack against the town. Von Trier wrote the part with Nicole in mind after he received word that she wanted to be in one of his films. He was surprised by her acceptance of the role, because *Dogville*, which is about as character-driven as a story can become, is closer to being an art-house film than a Hollywood blockbuster.

Nicole had no sooner returned to Sweden than reviews of *Birthday Girl* began surfacing. To her disappointment, the critics were not dazzled. Wrote Joe Leydon of the *San Francisco Examiner*: "Nicole Kidman is radiantly beautiful, even while dressed in frumpy Russian frocks and wearing enough eye shadow to suggest an unusually sexy racoon... *Birthday Girl* may be intended as a romantic thriller, but it is sorely lacking in romance and thrills. It's the closest thing to a totally useless movie that you'll find at megaplexes this weekend."

The *New York Times* critic Elvis Mitchell was impressed by Nicole's "high-hurdle sprinter's figure," but found the plot insubstantial: "By the end, all *Birthday Girl* does is toss off a few sparks. It doesn't generate enough down-and-dirty firepower to burst into flames."

The *Sydney Morning Herald* was more encouraging. Commenting on the criticism that Nicole seldom seems to connect emotionally with her male leads, critic Paul Byrnes found her on-screen relationship with Chaplin refreshing: "The tagline would have echoed that famous earlier one, 'Garbo talks.' As in 'Kidman loves!' She gets to show a tenderness we've rarely seen, but it's combined with the comic skills we saw in *To Die For*. It's a great part and a great performance."

It wasn't the reception she had hoped for the film, but she didn't let it get her down. What was weighing on her more heavily was the fact that for the first time since her marriage to Tom, she was going to be spending Valentine's Day alone.

Ever since their reunion at the Sundance festival, Russell Crowe had called her almost every day. When he realized how despondent she was about spending Valentine's Day alone, he flew to Sweden on his private jet to be with her. They had champagne and caviar dinner at the hotel, according to the manager—and then Crowe flew to London, where he met his Australian girlfriend, Danielle Spencer, so that they could attend the British Academy Awards (BAFTA) together.

Nicole also went to the awards show, arriving alone. She sat at the table next to where Crowe and his date were seated, and when Danielle got up to go to the bathroom, Nicole scooted over into her seat. When Danielle returned, she saw Nicole in her seat and Crowe's arm wrapped around her, so she took an even better seat—on Crowe's lap.

*Dogville* was wrapped in plenty of time for Nicole to return to Los Angeles for the Academy Awards ceremony on March 24, 2002. Nicole was nominated for an Oscar in the best actress category for her role in *Moulin Rouge*, but, unlike the Golden Globes, which saw her nominated for both *Moulin Rouge* and *The Others*, the Academy Awards nominating committee overlooked the latter film. *Moulin Rouge* was also nominated in the best picture category and six additional minor categories, though Baz Luhrmann did not make the director's list.

The week before the awards ceremony, Nicole made her obligatory visit to *The Tonight Show with Jay Leno*. Wearing a tight-fitting black dress, she walked out onto the stage to a standing ovation, which seemed to make her even more nervous. She longs for public adoration, yet when she receives it, it always makes her feel uncomfortable, as if she doesn't really deserve it.

Nicole talked about *Moulin Rouge*, about how Luhrmann first approached her to discuss the role—and later in the show Luhrmann joined her onstage to talk about the film from his vantage point—but the highlight of the interview was her revelation about her family's penchant for gambling. She explained that she had just returned from a movie distributors' exhibition in Las Vegas, where she had had a good time at the gaming tables.

Leno asked her if she lost big money, to which she responded, "No, not very much. I'm actually like a little old woman when I gamble. I sit there and I put my glasses on and I watch the cards and I hate for anybody to talk to me. So, I'm not a lot of fun—and I have a limit and as soon as I hit the limit, you have to walk away. That's how you win when you gamble. Yes, because gambling can be an addiction, so if you don't allow it to be an addiction, you can actually win at it."

Nicole went on to explain that she was careful about gambling because members of her family had found it addictive. "I've been warned that I may have it in my blood—so I'm fighting it."

The Leno interview confirmed what was becoming increasingly apparent—namely, that despite her great beauty and charm, she was ill at ease in social situations. She performed well when she did question-and-answer interviews that focused on her movie projects, but when it came to chitchat she had a difficult time keeping the conversation flowing with inane batter, the mainstay of all social interactions.

When placed in social situations, such as free-ranging television interviews, she tended to use hot-button topics such as gambling addiction or trolls with big penises to attract attention. That was the biggest change in her life, not having Tom at her side to glide her through anxiety-provoking situations.

On the night of the Oscars, that became even more apparent when she and actress Renee Zellweger, an adoring Tom Cruise supporter, were corralled by a television interviewer outside the Kodak Theatre, the new, 3,300-seat home of the Oscars.

When asked if they were sweating in their "fabulous dresses," Nicole committed a Hollywood gaffe and glanced down at her armpits (she had on a bare-shoulder pink gown) and answered that she was indeed sweating.

Nicole seemed very nervous and ill at ease, as if she might explode into a full-blown panic attack, the realization of which probably promoted the interviewer to address the remainder of his questions to a radiant Zellweger. It was a scenario that made Nicole's supporters cringe, for she seemed jittery and in a near panic as she watched Zellweger finish the interview.

Inside the theater, Nicole settled down amid the elegant cherry wood moldings and the walls lined with ornate opera boxes. She felt safe in the auditorium, where reporters could not rush her seat and ask her unwanted questions. Within seconds of sitting down, she was again glowing with regal self-confidence.

Though she never let her smile drop, it turned out to be a disappointing night for both her and Luhrmann. In the best picture category, *Moulin Rouge* lost to director Ron Howard's *A Beautiful Mind* (Howard also won for best director) and Nicole lost to Halle Berry for her role in *Monster's Ball*.

Nicole kept smiling when presenter Russell Crowe gave the award to Berry, but she must have felt humiliated when Berry turned what was supposed to be a brief moment of glory into an emotional, second-dragging tribute to "every nameless, faceless woman of color who now has a chance [to win an Oscar]."

For *Moulin Rouge* to win no Oscars in the major categories (Luhrmann's wife, Catherine Martin, won two Oscars for costume design and art direction) was a shock to Nicole, for in the weeks leading up to the event, some writers had proclaimed her the sentimental favorite.

Reuters news service had gushed one week before the ceremony, "If life was a Hollywood movie, Nicole Kidman would crown a year of personal woes and professional triumph by walking off into the sunset with her first Oscar. And the audience would stand up and cheer because when it comes to sympathy votes, Kidman's already a winner."

The loss was a blow to Nicole, who had thought that if she ever won an Oscar it would be for *Moulin Rouge*. The news media was obviously rooting for her, as was the public, but neither had a vote in the proceedings. The

Oscars are more about money than they are about popularity, unless, of course, the popularity is accompanied with money.

Nicole could be forgiven if she thought that her poor showing at the Oscars was a product of her divorce from Tom. He was the all-American poster boy for establishment Hollywood, while she had a reputation for preferring the less glossy films produced and directed by Europeans and Australians. He made $20 million per film and she made $2 million per film. He was one of *them*, so when academy members cast their votes for Oscars, why would they express their support of his ex-wife?

The one thing Nicole could take away from the event was the satisfaction that, for the first time, she had outgrossed Tom at the box office by a wide margin. Her two 2001 films, *Moulin Rouge* and *The Others*, grossed a total of $343.6 million worldwide, compared to *Vanilla Sky*'s worldwide gross of $183.4. She had beaten Tom where it counted the most—at the box office.

Whether it was a sign of her growing emotional maturity, or another symptom of her increasingly obsessive work habits, Nicole did not spend much time grieving over not winning an Oscar—instead she jumped into another movie project.

*The Human Stain*, which was directed by Robert Benton (with whom Nicole worked on *Billy Bathgate*) is about a classics professor named Coleman Silk (played by Anthony Hopkins) who has a secret affair with a much younger woman named Faunia Farley (played by Nicole). Based on the 2000 novel of the same title by author Philip Roth, the story centers on a colleague's reconstruction of Silk's illustrious career as an educator.

For the first time since *Eyes Wide Shut*, Nicole consented to engage in raunchy, on-screen sex with Hopkins, who, at sixty-four, was nearly twice her age. The actor said that despite his age, he had no problems doing the sex scenes with Nicole. "After all, what can they do?" he told reporters, "—put me in jail!"

Most of *The Human Stain* was filmed in Canada, primarily in Montreal, so Nicole did not have to travel extensively during production. She didn't discuss the film much during production, but that was probably because she was doing nude scenes reported to be as steamy as those she did in *Eyes Wide Shut*. Why would she refuse to do nude scenes without a bodysuit in *The Hours* and then do nude scenes in *The Human Stain* and not request a bodysuit? With Nicole, one never knows.

While Nicole worked on the film, Connor and Bella stayed with Tom, who was between projects. Interviewed during that time by a reporter from *Time* magazine, he stopped the conversation to take a telephone call from the children and then knelt close to the ground and whispered into the telephone so that the reporter could not hear.

Later, asked by the reporter what he thought about a comment that Nicole made on the *Late Show with David Letterman*—she had held up her foot and told the host that she could wear heels again, eliciting loud laughter from the audience at Tom's expense—he said he wasn't offended by the comment, adding, "She always wore heels. Truly I like her in heels. That's never been a problem for me."

Tom was surprised by the question, especially since Nicole's comment had been made more than a year earlier; his divorce from Mimi had created a media buzz, but it had died down quickly. His divorce from Nicole, he now understood, was not going to simply vanish from the public eye.

From Canada, Nicole flew to New York, where she spent a couple of days with Baz Luhrmann (gossips wondered if the meeting meant that there was going to be a *Moulin Rouge II*) and visited the set of *In the Cut*, which starred Meg Ryan. Nicole was not a tourist; she was the producer of the film. Nicole had purchased the rights to the novel written by Susanna Moore six years earlier and had persuaded her longtime friend Jane Campion to be the director.

Some people were surprised that Nicole asked Ryan to star in the film, considering their mutual connection to Russell Crowe (Ryan had dated him in 2001 and Nicole was linked to him after the breakup), but Nicole thought Ryan would be perfect for the part and Ryan, best known for her flair for chick-flicks, was flattered to be asked to star in an erotic thriller. Observers said the two women got along quite well.

From New York, it was then on to Romania for Nicole, to begin work on yet another film—*Cold Mountain*, a Civil War–era film adapted from Charles Frazier's best-selling novel of the same title, to be directed and written by Anthony Minghella, the Oscar-winning director of *The English Patient*. Nicole played the role of Ada, working opposite Jude Law, Renee Zellweger, Natalie Portman, and Donald Sutherland.

Nicole arrived in Romania in early August, about a week late for production, but her tardy arrival didn't matter because the remote village where they were to begin filming was hit by heavy rains and flooding, devastating large sections of the countryside. With her were seven-year-old Connor and a small army of bodyguards and trainers. They stayed in a villa with ten other actors.

*Cold Mountain* is the story of a wounded Confederate soldier named Inman (played by Jude Law) and his attempt to return to the woman he loves, Ada. Tom Cruise was originally scheduled to play the part of Inman, but he withdrew from the project after separating from Nicole.

"I feel so privileged to be in it," Nicole told the *Sydney Morning Herald*. "Anthony Minghella is a very spiritual, very kind man, and that infiltrates his work. He's also very smart, and he's written a beautiful script. And the people have been lovely, they've really embraced the film crew, which doesn't always happen. And the locations are just glorious—although it is very hot."

When not filming in and around the village—Minghella reportedly paid local farmers about $300 per cow for the inconvenience of relocating their livestock—Nicole flew to London or Budapest until called back to production. It was on one such trip to London that she encountered Adrian Deevoy, GQ magazine's editor at large, who subsequently wrote a wildly enthusiastic article about falling in love with the actress, thus proving, once again, that the actress has a strange rapport with writers.

"As any man with a beating heart knows, when she dresses down she looks gorgeous and when she dresses up it's just off the scale," wrote Deevoy. "The first time we meet formally she is wearing an antique T-shirt, old Levis and perfectly weathered loafers. Out initial conversation is about perfume. She makes her own.

"'Here,' she smiles, offering a slender wrist for a detailed olfactory inspection. The smell is reminiscent of home-made custard and autumnal woodland, subliminally sweet and deceptively powerful. Although you're never fully aware of it, her scent can subtly fill a room."

Considering the mysterious, breathtaking effect Nicole has on writers—and the effect that muse peddlers seem to have on her—oddsmakers would be well advised to chalk up a working scribe on her potential list of suitors-to-be, especially since, for the past five years, she has been secretly trying her hand at writing. Her first project as a writer? She worked on the Meg Ryan film, *In the Cut*, with director and longtime friend Jane Campion, though she didn't ask for screen credit.

Nicole's love life was the subject of intense speculation throughout 2001 and 2002. In May 2001, while in Cannes, she was reported to be dating Italian movie producer Fabrizio Mosca, who debuted his first film, *The Hundred Steps*, at the film festival. Then, there was Adam Duritz, the lead singer of Counting Crows, followed by Tobey Maguire, the star of *Spider-Man*. Nicole and Maguire, who is eight years younger and several inches shorter, were spotted at a Brentwood restaurant cuddling over breakfast. Sometime after that she was spotted at the Beverly Hills Hotel's Polo Lounge with actor Vin Diesel.

By 2002, it was Russell Crowe who seemed to attract the most headlines as a possible suitor. In June, Nicole flew to Mexico, where Crowe was filming *Master and Commander: The Far Side of the World,* and stayed overnight at the Club Marena, where Crowe also was registered as a guest. They met again in September at Crowe's usual suite at the Hotel Bel-Air in Los Angeles, according to *US* magazine, where they enjoyed a $240 room-service lunch that lasted four hours.

The following month, fresh back from Romania, Nicole flew to Mexico to visit Crowe again. This time they were spotted at a private lounge having what the bartender described to reporters as a "romantic evening for two."

Was Nicole actually dating Crowe or Duritz or Maguire or Mosca? In each instance, her publicist denied that was the case, saying that they were merely friends, but the truth hardly mattered at that point. America wanted Nicole to be with *someone*—exactly who didn't seem to matter.

"I've had a very strange life the past three years," Nicole told *In Style* magazine. "I think I was very naïve. Over [that time period] I've had to encounter death [a reference to Stanley Kubrick's passing]. I loved Stanley. It was very tough to lose him. And then divorce. All the things you think you're never going to have to do. But, hey—other people are battling cancer, so in terms of the big picture, I go, 'Pull yourself together, Nicole.'"

Nicole was able to pull herself together by focusing on her children, allowing her mother and sister to comfort her during the really hard times, taking her psychologist father's advice—"when individuals are in the process of divorcing, they need to practice risk taking if they wish to establish new relationships; of course, you don't have to look for a new partner if you choose not to"—and, of course, by throwing herself, without mercy, some would say, into her work.

*Premiere* magazine put her career in perspective in May 2002 when it named Nicole to its "Power List 2002: The Lords of Hollywood," along with other movers and shakers such as Robert De Niro, Martin Scorsese, Cameron Crowe, and ex-husband Tom Cruise. Describing her as a "plucky divorcee," who had thawed her icy image by the very human way in which she handled her divorce, the magazine gave her credit for singing her way to the Oscars in *Moulin Rouge* and for carrying *The Others*, but it also looked to the future by noting her willingness to get raped in *Dogville* (2002), her pluck to play a janitor opposite Anthony Hopkins in *The Human Stain* (2003), and her willingness to wear a prosthetic nose as Virginia Woolf in *The Hours* (2002).

The magazine also might have credited her unmitigated gall to play a Southerner in *Cold Mountain* and her fearlessness to leap into the role of the nose-twitching witch Samantha in the film version of the popular 1960s television show, *Bewitched*.

Incredibly, as 2002 wore on, Nicole was able to reestablish a civil, sometimes surprisingly warm relationship with Tom, with the common denominator being their children. It is not uncommon for parents to become closer to their children during and immediately after divorces—and Tom and Nicole were no exception.

Nicole took new delight in sharing stories about her children, especially if the stories were risqué. She told *Rolling Stone* about riding in a chauffeur-driven car in Vienna with Bella and several other people. Without warning, Bella suddenly broadcast that "my mommy has a vagina," to which Nicole responded with a parental warning that it was not a subject she should be discussing. But before the warning sank in, Bella countered with, "It has fur on it. Some vaginas don't have fur, and some do."

The driver burst out laughing, as did Nicole and everyone else. At a time in her life when her emotional connection to Tom was being rendered, she discovered new joys and possibilities in her children. Bella, she learned, had a talent for painting. When she told the child that there might be money in painting, the little girl's eyes lit up and before Nicole knew what had happened she had produced eight paintings, all of animals. Nicole promised to have an exhibition at which she would serve lemonade and cookies.

For whatever reason, Nicole decided to start downplaying her presence in Los Angeles. In September 2002, she purchased a four-thousand-square-foot condo in Manhattan's West Village for a cool $8 million (her new neighbors are Calvin Klein and Martha Stewart) and she expressed interest in making London her permanent home. She told the British magazine *Hello* that she thought the children would be better off there, where the schools are better and the air somewhat cleaner.

"You can't go for a walk in Los Angeles," she lamented. "I will rent a house [in London] for a while and see what happens. I would like to buy somewhere in London, but I bet they put the prices up when they realize it's me."

In late 2002, Nicole severed her final link to Los Angeles by selling the Pacific Palisades home she had shared with Tom. At the time of the divorce, the house was valued at $4.3 million. Nicole received a cool $12 million for the house, proving that she did indeed have an eye for business.

Nicole underwent many changes during and after her divorce, some good and some bad, but as she emerged from those dark, pain-ladden days, she made it clear to everyone around her that though she has no intention of giving up on romance, she plans to proceed ever so slowly into that brave new world.

# Filmography

## Bush Christmas
## (a.k.a. Prince and the Great Race) (1983)

### CAST

John Ewart
John Howard
Mark Spain
James Wingrove
Peter Summer
Nicole Kidman
Manalpuy
Vineta O
Malley
Maurice Houghes
Bob Hunt

Producers: Giolda Baracchi, Paul D. Barron
Director: Henri Safran
Writer: Ted Roberts

Nicole Kidman's character is one of three children in the Thompson household. As Christmas approaches, the family learns that it will lose its farm on January 1 unless it can raise enough money to pay the mortgage. One night, as the family sleeps, thieves steal the family's prize possession, a spirited racehorse named Prince. The following morning Nicole, along with her two brothers and an aborigine named Manalpuy, sneak away from the farm to go after the horse. They undergo many adventures before they finally catch up with the horse thieves. This well-directed film provides excellent family entertainment; it is aired every Christmas on Australian television.

# BMX Bandits (1983)

## CAST

Nicole Kidman
David Argue
John Ley
Angelo D'Angelo
James Lugton
Bryan Marshall
Brian Sloman
Peter Browne
Bill Brady
Linda Newton
Bob Hicks
Guy Norris
Chris Hession

Producers: Tom Broadbridge, Paul F. Davies
Director: Brian Trenchard-Smith
Writers: Patrick Edgeworth, Russell Hagg

The BMX Bandits is a teen bicycle club. Nicole Kidman, who plays Judy, meets the bikers when the rowdy teens crash into grocery carts at the store where she works. She gets fired because of the incident and joins the biker club. Their paths cross with a gang of bank robbers when they accidentally discover a cache of high-tech radios that were meant for the robbers. They sell the radios, one at a time, as the robbers track them down. Much of the film is about the bikers' efforts to escape from the robbers. At one point, the robbers corner Nicole in a warehouse and it looks bleak for her for a moment; then she escapes and leads the robbers on a chase through the city. Nicole handles her part beautifully, but she often seems ill at ease with her body. She is taller than most of the men in the movie and her physical presence is a factor in every scene in which she appears.

## Archer's Adventure (1985)

### CAST

Nicole Kidman
Brett Climo
Ernie Gray
John Flaus
Ned Lander
Tony Barry
Paul Bertram
Robert Coleby
Anna Maria Monticelli

Producer: Moya Iceton
Director: Denny Lawrence
Writer: Anne Brooksbank

Brett Climo plays the role of a stable boy who talks his employer into letting him take one of his best horses, Archer, on a five-hundred-mile journey to enter a prestigious race in Melbourne. On his first day on the road, he is robbed of his money. On the second day, he comes across a farm, where he asks for food and lodging. He meets Nicole Kidman, who is there to visit her uncle. They become friends and then part when he resumes his journey and she goes home to her own family.

After another adventure or two, Climo meets Nicole again when his travels take him to her parents' farm. He leaves Archer in the barn so that he can attend a wedding party in the house. While he dances with Nicole, Archer breaks free and joins a herd of wild horses. Climo tracks Archer down and resumes his journey to Melbourne.

This is a good family film that capitalizes on spectacular scenery. Nicole does not have a large impact on the film, but she shows incredible poise in her scenes with Climo and that, in itself, attracts attention to her character.

# *Wills & Burke (1985)*

## CAST

Nicole Kidman
Garry McDonald
Kym Gyngell
Peter Collingwood
Jonathan Hardy
Roderick Williams
Mark Little
Roy Baldwin
Alex Menglet
Tony Rickards
Simon Thorpe

Producers: Margot McDonald, Bob Weis
Director: Bob Weis
Writer: Philip Dalkin

This is a comedy that depicts the final stretch of William Wills's and Robert Burke's crossing of the Australian outback. No one associated with the film was willing to discuss it with the author and all video copies of the film seem to have vanished.

# *Windrider (1986)*

## CAST

Nicole Kidman
Tom Burlinson

Jill Perryman
Charles "Bud" Tingwell
Simon Chilvers
Kim Bullad
Stig Wemyss
Mark Williams
Alastair Cummings
Robin Miller

Producer: Paul D. Barron
Director: Vincent Monton
Writers: Everett De Roche, Bonnie Harris

Nicole Kidman plays a strong-willed rock singer who falls for a windsurfer (Tom Burlinson) who works at his father's engineering firm. There is not much of a plot, except for a windsurfing contest, and most of the dialogue between Nicole and Burlinson is uninspiring. The movie's chief importance is related to the fact that Nicole undertakes her first nude scene at the age of nineteen (she showers with Burlinson and can be seen jumping in and out of bed a couple of times). It was also the first time Nicole attempted to create a character with a punk attitude. She wasn't entirely successful, but the energy she put into the role was admirable.

# Nightmaster (a.k.a. Watch the Shadows Dance) (1986)

## CAST

Nicole Kidman
Tom Jennings
Joanne Samuel
Vince Martin
Craig Pearce
Doug Parkinson
Jeremy Shadlow

Alexander Broun
Laurence Clifford
Paul Gleeson

Producers: Jan Tyrrell, James Michael Vernon
Director: Mark Joffe
Writer: Michael McGennan

Nicole Kidman plays a student who falls in with a group that engages in war games with paint guns. The plot revolves around a karate teacher, a crazed war veteran and cocaine addict, who kills a drug dealer. The only witness to the murder is a member of the war games group. When the karate teacher goes after the witness, everyone gets involved in the action. Nicole has no decent lines in this movie, but watching her is a treat, especially when she loosens the throttle on a very heavy Australian accent. Movie fans will find little to satisfy them in this film, but Nicole fans will enjoy watching her maneuver with energetic grace through a very bad script.

# The Bit Part (1987)

## CAST

Chris Haywood
Katrina Foster
Nicole Kidman
John Wood
Maurie Fields
Brian Mannix
Deborra-Lee Furness
Ian McFadyen
Maggie Millar
Mauren Edwards
Wilbur Wilde

Producers: Frank Brown, John Gauci, Peter Herbert, Ian Rogers, Steve Vizard

Director: Brendan Maher
Writers: Peter Herbert, Ian McFadyen

The *Bit Part* is a comedy that was released in Australia and then quickly died a painless death. No one associated with the film was willing to discuss it, a commentary all unto itself, and no video copies of the film could be located by the author for review.

# Dead Calm (1989)

## CAST

Nicole Kidman
Sam Neill
Billy Zane
Rod Mullinar
Joshua Tilden
George Shevtsov
Michael Long
Lisa Collins
Paua Hudson-Brinkley
Sharon Cook
Malinda Rutter

Producers: Terry Hayes, George Miller, Doug Mitchell
Director: Phillip Noyce
Assistant Director: Stuart Freeman
Writers: Charles Williams, Terry Hayes

Nicole Kidman plays the part of a woman who loses her young son in an automobile accident and then goes on a cruise with her husband (Sam Neill) to recover from the loss. After three weeks at sea, they spot their first ship, a schooner that looms ahead, dead in the water. As they stare at the schooner, they see a man in a dinghy rowing toward them. Played by Billy Zane, the man tells them that the ship is sinking and that all aboard are dead of food poisoning. At that point, the plot takes a wicked turn in this suspenseful psychological thriller, and Nicole, giving a flawless performance, shines as a woman who must fight to keep herself and her husband alive. This is a first-rate movie, though the ending did bother some critics who thought it was just a tad over the top.

# *Emerald City (1989)*

## CAST

Nicole Kidman
John Hargreaves
Chris Haywood
Dennis Miller
Robyn Nevin
Bruce Venable
Michelle Torres
Ella Scott
Jan Ringrose
Dar Davies

Producer: Joan Long
Director: Michael Jenkins
Writer: David Williamson

Nicole Kidman plays a woman who gets caught in a love triangle with a screenwriter and his wife (who expands it to a quadrangle when she falls for her boss). There is not much in the way of a plot in this Australian-made comedy, but Nicole did receive a nomination from the Australian Film Institute for best actress in a supporting role. The movie was released in the United States in 1992, but it quickly dropped from sight and never made it into video distribution.

# *Flirting (1991)*

## CAST

Nicole Kidman
Noah Taylor
Thandie Newton
Bartholomew Rose
Felix Nobis
Josh Picker
Kiri Paramore
Marc Gray
Gregg Palmer
Joshua Marshall
David Wieland
Craig Black
Les Hill

Producers: George Miller, Doug Mitchell, Terry Hayes
Director: John Duigan
Writer: John Duigan

This story takes place in 1965 at two exclusive private schools in Australia. Since one of the schools is for boys only and the other school is for girls only—and they are located in close proximity—it surprises no one that romances occur from time to time, especially since the schools encourage joint educational and social programs.

The plot of this coming-of-age drama centers on the character played by Noah Taylor, a somewhat nerdy white student who falls in love with a beautiful and eminently more sophisticated black student played by Thandie Newton. The interracial nature of the relationship is never a factor in the story. The dramatic tension is derived from the obstacles the two must overcome to explore their romance.

Nicole plays an older student who assumes responsibility for Newton's social development at the school. The romance presents a problem for Nicole at first, but she soon is won over by Newton's determination to break the rules in the pursuit of love. Nicole does a first-rate job of acting in this film and, for the first time, shows an engaging wrinkle in her on-screen sexuality, one that does not require nudity.

# *Days of Thunder* (1990)

## CAST

Tom Cruise
Robert Duvall
Nicole Kidman
Randy Quaid
Cary Elwes
Michael Rooker

Producers: Jerry Bruckheimer, Gerald R. Molen, Don Simpson
Director: Tony Scott
Writers: Robert Towne, Tom Cruise

*Days of Thunder* begins with a Daytona 500 race and the announcement that a driver has dropped out of the lineup. It is a setup for race team owner Tim Daland (Randy Quaid) to cajole Harry Hogge (Robert Duvall), a retired pit boss, to come out of retirement and build a car for him. Hogge, reluctant and a bit testy, tells him that he needs to first find a competent driver. Daland invites him out to the track to watch his driver, Cole Trickle (Tom Cruise), take a turn or two around the track. Impressed, Hogge agrees to build the car and work as pit boss.

After several unsuccessful races, Hogge and Trickle have a disagreement, after which Trickle admits that he is insecure because he can't "talk car." Hogge and Trickle patch up their areas of disagreement and Trickle goes on to become a winning driver. Nicole, who plays the role of Dr. Claire Lewicki, an Australian neurosurgeon, enters the picture when Trickle and another driver are involved in a serious accident.

The remainder of the movie deals with Trickle's ability to deal with his fears about racing, his confusion over his romantic relationship with Dr. Lewicki, and his discovery of a world that is essentially a subculture with its own rules and expectations.

# Billy Bathgate (1991)

## CAST

Dustin Hoffman
Nicole Kidman
Loren Dean
Bruce Willis
Steven Hill
Steve Buscemi
Billy Jaye
John Costelloe
Timothy Jerome

Producers: Robert F. Colesberry, Arlene Donovan
Director: Robert Benton
Writers: E. L. Doctorow (novel), Tom Stoppard

Organized crime has always done well at the box office, so who could blame director Robert Benton for taking a swing at the genre? Loosely based on the organized crime syndicates of the 1920s and 1930s, *Billy Bathgate* (the title role of which is played by Loren Dean) is about a young man's entry into a life of crime, from the ground floor.

His boss is Dutch Schultz (a real-life gangster played by Dustin Hoffman), whose fictionalized and romanticized life is used as a backdrop for Billy's coming-of-age story. It is a journey into manhood that gets a hormonal boost when he falls in love with Schultz's mistress, Drew Preston, a married woman (played by Nicole Kidman).

As the characters move through assorted violence and nudity (all Nicole's doing), it becomes apparent that the real theme of the movie is survival—that is, who will be left standing at the end of the movie.

# *Far and Away (1992)*

## CAST

Tom Cruise
Nicole Kidman
Thomas Gibson
Robert Prosky
Barbara Babcock
Cyril Cusack
Eileen Pollock
Colm Meaney
Douglas Gillison
Michelle Johnson

Producer: Ron Howard, Brian Grazer
Director: Ron Howard
Writers: Ron Howard, Bob Dolman

The story begins in the 1890s in Ireland, where Joseph Donnelly (Tom Cruise), the impoverished son of a farmer, is forced to flee his homeland after the death of his father, to make a new life for himself in America. Accompanying him is Shannon Christie (Nicole Kidman), the daughter of the well-to-do landowner who owned the land that Donnelly's family farmed.

In the beginning, the couple has a strictly platonic relationship (both are suspicious of the other's intentions), but after suffering a series of hardships in America they discover that they are meant for each other. They break up after Christie is shot in a bungled robbery attempt (they were starving and only broke into the house to find food).

Donnelly leaves her behind with her former suitor, who has followed her to America, and he goes out west to make his fortune. This is a slow-moving film that does not get its legs until the end, when Donnelly and Christie find themselves competing for property in the same land rush. Nicole seems uninspired by the script and Tom seems confused about his character's motivation.

# *Malice (1993)*

## CAST

Alec Baldwin
Nicole Kidman
Bill Pullman
Bebe Neuwirth
George C. Scott
Anne Bancroft
Gwyneth Paltrow
Peter Gallagher

Producers: Rachel Pfeffer, Charles Muloehill, Harold Becker
Director: Harold Becker
Writers: Aaron Sorkin, Scott Frank

In this heavily layered thriller, Nicole Kidman plays the role of Tracy Kennsinger, a teacher who seemingly is enjoying the good life with her husband, Andy (played by Bill Pullman), a dean at a women's college. The story gets complicated at the get-go, with the rape of a student at the college and with the introduction into their household of Dr. Jed Hill, a surgeon played by Alec Baldwin. Tracy's husband rents Hill a room because the surgeon has just moved to town and needs a place to stay—and because he and Tracy need the money to renovate their three-story home. Tracy professes to be unhappy with her new tenant, but she has a secret agenda that is slowly revealed through misdirection. Toward the end, there is one surprise after another as nothing is ever quite what it seems.

# *My Life (1993)*

## CAST

Michael Keaton
Nicole Kidman
Bradley Whitford

Queen Latifah

Producers: Herry Zucker, Bruce Joel Rubin, Hunt Lowry
Director: Bruce Joel Rubin
Writer: Bruce Joel Rubin

Bob Jones (Michael Keaton) is a public relations executive who learns that he has cancer. When doctors give him no hope of a remission, he decides to compile a video history of his life for his unborn child. He interviews himself, he interviews his family and his friends from grammar school—and he interviews his wife, Gail (Nicole Kidman). Most of the film deals with Jones's lame attempts to get in touch with his feelings about his impending death. Nicole has a presence in the film, but since she whispers most of her lines, presumably to show respect for her husband's affliction, she barely seems to matter in the story's narrative development. This is one of her weakest performances, but that is due to the direction that she received and has little to do with her acting skills. Keaton's character is so unsympathetic that by the end of the film, you are happy to see him go.

## *Batman Forever* (*1995*)

### CAST

Val Kilmer
Tommy Lee Jones
Jim Carrey
Nicole Kidman
Chris O'Donnell
Drew Barrymore

Producers: Tim Burton, Peter MacGregor-Scott
Director: Joel Schumacher
Writers: Lee Batchler, Janet Scott Batchler, Akiva Goldsman

This is the third *Batman* epic, with Val Kilmer replacing Michael Keaton as the Caped Crusader and Jim Carrey taking on the role of the obnoxious

Riddler. Nicole Kidman plays Batman's love interest, psychologist Dr. Chase Meridian. There's not much plot to the movie—Batman goes up against two adversaries, the Riddler and Tommy Lee Jones's Harvey Two-Face—but plot and character development are not at the core of the franchise's success with moviegoers. Nicole delivers her lines well and she looks great, but that's about all you can say about her performance in a movie that is all about Zap! Bam! Boom!

## To Die For (1995)

### CAST

Nicole Kidman
Matt Dillon
Joaquin Phoenix
Casey Affleck
Illeana Douglas
Buck Henry
Wayne Knight

Producers: Laura Ziskin, Jonathan Taplin, Joseph M. Caracciolo
Director: Gus Van Sant
Writers: Joyce Maynard, Buck Henry

*To Die For* begins with news coverage of a murder. As it turns out, the prime suspect is the local cable-television weather girl, Suzanne Stone Maretto (Nicole Kidman). She is charged with enlisting the help of three teenagers to kill her husband. This is not so much a murder mystery, since viewers have a good grasp of the situation early on, as it is a fascinating glimpse into the distorted mind of the supremely ambitious weather girl.

Nicole Kidman does an amazing job with this character, making her lovable, yet despicable, diabolically brilliant, yet simple-minded beyond belief—and perhaps best of all, icy cold, yet sensual. In one scene she dances to the music of "Sweet Home Alabama" in the headlights of her teenage boyfriend's car, providing the sexiest cinematic moment of 1995. This movie is a must-see for Nicole Kidman fans.

# The Leading Man (1996)

## CAST

Jon Bon Jovi
Anna Galiena
Lambert Wilson
Thandie Newton
Nicole Kidman

Producers: Paul Raphael, Bertil Ohlsson
Director: John Duigan
Writer: Virginia Duigan

*The Leading Man* is about an arrogant American actor, Robin Grange (Jon Bon Jovi), who goes to London to star in a new play written by Felix Webb (Lambert Wilson). Felix is having an adulterous affair with Hilary Rule (Thandie Newton), the female lead in his play. When Felix's wife learns of the affair, she makes life miserable for her husband, so much so that he persuades Robin to seduce her. A romantic quadrangle develops when Robin also seduces Hilary. The movie is very slow moving, but it has its moments. Nicole Kidman has a cameo role as an Oscar presenter.

# The Portrait of a Lady (1996)

## CAST

Nicole Kidman
John Malkovich
Barbara Hershey
Mary-Louise Parker
Martin Donovan II
Shelley Winters
Shelley Duvall
John Gielgud

Producers: Monty Montgomery, Steve Golin
Director: Jane Campion
Writer: Laura Jones (based on the Henry James novel)

Isabel Archer (Nicole Kidman) is an American who goes to England to visit her wealthy uncle, Mr. Touchett (John Gielgud). When he dies, he leaves her a fortune, setting her up for two predators who want to take advantage of her in her position with newfound wealth. John Malkovich plays the cold-hearted Gilbert Osmond, who marries her for reasons that are not entirely clear at first. Nicole's Isabel Archer is a little on the cool side, but she is still the best thing about the movie.

## The Peacemaker (1997)

### CAST

George Clooney
Nicole Kidman
Marcel Iures
Aleksandr Baluyev
Rene Medvesek

Producers: Walter Parkes, Baanko Lustig
Director: Mimi Leder
Writer: Michael Schiffer

Nicole Kidman plays Julia Kelly, a nuclear scientist who heads up a government operation to investigate a nuclear explosion that occurs in Russia after a train accident. She soon learns that it was no accident and was staged to conceal the theft of nuclear devices being transported on the train. She teams up with Thomas Devoe, a U.S. army colonel played by George Clooney, in an effort to recover the devices before they can be used by terrorists. It was Nicole's most physical role to date.

# Practical Magic (1998)

## CAST

Sandra Bullock
Nicole Kidman
Stockard Channing
Dianne Wiest
Goran Visnjic
Aidan Quinn
Evan Rachel Wood
Alexandra Artrip
Mark Feurerstein
Caprice Benedetti
Producer: Denise DiNovi
Director: Griffin Dunne
Writers: Robin Swicord, Alice Hoffman (book)

*Practical Magic* is about two sisters, Sal Owens (Sandra Bullock) and Gilly-Bean Owens (Nicole Kidman), who must live with the curse of family witch-dom handed down to them from Puritan days. Each sister handles it differently: Sal marries and settles down, while Gilly-Bean falls in love with every man that comes her way. Their lives are complicated when they kill—sort of by accident—one of Gilly-Bean's suitors. When the sisters try to use black magic to bring him back to life, the situation only gets worse. Their situation becomes complicated further when Sal falls in love with the police detective sent to investigate the man's disappearance.

# Eyes Wide Shut (1999)

## CAST

Tom Cruise
Nicole Kidman
Madison Eginton

Jackie Sawiris
Sydney Pollack
Leslie Lowe
Peter Benson
Todd Field
Michael Doven
Sky Dumont
Louise J. Taylor
Gary Goba

Producer: Stanley Kubrick
Director: Stanley Kubrick
Writers: Frederic Raphael, Stanley Kubrick (based on an Arthur
Schnitzler novel)

Tom Cruise plays Bill Harford, a doctor who samples the sexual offerings of
New York City, always as a voyeur and never as a participant, after his wife,
Alice (Nicole Kidman), tells him that she once fantasized about having a
sexual affair with a naval officer they met in passing while on vacation. There
is no plot, per se—only the impressions of Bill and Alice as they deal with
the realities of their marriage, realities that are complicated by a mysterious
death and a descent into the secret sexual rituals of the city's social elite.
Nicole performs the most sexually explicit scenes of her career in this movie.

## *Moulin Rouge (2001)*

### CAST

Nicole Kidman
Ewan McGregor
Jim Broadbent
John Leguizamo
Richard Roxburgh
Kylie Minogue
Jacek Koman

Caroline O'Connor
Matthew Whittet
Kerry Walker
Garry McDonald

Producers: Steve E. Andrews, Fred Baron, Martin Brown, Catherine
    Knapman, Baz Luhrmann, Catherine Martin
Director: Baz Luhrmann
Writers: Baz Luhrmann, Craig Pearce

Impoverished writer Christian (Ewan McGregor) goes to Paris to write about
love, even though he has never experienced it. He quickly falls in with
Toulouse-Lautrec and a rowdy band of bohemians who want to sell a show to
the Moulin Rouge nightclub.

As it happens, the club's owner Harold Zidler (Jim Broadbent) needs a financial backer and decides to use the proposed show to attract the Duke of
Monroth. The story gets complicated when both Christian and the duke fall
in love with the nightclub's consumptive star Satine (Nicole Kidman).

Nicole sings and dances her way through the movie, giving one of the
most energetic performances of her career, one that earned her a nomination
for an Academy Award.

# The Others (2001)

## CAST

Nicole Kidman
Fionnula Flanagan
Alakina Mann
James Bentley
Christopher Eccleston
Eric Sykes
Elaine Cassidy
Renee Asherson
Gordon Reid
Keith Allen
Michelle Fairley

Producers: Fernando Bovaira, Jose Luis Cuerda,
   Sunmin Park
Director: Alejandro Amenabar
Writer: Alejandro Amenabar

Grace Stewart (Nicole Kidman) lives in a darkened house with her two children, convinced that they will die if exposed to sunlight. Her husband has gone off to war and not returned, and her servants have disappeared without warning. Just getting by day to day is all she can manage. Luckily, three servants appear at Grace's door one day and take over her household duties. Soon it becomes clear that Grace is in for the fight of her life, though what that fight is does not become clear until the final scenes.

## *Birthday Girl (2002)*

### CAST

Nicole Kidman
Ben Chaplin
Vincent Cassel
Mathieu Kassovitz
Kate Lynn Evans
Stephen Mangan
Alexander Armstrong
Sally Phillips
Jo McInnes
Ben Miller

Producers: Eric Abraham, Steve Butterworth, Julie Goldstein, Colin
   Leventhal, Diana Phillips, Sydney Pollack, Paul Webster
Director: Jez Butterworth
Writers: Tom Butterworth, Jez Butterworth

Nicole Kidman plays a Russian mail-order bride, Nadia, who travels to England to marry a mild-mannered bank teller named John (Ben Chaplin). He is distressed to learn that she speaks no English and he tries to send her back, only the Internet dating service that connected them will not return his telephone calls. He learns to make the most of it and things seem to be progressing well until Nadia's cousin Alexei shows up with his friend Yuri. One thing leads to another, and before John knows what has happened he is robbing his own bank to keep Yuri from hurting Nadia. It is at that point that the story takes a wicked turn and heads into unforeseen territory.

## The Hours (2002)

### CAST

Nicole Kidman
Julianne Moore
Meryl Streep
Eileen Atkins
Toni Collette
Claire Danes
Stephen Dillane

Producers: Robert Fox, Scott Rudin
Director: Stephen Daldry
Writers: Michael Cunningham (novel), David Hare

Nicole Kidman plays lesbian writer Virginia Woolf in this film based on the Pulitizer Prize–winning novel, *The Hours*. It is about women living in different eras who are affected by the feminist's writing. Julianne Moore plays a housewife who is influenced by Woolf's novel *Mrs. Dalloway*. Meryl Streep plays a contemporary woman who throws a party for a friend who is dying of AIDS. Nicole changed her appearance drastically to play the role and preview audiences did not recognize her.

## Dogville (2003)

### CAST

Nicole Kidman
Stellan Skarsgard

Siobhan Fallon
Chloe Sevigny
James Caan
Patrica Clarkson
Blair Brown
Jeremy Davies
Philip Baker Hall
Paul Bettany
Lauren Bacall

Producers: Gillian Berrie, Peter Aalbaek Jensen, Lars Jonsson, Vibeke
   Windelov
Director: Lars von Trier
Writer: Lars von Trier

Grace (Nicole Kidman) is a woman who moves to a small town in the Rocky
Mountains in the 1930s and finds herself treated as an outsider. Based on the
song "Pirate Jenny" from *The Threepenny Opera*, in which a town is attacked by
its enemies and leaves an unwanted woman as the only survivor, it deals with
themes of violence and vengeance. It was filmed in Sweden entirely on sets.

## *The Human Stain (2003)*

### CAST

Anthony Hopkins
Nicole Kidman
Ed Harris

Producers: Ronald M. Bozman, Andre Lamal, Gary Lucchesi, Michael
   Ohoven, Tom Rosenberg, Scott Steindorff
Director: Robert Benton
Writers: Philip Roth (novel), Nicholas Meyer

Based on Philip Roth's novel, *The Human Stain* is about a college professor,
Coleman Silk (Anthony Hopkins), whose life is shattered when it is dis-

closed that he had an affair with a young, female janitor, Faunia Farley (Nicole Kidman). The film contains Nicole Kidman's most explicit sex scenes since *Eyes Wide Shut*.

# Cold Mountain (2003)

## CAST

Jude Law
Nicole Kidman
Renee Zellweger
Natalie Portman
Philip Seymour Hoffman
Giovanni Ribisi
Brendan Gleeson
Charlie Hunnam
Ray Winstone
Donald Sutherland
Jena Malone

Producers: Steve Andrews, Albert Berger, Tim Bricknell, William Horberg, Sydney Pollack, Iain Smith, Ron Yerxa
Director: Anthony Minghella
Writers: Charles Frazier (novel), Anthony Minghella

Jule Law plays the role of Inman, a wounded Confederate soldier who makes a journey back to his mountain community to reunite with his pre–Civil War sweetheart, Ada (Nicole Kidman). It was filmed in Romania.

# Bibliography

## BOOKS

Cader, Michael, ed. *2000 People Entertainment Almanac*. New York: Cader, 1999.

Hubbard, L. Ron. *Scientology: The Fundamentals of Thought*. Los Angeles: Bridge Publications, 1983.

Kidman, Anthony, Ph.D. *From Thought to Action: A Self Help Manual*. St. Leonards, Australia: Biochemical and General Services, 1988.

———. *Family Life: Adapting to Change*. St. Leonards, Australia: Biochemical and General Services, 1995.

Kubrick, Stanley, and Frederic Raphael. *Eyes Wide Shut: A Screenplay by Stanley Kubrick and Frederic Raphael*. New York: Warner Books, 1999.

Pike, Jeffrey. *Australia*. London: Insight Guides, 2002.

Raphael, Frederic. *Eyes Wide Open: A Memoir of Stanley Kubrick*. New York: Ballantine Books, 1999.


## MAGAZINE AND NEWSPAPER ARTICLES

Aitchison, Diana. "There's Good Cruise and Bad Cruise." *The Commercial Appeal*, December 5, 1992.

Andrew, Geoff. " 'Portrait of a Lady.' " *Time Out*, January 1996.

Angeli, Michael. "Screaming Mimi!" *Playboy*, March 1993.

Ansen, David. "Kidman's a Comedienne." *Newsweek*, October 2, 1995.

Atkinson, Michael. "The Naked Truth." *Movieline*, April 2000.

Barron, James. "Boldface Names." *New York Times*, April 19, 2001.

Beitks, Edvins. " 'Practical Magic' Weaves a Fun Spell." *San Francisco Examiner*, October 16, 1998.

Blowen, Michael. "Howard's 'Far and Away' Doesn't Come Close." *Boston Globe*, October 30, 1992.

————. "Kubrick's Final Film Generates Juicy Rumors." *Boston Globe*, March 10, 1999.

Brantley, Ben. "Fool's Gold in the Kingdom of Desire." *New York Times*, December 14, 1998.

Brown, Joe. " 'The Firm.' " *Washington Post*, July 2, 1993.

Brown, Scott. "Marriage Impossible." *Entertainment Weekly*, May 11, 2001.

Byrnes, Paul. "Birthday Girl." *Sydney Morning Herald*, August 10, 2002.

Cagle, Jess. "Madame Moulin." *Time*, May 13, 2001.

————.

Campbell, Caren Weiner. "Honeymoon Cruises." *Entertainment Weekly*, September 18, 1998.

Carr, Jay. " 'Billy Bathgate': Unrealized Underworld." *Boston Globe*, November 1, 1991.

————. "Cruise Holds 'Firm': The Movie Isn't a First-Rate Thriller, But It's Slick Enough to be Satisfying." *Boston Globe*, June 30, 1993.

————. "Oscar Night '97." *Boston Globe*, March 25, 1997.

————. " 'Practical Magic' Doesn't Cast a Spell." *Boston Globe*, October 16, 1998.

Clark, Mike. "Long Life Ahead for Darkly Comic 'To Die For.' " *USA Today*, December 1, 1998.

Collins, Nancy. "Lust & Trust." *Rolling Stone*, July 8, 1999.

Connelly, Christopher. "Tom Cruise," *Rolling Stone*, 1986.

Corliss, Richard. "An Actress to Die For." *Time*, October 9, 1995.

Cruz, Clarissa. "All the Right Moves." *Entertainment Weekly*, June 1, 2001.

Deevoy, Adrian. "The Real Nicole." GQ (UK), August 2002.

Demick, Barbara. "Scientology Throws Germany into a Panic." *Philadelphia Inquirer*, August 19, 1996.

Dolen, Christine Arnold. "Grisly Effects Sink Dead Calm." *Miami Herald*, April 7, 1989.

Dunne, Dominick. "Smoke and Murders." *Vanity Fair*, July 2001.

Ebert, Roger. "Dead Calm." *Chicago Sun-Times*, April 7, 1989.

———. "Flirting." *Chicago Sun-Times*, November 20, 1992.

———. "A Few Good Men." *Chicago Sun-Times*, December 11, 1992.

———. "Malice." *Chicago Sun-Times*, October 1, 1993.

———. "My Life." *Chicago Sun-Times*, November 12, 1993.

———. "To Die For." *Chicago Sun-Times*, October 6, 1995.

———. "The Leading Man." *Chicago Sun-Times*, March 3, 1998.

———. "Risqué Business." *Nashville Tennessean*, July 16, 1999.

Errico, Marcus. "Cruise Files for Divorce." *E! Online*, February 7, 2001.

Evans, Martin. "Why Nicole Adored Singing Ewan." *Sydney Morning Herald*, May 10, 2001.

Farache, Emily. "Foster: Au Revoir Cannes, Hello, 'Panic.' " *E! Online*, February 5, 2001.

Fernandez, Jay A. "Thandie Newton." *Premiere*, September 2002.

Figueroa, Ana. "He Said, She Said." *Newsweek*, May 4, 2001 [www.msnbc.com/news/569053.asp]

Germain, David. " 'Moulin Rouge.' " Associated Press, May 14, 2001.

Gilbert, Matthew. "Nicole Kidman: The Candid Portrait of a Lady on Her Own." *Boston Globe*, January 12, 1997.

Ginna, Robert Emmett. "The Odyssey Begins." *Entertainment Weekly*, April 9, 1999.

Gleiberman, Owen. "Ghost Worlds." *Entertainment Weekly*, August 17, 2001.

Gould, Martin, and Gary Morgan. "Nicole Triumphs in Divorce Case." *Star*, July 17, 2001.

Gould, Martin, and Peter Kent. "Nicole's Cancer Ordeal." *Star*, January 22, 2002.

Gray, Marianne. "Nicole Kidman Is the Latest Hollywood Star to Tread a London Stage." *London Evening Standard*, September 3, 1998.

Gritten, David. "Portrait of a Lady." *Telegraph Magazine*, February 1996.

Grobel, Lawrence. "Nic at Twilight." *Movieline*, October 1998.

Harris, Mark. "Entertainer of the Year." *Entertainment Weekly*, December 21, 2001.

Hinson, Hal. "Far and Away." *Washington Post*, May 22, 1992.

———. "Flirting." *Washington Post*, November 20, 1992.

Hiscock, John. "We Didn't Need Sex Lessons, Say Cruise and Kidman." *London Telegraph*, April 24, 1999.

———. "We're So Tired We May Quit, Says Kidman." *Content*, June 23, 1999.

———. "Kubrick Film Gave Cruise an Ulcer." *Content*, June 30, 1999.

Honeycutt, Kirk. " 'Moulin Rouge.' " *Hollywood Reporter*, May 10, 2001.

Howe, Desson. " 'Dead Calm.' " *Washington Post*, April 7, 1989.

———. " 'Days of Thunder.' " *Washington Post*, June 29, 1990.

———. " 'My Life.' " *Washington Post*, November 12, 1993.

———. "An Unflattering 'Portrait.' " *Washington Post*, January 17, 1997.

Hunter, Stephen. "No Candles for This 'Birthday Girl.' " *Washington Post*, February 1, 2002.

Hutton, Punch. "Nicole Kidman: The Legends of Hollywood." *Vanity Fair*, April 2001.

Jablon, Robert. "Kidman, Cruise Arrive Separately." Associated Press, August 8, 2001.

Jacobson, Harlan. "Kidman Plays Fame Game, But Craves Privacy." *USA Today*, May 14, 2001.

Janos, Leo. "Nicole Kidman." *Cosmopolitan*, July 1991.

Jensen, Jeff. "First Tango in Paris." *Entertainment Weekly*, May 25, 2001.

Junod, Tom. "A Bridge, a Bed, a Bar, and One Real Ozzie Gull." *Esquire*, August 1999.

Kempley, Rita. " 'Billy Bathgate.' " *Washington Post*, November 1, 1991.

———. " 'A Few Good Men.' " *Washington Post*, December 11, 1992.

Kennedy, Mark. "Kidman Relishes Chance to Play a Complicated Lady." *Atlanta Journal-Constitution*, January 17, 1997.

Kroll, Jack. "Nicole Takes Off." *Newsweek*, December 14, 1998.

———. "Kubrick's View." *Newsweek*, March 22, 1999.

La Badie, Donald. "Pollack Peels Away Actors' Artifice." *The Commercial Appeal*, June 26, 1993.

Lagerfeld, Karl. "Nicole Kidman." *Interview*, February 2002.

LaSalle, Mick. "Kidman Monstrously Good in 'To Die For.' " *San Francisco Chronicle*, October 6, 1995.

———. " 'Batman' Entertains, Again." *San Francisco Chronicle*, October 27, 1995.

———. "Terrorism X Two: George Clooney Makes a Fretful 'Peacemaker.' " *San Francisco Chronicle*, September 26, 1997.

Laville, Sandra. "Tom Cruise Wins Libel Case Over 'Lies About Family.' " *London Telegraph*, October 30, 1998.

Lee, Luaine. "For Nicole Kidman Life Is a Blast." *Detroit Free Press*, September 29, 1997.

Lollar, Michael. "A Final Firm Farewell, It's a Wrap: Cast and Crew Say Goodby to the Memphis Scene." *The Commercial Appeal*, February 23, 1993.

Long, Gary. "Passing Grades: Nascar 'Critics' Give Thumbs Up to 'Thunder.' " *Miami Herald*, July 6, 1990.

Lowing, Rob. "Nicole: How Mum Eased My Pain." *Sydney Morning Herald*, May 20, 2001.

Luhrmann, Baz. "Nicole Kidman." *Interview*, May 2, 2001.

Lyman, Rick. "A Perfectionist's Pupil with a Major in Creepy." *New York Times*, February 22, 2002.

———. " 'Beautiful Mind' Wins; Best Actress Goes to Halle Berry." *New York Times*, March 25, 2002.

Maddox, Garry. "Kidman's Toughest Challenge." *Sydney Morning Herald*, n.d.

Marshall, Leslie. "Things You Don't Know About Nicole." *In Style*, June 2001.

Mitchell, Elvis. "Shy Neat-Freak With Kinky Leanings? Sounds Like the Perfect Victim." *New York Times*, February 1, 2002.

———. " 'Moulin Rouge': An Eyeful, an Earful, Anachronism." *New York Times*, May 18, 2001.

Morris, Wesley. "Unmasking Kubrick's Eyes." *San Francisco Examiner*, July 16, 1999.

Nugent, Benjamin. "Show Business." *Time*. [www.time.com/time/europe/magazine/2002/0701/cruise/story3.html]

O'Donnell, John. "Flaming Star." *Rolling Stone* (Australian edition), June 1989.

Oldenburg, Ann. "Unexpected 'Portrait' of Nicole Kidman." *USA Today*, January 2, 1997.

Pacheco, Patrick. "Kidman and 'Blue Room' Generate a Red-Hot Buzz." *Los Angeles Times*, November 16, 1998.

Patterson, Troy. "Sexual Healing." *Entertainment Weekly*, July 1999.

Peretz, Evgenia. "The Naked Truth." *Vanity Fair*, January 2002.

Pond, Steve. "Oscar Finds a New Home." *Premiere*, January 2002.

Potter, Jerry. " 'Days of Thunder' Isn't Taking World by Storm." *USA Today*, February 15, 1991.

Rea, Steven. "An Aussie Adventure in Making Movies." *Philadelphia Inquirer*, April 20, 1989.

———. "Director Ron Howard, On What His 'Far and Away' Has to Offer." *Philadelphia Inquirer*, May 31, 1992.

———. "Shut Your Eyes: Kubrick's Final Film Long, Dull." *Philadelphia Inquirer*, July 16, 1999.

Rebello, Stephen. "All that Baz." *Movieline*, June 2001.

Reynolds, Nigel. "Kidman Strips Off on London Stage for 250 Pounds a Week." *London Telegraph*, September 23, 1998.

———. "Kidman Wants to Make London Her Main Home." *London Telegraph*, January 26, 2002.

Rickey, Carrie. "A Media Star Is Born: Nicole Kidman in 'To Die For.' " *Philadelphia Inquirer*, October 6, 1995.

Ridley, Clifford A. "Nicole Kidman Delivers in 'The Blue Room.' " *Philadelphia Inquirer*, December 14, 1998.

Rochlin, Margy. "Nicole." *US*, December 1996.

———. " 'Moulin Rouge': Think Bollywood, Australia and Paris in Song." *New York Times*, May 6, 2001.

Rommelmann, Nancy. "Nicole Kidman: Women Who Have Made Me the Person I Am Today." *Marie Claire*, May 2001.

Ryan, Desmond. "Surf's Up in Australian Effort." *Philadelphia Inquirer*, June 8, 1987.

———. " 'Female Thing' Surgery for Nicole Kidman." *E! Online*, February 20, 1998.

Sams, Christine. "When Nicole met Kevin . . . and Meg." *Sydney Morning Herald*, August 4, 2002.

Seiler, Andy. "Nudity Isn't New on Cruise, Kidman Resumes." *USA Today*, July 16, 1999.

Sessums, Kevin. "Lady of Spain." *Vanity Fair*, September 2001.

Shannon, Jeff. "Magic of 'Malice' is Clever Wickedness." *Seattle Times*, October 1, 1993.

Shulgasser, Barbara. "Little Life in Campion's Murky 'Portrait.' " *San Francisco Examiner*, January 17, 1997.

Siegel, Ed. "The Near-Perfect End of Kubrick's Odyssey." *Boston Globe*, August 1, 1999.

Silverman, Stephen. "Kidman and Cruise: Together, Briefly." *People*, August 8, 2001.

Smith, Liz. "Nicole Stands Tall." *Good Housekeeping*, November 2001.

Snead, Elizabeth. "Nicole Kidman: Stepping Out of Cruise's Shadow." *Seattle Times*, September 29, 1995.

Socol, Gary. "The Nicole Kidman Nobody Knows." *McCall's*, May 1998.

Spears, W. "McCall's Apologizes to Cruise." *Washington Post*, February 4, 1995.

———. "Nicole Kidman Stands Up for her Guy Tom Cruise." *Philadelphia Inquirer*, June 6, 1995.

———. "Cruise Wins Apology from German Mag." *Philadelphia Inquirer*, August 14, 1996.

Sterritt, David. "Cruise Takes a Wrong Turn, 'Thunder' Squanders Talent with Laughable Plot and Blatant Commercialism." *Christian Science Monitor*, July 3, 1990.

———. "Henry James's 'Portrait of a Lady': More Than Just a Pretty Picture." *Christian Science Monitor*, December 24, 1996.

Strauss, Bob. "All Eyes on Kidman." *Boston Globe*, July 15, 1999.

Strauss, Bruce. "Playing Complex Character May Boost Kidman's Career." *Atlanta Constitution*, October 9, 1995.

Svetkey, Benjamin. "Eyes of the Storm." *Entertainment Weekly*, July 23, 1999.

Tauber, Michelle et al. "Sealed With a Hug." *People*, December 3, 2001.

Thomas, Karen. "Child's Play with Cruise, Kidman." *USA Today*, January 14, 1992.

———. "Cruise, Kidman Cancel Adoption." *USA Today*, December 24, 1992.

Thomas, Kevin. " 'The Leading Man.' " *Los Angeles Times*, March 6, 1998.

Travers, Peter. " 'A Few Good Men.' " *Rolling Stone*, 1992.

———. " 'Malice.' " *Rolling Stone*, 1993.

———. " 'Batman Forever.' " *Rolling Stone*, 1995.

Turan, Kenneth. " 'Batman Forever.' " *Los Angeles Times*, June 16, 1995.

———. " 'The Portrait of a Lady.' " *Los Angeles Times*, December 24, 1996.

———. " 'The Peacemaker.' " *Los Angeles Times*, September 26, 1997.

———. "Tripping the Light." *Los Angeles Times*, May 18, 2001.

———. "Kidman Proves Haunting." *Los Angeles Times*, August 10, 2001.

Unreich, Rachelle. "Woman on the Verge." *Juice*, March 1996.

Unsigned. "Alleged Stalker Targets Kidman." *E! Online News* [entertainment. msn.com/news/eonline/050901_nkidman.asp].

Voorhees, John. " 'Bangkok Hilton' Restores Your Faith in the Miniseries Genre." *Seattle Times*, October 8, 1990.

Walker, Alexander. "By Jovi! It's So Terribly English." *London Evening Standard*, Sept. 9, 1997.

Weintraub, Bernard. "Cruise Talks But Cat Stays in the Bag." *New York Times*, September 15, 1998.

———. "All Eyes for a Peek at Kubrick's Final Film." *New York Times*, March 10, 1999.

Welkos, Robert W. " 'Eyes' Keeping Cruise Out of Sight." *Los Angeles Times*, May 1, 1998.

Werner, Laurie. "Portrait of an Iron Lady." *Los Angeles Times*, October 1, 1995.

Williams, Jeannie. "Cruise Marriage on the Rocks." *USA Today*, January 17, 1990.

———. "Cruise and Kidman's Irish Epic." *USA Today*, August 22, 1991.

———. "Cruise and Kidman Try New Roles: Parents." *USA Today*, January 22, 1993.

———. "Kidman: Australian for Flirt." *USA Today*, July 7, 1999.

Winer-Bernheimer, Linda. "More Than Just the Bare Basics." *Los Angeles Times*, December 14, 1998.

Wloszczyna, Susan. " 'Magic' Is What's Missing from Witch Tale." *USA Today*, December 17, 1999.

Wolk, Josh. "Days of Asunder." *Entertainment Weekly*, February 16, 2001.

Wright, David, Marc Cetner and John South. "Tom: Why I Divorced Nicole." *National Enquirer*, April 24, 2001.

Wyatt, Gene. "Risky Business." *Nashville Tennessean*, June 1, 2001.

Young, Josh. "Mystery Movie." *Entertainment Weekly*, October 2, 1998.

Zoglin, Richard. "Room for Improvement." *Time*, December 28, 1998.

———. "Nicole Kidman Miscarriage Confirmed." *Associated Press*, March 30, 2001.

———. "Tom Cruise Sues Porn Actor Over Gay Affair Story." *Associated Press*, May 3, 2001.

———. "Nicole Kidman Wants Joint Custody." Associated Press, May 4, 2001.

———. "Nicole and Spider-Man Red-Hot Romance!" *Star*, May 21, 2002.

———. "Kidman Gets Break from Alleged Stalker." Associated Press, May 30, 2001.

———. "Cruise in Fiji: Nicole Takes Kids." Associated Press, July 18, 2001.

———. "Cruise-Kidman Divorce Near Final." Associated Press, July 31, 2001.

———. "Cruise Drops Suit Against Publisher." Associated Press, December 1, 2001.


## TELEVISION

*Oprah Winfrey Show*, May 18, 2001.
*Ray Martin Show*, November 5, 2001.
*The Tonight Show with Jay Leno*, January 18, 2002.
*The Tonight Show with Jay Leno*, March 2002.

# Index

NOTE: **Bold page numbers** indicate Nicole Kidman filmography.

Academy Awards, 91, 97, 149, 167–70
Acting lessons, 8–9, 77
*Actustar* (magazine), 156
Adoption (adopted children), 68, 70–71, 79,
    96, 143–44. *See also* Cruise, Connor Antony
    Kidman; Cruise, Isabella Jane Kidman
*A Few Good Men* (movie), 65–67
Alley, Kirstie, 48–49
Amenabar, Alejandro, 145; *The Others*,
    140–42, 158, 170, **196–97**
Amsterdam, 13–14
Anderson, Paul Thomas: *Magnolia*, 129
Ansen, David, 88
*Archer's Adventure* (movie), 15–17, **179–80**
Atkinson, Michael, 125
Australian Film Institute (AFI), 18, 35

Bacon, Kevin: *A Few Good Men*, 65–67
Baker, Tom, 76
Baldwin, Alec: *Malice*, 68–70, **189**
Ballet lessons, 8
Bancroft, Anne: *Malice*, 68–70, **189**
*Bangkok Hilton* (TV series), 35
*Batman Forever* (movie), 80–82, **190–91**
Beck, Marilyn, 160–61
Becker, Harold: *Malice*, 68–70, **189**
Benton, Robert: *Billy Bathgate*, 54–58, **187**; *The
    Human Stain*, 170, 174, **199–200**
Berry, Halle, 169
*Bewitched* (movie), 174
Bibliography, 201–9
*Billy Bathgate* (movie), 54–58, **187**

*Birthday Girl* (movie), 130–32, **197–98**; reviews,
    166–67; at Sundance Film Festival, 164
*Bit Part, The* (movie), 24, **182–83**
*Blue Room, The* (play), 119–22
*BMX Bandits* (movie), 12–13, **178–79**
Bon Jovi, Jon: *The Leading Man*, 94–96, **192**
Boyfriends, 10–11, 13–14, 19–20. *See also*
    Graham, Marcus
Brantley, Ben, 121
British Academy Awards (BAFTA), 167
Broadbent, Jim: *Moulin Rouge*, 132–39, **195–96**
Brown, Joe, 77
Bruckheimer, Jerry, 42–43, 46
Bullock, Sandra, 80; *Practical Magic*, 116–19,
    **194**
Bunton, Phil, 124–25
Burlinson, Tom: *Windrider*, 19–20, **180–81**
Burr, Ty, 125
*Bush Christmas* (movie), 11–12, **177–78**
Butterworth, Jez: *Birthday Girl*, 130–32, 166–67,
    **197–98**
Byrnes, Paul, 167

Cage, Nicholas, 157
Caine, Michael, 165
Campion, Jane, 9; See also *Portrait of a Lady*
Cannes Film Festival, 145, 151–53
Carr, Jay, 57, 77, 119
Carrey, Jim, 156; *Batman Forever*, 80–82,
    **190–91**
Cassel, Vincent: *Birthday Girl*, 130–32, 166–67,
    **197–98**

Catholicism, 5, 52
Chaplin, Ben: *Birthday Girl*, 130–32, 166–67, **197–98**
Church of Scientology, 48, 52–54, 93, 97, 159
Climo, Brett, 18; *Archer's Adventure*, 15–17, **179–80**
Clooney, George, 99, 146; *The Peacemaker*, 97–99, **193**
Cohen, Sam, 42
*Cold Mountain* (movie), 171–72, 174, **200**
Cook, Alyssa-James, 18, 24
Crowe, Cameron, 156, 157, 174; *Jerry Maguire*, 91–92, 94, 97; *Vanilla Sky*, 145, 156, 170
Crowe, Russell, 156, 160, 164, 166, 167, 169, 171, 173
Cruise, Connor Antony Kidman (son), 79, 96; *Cold Mountain* set, 172; divorce and, 146, 156, 159, 171; Mediterranean cruise, 92; *Moulin Rouge* set, 138; music lessons, 92; in Prague, 87
Cruise, Isabella Jane Kidman "Bella" (daughter), 71; *Cold Mountain* set, 174; divorce and, 146, 156, 159, 171; Mediterranean cruise, 92; *Moulin Rouge* set, 138; music lessons, 92; in Prague, 87
Cruise, Tom, 37–54, 174; background of, 39–41; *Days of Thunder*, 37–38, 42–46, 47–48, **186–87**; divorce: from Mimi Rogers, 45–49; from Nicole, 145–50, 155–59, 162–63, 171; *Eyes Wide Shut*, 100–116, 122–28, **194–95**; *Far and Away*, 61–64, **188**; *A Few Good Men*, 65–67; *The Firm*, 75–77; gay allegations, 49, 58, 79–80, 96, 118–19, 155–56; *Interview with the Vampire*, 75, 77–78; *Jerry Maguire*, 91–92, 94, 97; *Magnolia*, 129; married life, 59–61, 64–65, 68, 77, 90, 92–93, 124–25, 128–29, 140, 143–45; Mediterranean cruise, 92; *Mission: Impossible*, 87–88; *Mission Impossible II*, 123, 130, 135–36, 139–40; *Vanilla Sky*, 145, 156, 170; wedding to Nicole, 52
Cruz, Penelope, 145, 148–49, 156–57, 162–63

Daldry, Stephen: *The Hours*, 153–54, 170–71, 174, **198**
Damon, Matt, 157
Dance lessons, 8
Dating, 10–11, 19–20, 61, 160, 173
Davis, Michael, 155–56
*Days of Thunder* (movie), 42–46, 47–48, **186–87**; audition, 37–38; reviews, 45–46
*Dead Calm* (movie), 28–34, 37, **183–84**
Dean, Loren: *Billy Bathgate*, 54–58, **187**
Deevoy, Adrian, 172
De Palma, Brian: *Mission: Impossible*, 87–88
*Dianetics* (Hubbard), 53

Diesel, Vin, 173
Dillon, Matt: *To Die For*, 84–88, 91, **191**
Divorce, 145–50, 155–59, 162–63, 171
Doctorow, E. L., 54, 57
*Dogville* (movie), 163–65, 174, **198–99**
*Dream Story* (Schnitzler), 101
Duffield, Wendy and Tony, 124–25
Duigan, John: *Flirting*, 25–27, **185–86**; *The Leading Man*, 94–96, **192**
Dunne, Dominick, 152
Dunne, Griffin: *Practical Magic*, 116–19, **194**
Duritz, Adam, 173
Duvall, Robert: *Days of Thunder*, 43–46

Ebert, Roger, 27, 34, 63, 67, 70, 74, 88, 95–96
Education, 5–6, 9–10
Elliott, Denholm, 35
*Emerald City* (movie), 35–36, **184**
*Entertainment Weekly*, 160–61
*Esquire*, 128–29
Estevez, Emilio, 52, 156
*Eyes Wide Shut* (movie), 100–116, 122–28, **194–95**; production, 104–7, 118, 126–27; sex scene with Goba, 109–15, 118, 123; reviews, 125–26; screening for Tom and Nicole, 122–23; screenplay for, 101–4; synopsis, 107–9

*Family Life: Adapting to Change* (Kidman), 7, 22, 64–65, 147
*Far and Away* (movie), 61–64, **188**
Feminism, 2, 4–5
*Few Good Men, A* (movie), 65–67
Filmography, 177–200. *See also specific films*
Fincher, David, 145
*Firm, The* (movie), 75–77
*Flirting* (movie), 25–27, **185–86**
Foster, Jodie, 145
Freeman, Stuart, 30–33, 34

Gleiberman, Owen, 158
Glen, Iain: *The Blue Room*, 119–22
Goba, Gary: *Eyes Wide Shut*, 109–15, 123, 126, 127, **194–95**
Golden Globes, 91, 164–66
Gooding, Cuba, Jr., 156; *Jerry Maguire*, 91–92, 94, 97
Graham, Bob, 129
Graham, Marcus, 20, 36, 41–42, 47, 51, 145, 146

Haberman, Clyde, 121
Hair color, 6
Hayes, Terry, 35
Haywood, Chris, 35
Hendrick, Rick, 42, 46

Henry, Buck, 84
Hinson, Hal, 27, 63
Hoffman, Dustin, 52; *Billy Bathgate*, 54–58, **187**
Hooker, Matthew, 150–51
Hopkins, Anthony: *The Human Stain*, 170, 174, **199–200**
*Hours, The* (movie), 153–54, 170–71, 174, **198**
Howard, Ron: *Far and Away*, 61–64, **188**
Howe, Desson, 34, 45–46, 74, 93
Hubbard, L. Ron, 52–54
*Human Stain, The* (movie), 170, 174, **199–200**

*Interview with the Vampire* (movie), 75, 77–78
*In the Bedroom* (movie), 165
*In the Cut* (movie), 171, 172

Jennings, Tom: *Watch the Shadows Dance*, 22–23, **181–82**
*Jerry Maguire* (movie), 91–92, 94, 97
Joffe, Mark: *Nightmaster*, 22–23, **181–82**
Jones, Tommy Lee: *Batman Forever*, 80–82, **190–91**
Junod, Tom, 128–29

Kassovitz, Mathieu: *Birthday Girl*, 130–32, 166–67, **197–98**
Keaton, Michael, 81; *My Life*, 71–74, **189–90**
Keitel, Harvey, 107, 122
Kempley, Rita, 67
Kidman, Antonia (sister), 3, 5, 6, 52; divorce and, 147–48
Kidman, Antony (father), 1–5, 7–8, 97; breast cancer and, 21–22; dating and, 11; divorce and, 147–48; *Family Life: Adapting to Change*, 7, 22, 64–65, 147; at Golden Globes, 165; on marriage, 60; panic attacks and, 50, 120; wedding and, 52
Kidman, Janelle (mother), 1–5, 7, 8, 97; breast cancer and, 20–22; dating and, 11; divorce and, 147–48, 153; Tom and, 50; wedding and, 52
Kidman, Sidney (great-grandfather), 3–4
Kilmer, Val: *Batman Forever*, 80–82, **190–91**
Kubrick, Stanley, 100–102, 173; death of, 123–24. See also *Eyes Wide Shut*

LaSalle, Mick, 82, 88, 99
*Late Show with David Letterman*, 171
Lawrence, Denny: *Archer's Adventure*, 15–17, **179–80**
*Leading Man, The* (movie), 94–96, **192**
Leder, Mimi: *The Peacemaker*, 97–99, **193**
Ledger, Heath, 134
Leguizamo, John: *Moulin Rouge*, 132–39, **195–96**
Leibovitz, Annie, 148–49

Leno, Jay, 164–65, 168
Levdon, Joe, 166–67
Luhrmann, Baz, 132–33, 171. See also *Moulin Rouge*

McGregor, Ewan, 139, 146. See also *Moulin Rouge*
*Magnolia* (movie), 129
Maguire, Tobey, 173
*Malice* (movie), 68–70, **189**
Malkovich, John: *Portrait of a Lady*, 82–84, 89–91, 93–94, **192–93**
Mapother, Mary Lee, 39–41, 52
Married life, 59–61, 64–65, 68, 77, 90, 92–93, 124–25, 128–29, 140, 143–45, 157
Martin, Ray, 160
Minghella, Anthony: *Cold Mountain*, 171–72, **200**
Miscarriage, 146–47
*Mission: Impossible* (movie), 87–88
*Mission Impossible II* (movie), 123, 130, 135–36, 139–40
Mitchell, Elvis, 154, 167
Monton, Vincent: *Windrider*, 19–20, **180–81**
Moore, Demi: *A Few Good Men*, 65–67
Moore, Julianne: *The Hours*, 153–54, 170–71, **198**
Morris, Wesley, 158
Mosca, Fabrizio, 173
*Moulin Rouge* (movie), 132–39, 149, **195–96**; Academy Awards and, 167–70, 174; Cannes Film Festival and, 151–53; casting, 134–35; Golden Globes and, 164–66; production, 135–36, 137–39; reviews, 154–55; synopsis, 133–34, 136–37
*My Life* (movie), 71–74, **189–90**

Neill, Sam, 35; *Dead Calm*, 28–34, **183–84**
Nevin, Robyn, 35–36
Newton, Thandie: *Flirting*, 25–27, **185–86**; *The Leading Man*, 94–96, **192**
Nicholson, Jack: *A Few Good Men*, 65–67
*Nightmaster* (movie), 22–23, **181–82**
Noyce, Phillip, 38; *Dead Calm*, 28–34, **183–84**

*Oprah Winfrey* (TV show), 149–50
Oscars (Academy Awards), 91, 97, 149, 167–70
*Others, The* (movie), 140–42, 170, 174, **196–97**; premiere, 158
Outsider status, 5–7, 8, 12

Paltrow, Gwyneth: *Malice*, 68–70, **189**
Panic attacks, 50–51, 120, 163, 169
*Panic Room, The* (movie), 145
*Peacemaker, The* (movie), 97–99, **193**
Peretz, Evgenia, 162–63

Pfeiffer, Michelle, 99
Phillip Street Theater (Sydney), 8–9
Phoenix, Joaquin: *To Die For*, 84–88, 91, **191**
Pollack, Sidney, 107; *The Firm*, 75–77
*Portrait of a Lady* (movie), 89–91, **192–93**; audition, 82–84; reviews, 93–94
*Practical Magic* (movie), 116–19, **194**
*Premiere* (magazine), 174
*Prince and the Great Race* (movie), 11–12, 177–78
Pullman, Bill: *Malice*, 68–70, **189**

Quaid, Randy: *Days of Thunder*, 43–46

Raphael, Frederic: *Eyes Wide Shut*, 100–116, 122–28, **194–95**
Rea, Steven, 125
Red hair, 6
Reiner, Rob: *A Few Good Men*, 65–67
Religion, 5, 48, 52, 97. *See also* Scientology
Rice, Anne: *Interview with the Vampire*, 75, 77–78
Ridley, Clifford A., 121–22
Rogers, Mimi, 45–49, 60, 79
*Romeo and Juliet* (movie), 133, 134
*Room to Move* (TV series), 24, 25
Rubin, Bruce Joel: *My Life*, 71–74, **189–90**
Ryan, Meg, 171, 172–73

Samuel, Joanne: *Watch the Shadows Dance*, 22–23, **181–82**
Schnitzler, Arthur, 101, 119
Schooling, 5–6, 9–10
Schumacher, Joel: *Batman Forever*, 80–82, **190–91**
Scientology, 48, 52–54, 93, 97, 159
Scott, Tony: *Days of Thunder*, 43–46
Shannon, Jeff, 70
Shaw, Vinessa, 107
Shulgasser, Barbara, 94
Siegel, Ed, 125
Simpson, Don, 42–43, 46
Skaaren, Warran, 43
Skydiving, 49–50, 59
Slater, Chad, 156
Smith, Liz, 160
Smith, Stacy Jenel, 160–61
Spacek, Sissy: *In the Bedroom*, 165

Spencer, Charles, 120–21
Spencer, Danielle, 167
*Star Wars: Episode II* (movie), 139
Sterritt, David, 94
Stoppard, Tom, 55, 57
Streep, Meryl: *The Hours*, 153–54, 170–71, **198**
Sundance Film Festival, 164
Sydney Harbour Bridge, 3–4, 51

Taylor, Noah: *Flirting*, 25–27, **185–86**
Theater, 8–9; *The Blue Room*, 119–22
Thomas, Kevin, 95
*To Die For* (movie), 84–88, 91, **191**
*Tonight Show with Jay Leno*, 164–65, 168
*Top Gun* (movie), 42, 43, 46, 81
Towne, Robert, 43
Travers, Peter, 58, 66, 70, 82
Travolta, John, 54
Trenchard-Smith, Brian: *BMX Bandits*, 12–13, **178–79**
Trier, Lars von: *Dogville*, 163–65, 174, **198–99**
Turan, Kenneth, 82, 93–94, 99, 154–55, 158
*2001: A Space Odyssey* (movie), 102, 104

*Vanilla Sky* (movie), 145, 156, 170
*Vanity Fair*, 148–49, 157, 162–63
Van Sant, Gus: *To Die For*, 84–88, 91, **191**
*Vietnam* (TV series), 18, 25
Vietnam War, 1–2
Vitali, Leon, 109–11

Walker, Alexander, 96
*Watch the Shadows Dance* (movie), 22–23, **181–82**
Wedding to Tom Cruise, 52
Weis, Bob: *Wills & Burke*, 17–18, **180**
Willis, Bruce, 55
*Wills & Burke* (movie), 17–18, **180**
*Windrider* (movie), 19–20, **180–81**
Woo, John: *Mission Impossible II*, 123, 130, 135–36, 139–40

Zane, Billy, 34–35; *Dead Calm*, 28–34, **183–84**
Zellweger, Renee, 156, 165, 168–69; *Cold Mountain*, 171–72, **200**; *Jerry Maguire*, 91–92, 94, 97
Zeta-Jones, Catherine, 134